READING HEBREWS

SEARCH THE SCRIPTURES SERIES

READING HEBREWS

Your Guide to Reading and Understanding the Letter to the Hebrews

DAVID ADEEB

Copyright © 2024 by David Adeeb

Adeeb Christian Publishing, LLC, 38439 5th Ave, Unit 2822, Zephyrhills, FL 33542.
info@adeebchristianpublishing.com

All rights reserved. No part of this publication may be reproduced, stored, or transmitted in any form or by any means, electronic, mechanical, photocopying, recording, scanning, or otherwise, without written permission from the publisher. It is illegal to copy this book, post it to a website, or distribute it by any other means without written permission from the publisher.

Library of Congress Control Number: 2024909151
ISBN 978-1-964624-01-3 (hardcover)
ISBN 978-1-964624-00-6 (paperback)
ISBN: 978-1-964624-02-0 (eBook)

Unless otherwise noted, all Scripture quotations in this work are from the ESV® Bible (The Holy Bible, English Standard Version®), © 2001 by Crossway, a publishing ministry of Good News Publishers. Used by permission. All rights reserved. The ESV text may not be quoted in any publication made available to the public by a Creative Commons license. The ESV may not be translated in whole or in part into any other language.

Scripture quotations marked KJV are from The Authorized (King James) Version.

Scripture quotations marked LEB are from the *Lexham English Bible*. Copyright 2012 Logos Bible Software. Lexham is a registered trademark of Logos Bible Software.

Scripture quotations marked NASB are taken from the New American Standard Bible®, Copyright © 1995 by The Lockman Foundation. Used by permission. All rights reserved. lockman.org.

Scripture quotations marked NIV are taken from the Holy Bible, New International Version®, NIV®. Copyright © 2011 by Biblica, Inc.™ Used by permission of Zondervan. All rights reserved worldwide. www.zondervan.com. The "NIV" and "New International Version" are trademarks registered in the United States Patent and Trademark Office by Biblica, Inc.™

Scripture quotations marked NRSV are from the New Revised Standard Version Bible, copyright © 1989 National Council of the Churches of Christ in the United States of America. Used by permission. All rights reserved worldwide.

Scripture quotations marked RSV are from the Revised Standard Version of the Bible, copyright © 1971 National Council of the Churches of Christ in the United States of America. Used by permission. All rights reserved worldwide.

Scripture quotations marked YLT are from Young's Literal Translation.

Edited by David Adeeb and Jonathan Wright.

Cover art and design by KUHN Design Group | kuhndesigngroup.com.

Interior Design by David Adeeb.

Printed in the United States of America.

Soli Deo Gloria!

To my wife, Michelle, for supporting me through my master's studies and through the years to come!

Table of Contents

Preface   i

Acknowledgments   v

Introduction   1

The Authorship of Hebrews   7
   Who Is the Author of Hebrews?   8

The Audience, Purpose, and Date   13
   Who Were the Recipients of Hebrews?   14
   Why Was Hebrews Written?   15
   When Was Hebrews Written?   17
   Outline of Hebrews   18

The Superiority of the Son   25
   The Son as the Radiance of God's Glory (1:1–4)   26
   Jesus versus the Angels (1:5–14)   31
   Questions on This Chapter   36

Jesus Redeems His Brethren   41
   So Great a Salvation (2:1–4)   42
   Jesus as a Brother among Many (2:5–18)   46
   Questions on This Chapter   55

Greater Apostle, Greater Loss   59
   Moses a Servant, Jesus a Son (3:1–6)   60

Warning against Lack of Faith (3:7–19)	65
Questions on This Chapter	70

Entering God's Rest — 75
The Promise of Rest (4:1–13)	76
The Tempted High Priest (4:14–16)	83
Questions on This Chapter	87

The Ultimate High Priest — 91
A High Priest Called by God (5:1–10)	93
Milk for Infants, Solid Food for Adults (5:11–14)	101
Questions on This Chapter	103

Faith, Patience, and Attaining Promises — 107
The Consequences of Apostasy (6:1–12)	108
The Truthful Promises of God (6:13–20)	116
Questions on This Chapter	122

The True Melchizedek — 125
The Priesthood of Melchizedek	126
Melchizedek in Genesis 14	127
Melchizedek in Psalm 110	131
The Priesthood of Melchizedek in Hebrews	132
The Background of Psalm 110	136
The Significance of Melchizedek in Chapter 7	137
A Personal Note	141
Questions on This Chapter	142

The Minister of the New Covenant — 145
The Old as a Shadow of the New (8:1–6)	149
A New Covenant Ratified by Blood (8:7–13)	154
Jeremiah 31:31–34 in Its Old Testament Context	155
Fulfillment in the Old Testament	161
Fulfillment in the New Testament	161
Questions on This Chapter	164

A Sacrifice through the Eternal Spirit — 167
- Worship in the Earthly Tabernacle (9:1–10) — 168
- The Holy of Holies — 169
- The Holy Place — 173
- A Word of Edification — 176
- Ministry within the Tabernacle — 178
- Christ as the Mediator of the New Covenant (9:11–28) — 181
- Questions on This Chapter — 191

The First Abolished, the Second Established — 195
- The Single Sacrifice That God Desired (10:1–18) — 196
- Exhortation to Persevere (10:19–39) — 204
- Questions on This Chapter — 218

The Miracles and Tribulations of Faith — 221
- Faith Defined (11:1–3) — 222
- Abel, Enoch, and Noah (11:4–7) — 225
- Abraham (11:8–22) — 228
- Moses (11:23–28) — 235
- Other Heroes (11:30–32) — 239
- The Miracles of Faith (11:33–35) — 244
- Conquering Kingdoms — 245
- Quenching Fires — 247
- The Edge of the Sword — 248
- The Weak Made Strong — 249
- The Dead Received Alive — 252
- The Tribulations of Faith (11:35–40) — 253
- Accepting Torture — 253
- Chains and Imprisonment — 254
- Killed by the Edge of the Sword — 256
- Epilogue — 258
- Questions on This Chapter — 259

A New and Precious Covenant — 263
- God's Chastisement of His Children (12:1–13) — 264
- Holiness (12:14–17) — 268
- A Mountain Trembling (12:18–24) — 271

    Final Admonition (12:25–29)   276
    Questions on This Chapter   279

The Final Benediction   283
    Acceptable Sacrifices (13:1–6)   283
    Godly Leaders (13:7–9)   287
    A Different Altar (13:10–14)   289
    The Sacrifice of Praise (13:15–16)   291
    The Last Prayer and Benediction (13:17–25)   293
    Questions on This Chapter   296

Conclusion   297
    Questions on the Conclusion   302

My Personal Journey with Hebrews   305

About the Author   309

The Significance of the Book Cover   311

Scripture Reference Index   315

Subject and Name Index   325

Preface

The idea of writing this book has its roots in my coursework undertaken when I was a graduate student at Moody Theological Seminary in Chicago. As I spent countless hours researching various biblical topics, I consulted an enormous library of commentaries on every book of the Bible. One thing I noticed was that there were scarcely any books that aid Christian laity in understanding the biblical text without diving deeply into the original languages, theological and interpretive issues, or textual and literary criticism. Apart from commentaries, there was little the Christian reader could consult to help him or her understand the Bible with substance and simplicity.

During my studies, I compiled a writing body that included a few research papers on the Epistle of Hebrews. Before authoring those papers, I had not studied that epistle in depth. Though I was familiar with its content, Hebrews had not been among the books of the Bible that I focused on. By the end of my coursework, I had studied Hebrews more closely and eventually authored my final project on the theme of Jesus's priesthood in Hebrews. It was that paper that drew me closer to the heart of the epistle and to the heart of its author. It is to that pivotal moment in my journey to "search the Scriptures" that this book owes its origin.

The book you hold in your hands is not a commentary on Hebrews. Commentaries often include technical treatment of terms in their original languages. In this book you will not find many references to Hebrew or Greek except on a handful of occasions. Moreover, while most commentaries provide a verse-by-verse interpretation, this volume offers a chapter-by-chapter discussion of Hebrews. In other words, it is intended to serve as a reading companion for the epistle. In fact, I have written each chapter of this book as an expository sermon, the main emphasis of which is the biblical text itself. For this reason, I have provided practical applications for our lives today as modern-day Christians, whether in the body of each chapter or in the concluding questions.

In writing this book, I have one goal in mind: to help you read Hebrews with depth and understanding. Whether you are a teacher, preacher, or a member of the laity, it has something to offer you, provided you are looking to rise to new heights in your understanding of God's word. To do that, I have endeavored to help you connect Hebrews with the rest of the Bible. I believe that the best way to understand Scripture and appreciate its richness is to allow the Bible to interpret itself. One of the major obstacles Christians struggle with today is poor knowledge of Scripture. Our inability to connect various parts of the Bible to each other limits our understanding and prevents us from grasping the fullness of its beauty, the vibrance of its imagery, and the depth of its meaning.

Another area that I attempt to address in this book is our ability to read the Bible *critically*. By this I mean our ability to *interact* with the text as we read it. One way we may be able to interact with a text is to ask questions like: Why did the author choose to write this down? Why did he organize his thoughts this way? What is the link between this passage and the ones before and after it? Our ability to ask and answer these kinds of questions is what enables us to get into the mind of the author so we can understand what he intended to communicate.

We should recognize that the biblical authors did not just sit down and start writing. Though many of them, as far as we know, did not receive formal education in literature, theology, or hermeneutics, when we analyze the literary arrangement of their writings, it becomes evident that they were among the most talented writers ever known to mankind. Nothing of what they have written was arbitrary. They wrote with intentionality and organization that serve their overall message. For this reason, I have written this book not by tracing the topics or themes discussed in Hebrews but rather by following the biblical text as it appears in your Bible. In other words, I did not attempt to arrange the topics of Hebrews—the author has already done that for me; I only identified and traced them. Therefore, this book is not topical but textual.

As you read this book, I urge you to keep your Bible nearby. Before you begin reading each chapter, I encourage you to read the corresponding chapter of Hebrews first so that its content is fresh in your mind as you study it. This will allow you to get the most out of your reading experience. Reading this book in isolation of the biblical text would greatly compromise your ability to enjoy it. I assure you that I have kept my Bible open and close by on my desk as I wrote every word you are about to read.

Throughout this book I have used several modern Bible English translations, in each instance choosing what I felt was the best translation to capture the essence of the original text. All translations are noted with their acronyms, except verses quoted from the ESV, which is considered the default translation for this work. See the copyright page for a list of these acronyms. Italicized text within a biblical quotation is never italicized in the original. Such amendments are strictly mine and were added for emphasis.

To avoid confusing the chapter numbers from Hebrews with the chapter numbers from this book, I have divided the book into chapters that correspond to the chapter divisions of the epistle. Therefore, the first couple of sections of this book, which include introductory topics to the epistle, do not have chapter numbers. To allow for a fluid reading experience, I have used paragraph/section divisions that follow the sequence of each chapter of the epistle. In terms of style, capitalization, numbering, and formatting, I have adhered to the *Chicago Manual of Style* (17th edition) throughout this book.

Hebrews is a remarkably deep and rich epistle. I am often amazed at how the New Testament authors could pack so much depth and richness into just a couple of lines of text. Hebrews is what I would call a "heavyweight" epistle, comparable only to Romans in its theological richness and depth—but perhaps even more so. I have tried my best to articulate the biblical truth and synthesize major theological themes in as simple a manner as possible. As I firmly believe it is the written word of God, I approach the Bible with complete reverence; this has compelled me to give each chapter the thorough treatment it merits. Thus, you may find it necessary at times to read some chapters (or paragraphs) more than once to capture the full meaning of what I have attempted to articulate. I hope this book motivates you and sparks your interest to grab your Bible, "search the Scriptures," and do your own Bible study!

As we begin our journey, I encourage you to read this book prayerfully so that the LORD may speak to you personally through its words.

Acknowledgments

It would be remiss of me not to recognize all those who have contributed, in some capacity or another, to the writing and publishing of this book. First of all, I would like to thank the Lord, my rock and my strength, for supporting and leading me through this endeavor. Without the guidance of his Holy Spirit at every step, this book would never have come to light. I glorify his name and acknowledge his favor with every breath I take.

Second, I would like to thank my wife, Michelle, who has enormously helped in reviewing and proofreading, making suggestions along the way to help bring this book to its final form. Michelle has been a gift from the Lord in my life—my partner in doing his work.

I would also like to acknowledge both my parents, Albir and Isis, for their support and encouragement from the initial stages of this production and all along the way. Their reassurance was invaluable. They too were sent by God in my life to help guide me and lift me up when needed.

Finally, Jonathan Wright was instrumental in adding the final touches to the manuscript during the final editing process. His meticulousness and expertise were invaluable.

Introduction

The New Testament epistles are among the most frequently read and quoted books of the Bible. Yet they are among the least understood and the most misinterpreted. Much doctrine has been unearthed from these beautiful letters that contradicts sound biblical teaching found elsewhere in the Bible. This often stems from a serious lack of biblical knowledge and a deficiency in sound hermeneutics on the part of both the preachers and their audiences.

When reading Hebrews, this deficiency in scriptural knowledge plays an even more significant role. The epistle was written to converted Jewish Christians (equivalent to Messianic Jews in our modern day). Thus, it makes manifold references—either by allusion or direct quotation—to the Old Testament scriptures. Oftentimes, the author of Hebrews quotes the same passage from the Old Testament multiple times in the same chapter, and occasionally just a few verses later. In fact, Hebrews contains the single longest uninterrupted direct quotation of the Old Testament in the entire New Testament! Therefore, the reader's knowledge (or the lack thereof) of the Old Testament scriptures becomes vital when reading Hebrews. Hence, connecting Hebrews with its rich Old Testament context is key to understanding it. As a result and due to Hebrews' dense Old Testament theology, some portions of this book have been devoted to expositing the theological themes emerging from the Old Testament references in their original context. This will be essential to understanding the author's treatment of the Old Testament scriptures.

Since this book focuses on one of the epistles, it is important to state my position on the Bible as the word of God—especially since we live in an era when not every teacher or preacher of the Bible adheres to the same beliefs.

I wholeheartedly believe that the Bible we have today *is* the inerrant, unchangeable word of God, written by men of God under the inspiration of the Holy Spirit, and thus is God-breathed (2 Tim. 3:16). Although the Holy Spirit did not dictate the contents of the Bible word for word, he moved the biblical authors to pen what they wrote (2 Peter 1:20–21). Despite textual variants, the Bible is inerrant not only in the original autographs but also in the Bible we have today *to the extent* that it reflects the original writings. Any such variants do *not* invalidate the inerrancy of the Bible. God has preserved his written word, true and unchanged, for our generation and for the generations to come. Since it is the word of God, the Bible is unequivocally normative to the lives of all believers; it is true in all that it affirms, and none of it can be excluded, marginalized, or set aside as irrelevant or inapplicable in our modern day.

In terms of canonicity, I consider the canonical books of the Bible to be the thirty-nine books of the Old Testament from Genesis to Malachi. For the New Testament, they are the twenty-seven books from Matthew to Revelation. Though the Apocryphal books are valuable in terms of their historical and literary value, I do not consider them part of the biblical canon, nor do I believe they were inspired by God.

As you read Hebrews—or any other book of the Bible—remember that none of the books of the Bible were written with chapter or verse divisions.[1] The original audience read

---

[1] Chapters were introduced in the thirteenth century; verse divisions

the books of the Bible as free-flowing texts with no interruptions, the same way we read most other books today. These divisions—which are the addition of men—do not always coincide with units of thought. Oftentimes, a single unit of thought is divided between two verses, two chapters, or even two books with no regard to its unity. You will notice the effects of this throughout this book, but let me give you a few examples.

In Galatians 5, Paul lists nine manifestations of the fruit of the Spirit. Seven of them appear in verse 22 and two appear in verse 23. The last complete sentence in Psalm 10 speaks of the LORD inclining his ear to do justice on behalf of the orphan and the oppressed. In your Bible you will see that this complete sentence is inexplicably split between the end of verse 17 and the beginning of verse 18. The book of First Kings concludes by announcing Ahaziah as the king of Israel and as a successor to his father Ahab. Second Kings begins with the account of his falling through a lattice from his upper room and sustaining injuries. But perhaps there is no worse example than that of Acts 21 and 22. The conclusion of Acts 21 is Paul motioning with his hand to speak before a tumultuous crowd in Jerusalem. He begins speaking to them in the Hebrew language, "saying." (Acts 21:40). This is where the chapter inexplicably ends. What he said begins a new chapter (Acts 22). These thoughtless divisions of the biblical text interrupt the flow of thought as intended by the original authors, hinder our ability to follow their reasoning, and compromise our reading experience. Throughout this book it is my intention that we trace the common threads in the arguments presented by the author of Hebrews, regardless of chapter or verse divisions.

To clarify, in this work, I make a deliberate distinction between the all-caps "LORD" and "Lord." These terms are not synonymous in my writing. "LORD" refers specifically to the

were added in the sixteenth century.

personal name of God the Father as revealed to Moses in the Old Testament, often rendered as YHWH, in its Hebrew form, but properly pronounced *Adonai* (see Ex. 3:13–15; Isa. 42:8).[2] In contrast, "Lord" is primarily used in the New Testament to refer to our Lord Jesus Christ, derived from the Greek *kyrios*, which connotes *master* or a similar title. Thus, I have employed these terms with great care and precision throughout the book.[3]

Similarly, I draw a clear distinction between "the Word of God" and "the *word* of God." The former denotes the *person* of Jesus Christ, the second person of the Trinity, the Word of God, and the Son of God. The latter refers to the *written* word of God as conveyed in the Bible. While many within Western evangelical Christendom may not differentiate between these two terms, I find it crucial to do so, as they are not one and the same. For instance, our Lord Jesus has existed with the Father in eternity, as the Word of God, before the beginning of time (John 1:1; 17:5, 24). In contrast, the Bible was written by the hands of men, inspired by the Holy Spirit. Before Moses began writing Genesis, the written word of God did not yet exist. However, no Bible-believing Christian can (or should) say that there was ever a time when our Lord Jesus did not exist.

---

[2] In the Septuagint (the ancient Greek translation of the Old Testament), the Hebrew name YHWH is rendered as *ego eimi* (ἐγώ εἰμι), meaning "I am." (See chapter 10 for further discussion regarding the Septuagint translation and its influence on the New Testament writings.) As the Greek rendering of the Hebrew personal name of God, this phrase carries significant theological overtones. Since Jesus is fully God, sharing the same essence (being) with his Father, he shares all attributes, titles, and designations with the Father. In the Greek New Testament, *ego eimi* is used to refer to our Lord Jesus, often rendered as "I am he" or similar, thus affirming his deity by assigning to him the personal name of God in the Old Testament (see John 8:24; 13:19; Rev. 1:8).

[3] This distinction is observed in most English Bible translations. For example, in Psalm 110:1 God the Father (LORD) is speaking to God the Son (Lord), saying, "The LORD says to my Lord: 'Sit at my right hand, until I make your enemies your footstool.'"

Therefore, I have carefully and selectively used these terms as well.

We now turn to our study of Hebrews. We will start with a few introductory topics that will establish the context and the backdrop against which the epistle was written—all of which are crucial to understanding its content.

The Authorship of Hebrews

Before we begin reading Hebrews, some rather important questions must be addressed first. In many ways, Hebrews is more anonymous and mysterious compared to other epistles. For example, Hebrews does not tell us much about who wrote it, when it was written, or to whom it was addressed. I wish we had the usual Pauline-style introduction that specifies the author and his audience, but we do not have that luxury here. Therefore, some detective work is necessary to arrive at these answers.

Though some of the discussion below may seem unnecessary to some, I believe that a book about Hebrews (or any other book of the Bible for that matter) would not be complete without at least some high-level overview of these issues. I will not get into the details of the scholarly debates taking place in academic circles. (There are tons of books written on these topics!) Instead, I will briefly touch upon some of the key highlights and then move on to the content of the epistle itself.[4]

---

[4] The term *epistle* simply means "letter." Throughout this book I use both terms interchangeably.

Who Is the Author of Hebrews?

The first question we will address regarding Hebrews is its authorship. Since the letter itself does not name its author, this question goes back two thousand years. Quite early in the history of the church, we see this question being wrestled with, and several different proposals have been offered as to who the author may have been. In fact, Hebrews is unique in that it has more proposals for its authorship than any other book in the entire Bible! This is due, at least in part, to its importance in shaping New Testament theology.

When we look at the New Testament books, we notice that they are all authored by either a direct disciple of Jesus, such as John and Peter; an apostle, such as Paul; one of their close associates, such as Luke; or a close associate of Jesus himself, such as James and Jude. There is no New Testament book whose author falls outside these classifications. Thus, it is reasonable to assume that the author of Hebrews belongs to one of these categories as well.

In addition to being anonymous, Hebrews lacks a few other features when compared to other New Testament epistles, such as those of Paul's. For example, Hebrews does not specify its audience, it lacks the customary opening greeting common in other letters, and it does not open with the usual thanksgiving prayer. Though more succinct, its last chapter includes the typical Pauline conclusion, ending with exhortations, prayer requests, personal greetings, travel plans, and a mention of Timothy, Paul's close ministry and travel companion.

The first of the proposals put forth for Hebrews' authorship identifies Paul as the author. There is a strong early church tradition that asserts this view, especially among the Eastern church fathers. This proposal was postulated on the premise that Paul wanted to hide his identity as the author due to the animosity that the Jews of his time (his potential audience) harbored against him. This is unlikely, however, since Hebrews differs in style and language from that of Paul's as shown in his other, undisputed epistles. Some of these differences cannot be accounted for by simply assuming that Paul used a scribe or a writer. From its content, it is clear that the author of Hebrews knew his audience personally. This would be unlikely if Paul—being the author—intended to conceal his identity from the Jewish recipients of this epistle. Some early church fathers (as early as the second century) took the position that the thoughts and the theology of Hebrews belonged to Paul, but not its authorship.

The second of the proposals asserts that Luke was the writer of Hebrews. This is due to the well-refined Greek that appears in the epistle, since Hebrews has the most scholarly Greek found in all the New Testament. We know, however, that Luke wrote his gospel and Acts to the Gentile church, not to the Jews. Thus, this proposal remains a matter of pure speculation.

Others have proposed Clement of Rome as the author of Hebrews. Assuming he was the same Clement mentioned in Philippians 4:3, he was a close associate of Paul's. This remains a weak proposition since we know that Clement of Rome had written a letter to the Corinthians (not part of the New Testament) and that it lacks in style and eloquence when compared to Hebrews. Furthermore, we find no evidence among the writings of the Roman church fathers that Clement authored Hebrews (which we would expect to find had he indeed authored it).

Another proposal comes to us from an ancient church father by the name of Tertullian from the third century. Tertullian asserts that it was Barnabas who wrote Hebrews. His assertion is so matter-of-fact that he does not even give his readers any grounds for his claim. But this also remains highly speculative since we do not know any of what Barnabas may have written or spoken, as none of his writings or speeches (if there had been any) have survived. It is also significant that no other church father before or after Tertullian attached any importance to this claim. Apart from that, this view is unlikely for another reason. As a resident of Jerusalem, Barnabas likely saw and heard Jesus; but in speaking of the salvation we received, the author of Hebrews writes, "How shall we escape if we neglect such a great salvation? It was declared at first by the Lord, and it was attested to *us* by those who heard him" (Heb. 2:3). The pronoun *us* here implies that the author does not consider himself among those who saw the Lord in the flesh; this would not apply to Barnabas.

We now arrive at the last—and the most likely—proposal, and that is Apollos. We know Apollos from Paul's writings (1 Corinthians 1:12; 3:4, 22) and from Acts (see Acts 18:24–26; 19:1–2). It was Martin Luther who first made this appealing suggestion, and this view is the most widely accepted today. Apollos fits the description of being highly educated, eloquent, and well-versed in Scripture (see Acts 18:24–28). That he was well-versed in Alexandrian philosophy qualifies him to write with such reasoning and to craft such carefully constructed arguments. From the narrative we read in Acts, it is evident that Apollos had zeal for expounding and expositing the Old Testament scriptures, proving that Jesus is the Christ (Acts 18:28). This same zeal is what we read in Hebrews.

Given these proposals, then, who is the author of Hebrews? Some ancient and modern scholars adopt the view that we simply cannot say. Despite the difficulty in identifying the author, the epistle itself offers some clues to his background and his relationship to his readers. He knew his readers well and desired to be reunited with them again (Heb. 13:19). Both he and his audience knew Timothy (presumed to be the same Timothy associated with Paul. See Heb. 13:23). We also know that he was a male and from a Jewish background. Additionally, he was very well-schooled in the Old Testament and in the Jewish philosophical thinking of his time. He was also a talented writer of sophisticated Greek. Although his Greek is different from that of Paul's, his arguments bear many of the hallmarks of the Pauline theology. Thus, he must have been closely associated with Paul and well acquainted with his writings and thought.

While I cannot *name* the author of Hebrews for sure (to be Apollos or someone else), it seems plausible that Paul *supplied the ideas* contained in the epistle and that someone else put them into their present form (likely shortly after Paul's death). This suggests that the letter was composed from a then-recent (re)collection of Paul's teachings and thought. This explains the strong church tradition that intimately associates Paul with the author of Hebrews. It also explains the peculiarly similar theology between Hebrews and Paul's writings. Furthermore, it provides an adequate explanation of the differences in style and language between Hebrews and Paul's undisputed epistles. This view also accounts for the fact that the last chapter of the epistle is Pauline in style. For example, in 13:19 the author uses the first-person singular for the first time—something unique to Paul's writing style. The closing paragraph of the epistle is also distinctively Pauline. The final benediction in the last few verses is Paul's unique way of authenticating his epistles as his own writing. Although it may not be weighty evidence to many, the postscript appearing in some ancient translations (such as the KJV) suggests that the epistle was written from Italy by the hand of Timothy. If true, it is reasonable to assume that this epistle was written with Paul's involvement during his imprisonment in Rome, which further supports this view (see Acts 28). This is also sustained by the mention of "those from Italy" in 13:24.

Admittedly, all the proposals outlined above are exactly that—proposals. Except for Apollos, all other proposals do not explain the widespread, strong church tradition that Hebrews was a Pauline epistle (at least in its theology). This is a serious weakness in those proposals, given how pervasive that tradition was (though it was by no means universal). Even if Paul himself did not author the epistle, any acceptable suggestion must explain the presence of such a strong tradition in the early church. The most plausible proposal is the one that considers all the conflicting pieces of information and provides the best explanation for all of them.

Thus, we can conclude that whoever wrote Hebrews was remarkably close to Paul and drank from the fountain of knowledge of that great apostle! He was deeply familiar with Paul's theology and his intimate knowledge of the Scriptures, soaking it all like a sponge. Was it Apollos? Quite possibly. Was it someone else who traveled with Paul, heard him preach, read his other epistles, or even helped write them? Likely! Do we know who it was by name? No, we do not. Hence, for today's Christians, we can be confident that Hebrews was authored within the sphere of the apostolic tradition and affirmation. In other words, it falls within one of the categories of New Testament authors we identified at the beginning of this chapter. That we know with certainty! Thus, Hebrews is not an "exception" in terms of its authorship, nor is it *entirely* "anonymous." Therefore, today's church can be certain that what the first-century church left behind and documented for us in Hebrews is the inspired and authoritative word of God (2 Peter 1:20–21; 2 Tim. 3:16).

In the remainder of this book, I will refer to the author of Hebrews simply as "the author" or "the writer" interchangeably. Now that I have addressed the topic of authorship as it pertains to Hebrews, a couple of other topics remain that I must address first before we turn to the epistle itself.

The Audience, Purpose, and Date

Having now discussed the authorship of Hebrews, this chapter will examine other issues related to the epistle such as its original audience, date of writing, and purpose. Though in some cases the modern reader may not recognize the relevance and importance of these questions, they are crucial to understanding the content of the epistle itself.

To properly understand what any verse in the Bible means, we must first consider the author's intention when writing it and the perspective of his original audience. When reading any part of the Bible (or any other book for that matter), *the proper meaning of a sentence or a phrase cannot be something the author could not have intended to convey, or something his original audience could not have understood from the text.* Stated differently, whatever the intended meaning of the author is, it must be something that he could have conceivably had in view. It must also be something the original audience could have reasonably understood from the written text as it stands. This necessitates that we—as modern-day readers—assume the state of mind of both the author and his recipients in order for us to capture the proper meaning of the text as intended by its author. Thus, the importance of studying the circumstances that surrounded the writing process and the background of the audience cannot be overstated.

Who Were the Recipients of Hebrews?

From the context and the content of Hebrews, it is certain that the recipients were Jews who had converted to Christianity, leaving behind their Jewish faith and ritualistic practices. It is also evident that the original audience of the epistle was at risk of reverting to their previous Jewish tradition. It is not clear why they were at risk of this backsliding. They may have been under pressure from the Jewish community where they lived, or they may have been facing external persecution for being Christians. It is not clear. What is clear, however, is their familiarity with the Old Testament scriptures, as seen from the author's use of Old Testament references without needing to explain them. When we observe the depth of those references, it becomes evident that the original recipients were as familiar with the Old Testament scriptures—and their theology—as the author himself.

There is one small detail that may give us some indication of where the audience was located. In 13:24 the author writes, "Those from Italy send you greetings." The Greek of this verse could mean "those who *live* here in Italy," in which case the author would be writing from Italy to the Jewish Christians elsewhere (possibly Israel, since by that time it had a large Jewish Christian community). The phrase could also mean "those who *are* [originally] from Italy," in which case the author would be writing from outside Italy to an audience in Italy (or also elsewhere). The most natural interpretation, however, is that the author was writing from Italy to an audience located elsewhere. (See the previous chapter for our discussion on authorship.)

From the context of the letter, we know that the audience was not scattered over a large geographical area but was localized to a specific city or region. This can be discerned from the way the author addresses the audience as a specific group of people whom he knows. He also sends specific greetings to them from specific individuals (chapter 13). Moreover, he refers to the work and love they showed toward God by their serving his saints (Heb. 6:10). In 10:32 he exhorts his audience to recall their sufferings and struggles after they were enlightened (by the light of Christ). More importantly, he expresses his desire and intention to visit them (Heb. 13:19, 23). This specificity tells us that they lived in a particular locale and were not just a dispersed group. Thus, although we cannot pinpoint the exact audience of this epistle, we know they were Christians of Jewish descent residing in a specific locale.

But what prompted the author to compose this epistle and send it to them?

Why Was Hebrews Written?

Despite its heavy use of the Old Testament scriptures, Hebrews is the most Christ-centered book of the entire New Testament and the Bible at large! One cannot read Hebrews without noticing the predominance of Jesus as the Son of God and the sacrificial lamb. Without exception, every argument made throughout the entire letter has one aim and one aim only, and that is to show that the person of Jesus of Nazareth is the ultimate fulfillment of the Old Testament scriptures and is the center of God's redemptive plan for mankind.

Because it repeatedly makes use of Psalm 110, some interpreters have come to view Hebrews as a commentary on that psalm. But as we will see later, though he offers a thorough exposition on some key Old Testament passages, the intention of the author goes far beyond simply providing a commentary on those passages. Expositing these passages is a means to bolster his argument, but it does not constitute the core of his thesis. So what is the main purpose of the author for writing this letter?

I stated above that Hebrews was written to a group of Jewish Christians who were at risk of abandoning their faith and sliding back to Judaism. The writer's main concern (as will become evident) was to caution them against that backsliding and to provide them with a series of comparisons between Jesus and revered Old Testament figures such as Moses, Aaron, and the like. The author begins his argument by comparing Jesus to the angels of heaven, showing his infinite superiority. This superiority can be termed using the word *better*. Jesus offers his followers better hope, better covenant, better promises, better sacrifices, better plan for salvation, and so on. This "better" theme is designed to encourage the recipients to remain steadfast in their Christian faith and not revert to their former Jewish practices.

This hortatory tone is prevalent in many sections of Hebrews. The epistle is filled with moral exhortations urging the audience to maintain their Christian faith and values. In some instances, the author employs warnings and admonitions instead of encouragement to ensure that his message is conveyed as clearly and forcefully as possible. This approach underscores the depth of his concern for their salvation and spiritual well-being.

If I had to sum up what the letter to the Hebrews is in a single phrase, it would be this: a sermon of exhortation. When read in a single sitting (something I strongly encourage you to do), Hebrews does feel like a sermon.[5] But it is a sermon writ-

---

[5] Reading large sections or even entire books of the Bible uninterrupted by chapter and verse divisions is an experience I sincerely hope you will take time to enjoy. In addition to providing a pleasant reading experience, this approach allows you to absorb and comprehend Scripture in well-connected portions, discerning the literary and theological themes that weave them all together. In recent years, a few different formats of the Bible have been released that aim to provide their readers with this enjoyable experience. One such format that I highly recommend is the Biblio-

ten by a shepherd who is immensely concerned for the salvation of his readers (precisely how every good shepherd should be!)

When Was Hebrews Written?

Most New Testament books are hard to date; Hebrews is no different. Like the issue of authorship (addressed in the previous chapter), dating Hebrews has also been a subject of debate. Without delving into the complex scholarly debates surrounding the dating of Hebrews, it is reasonably concluded that it was written before the year AD 70. Why this date in particular? This is the date when Jerusalem and its temple were destroyed and burned to the ground by the hand of Titus, a Roman general—and later an emperor—who was put in charge by his father, Emperor Vespasian, of suppressing the Jewish revolt. Titus crushed the Jewish revolt, leveled Jerusalem to the ground, and burned its temple. His victory was later commemorated by the still-standing Arch of Titus (erected in AD 80) at the entrance to the Roman Forum.

This historical context is crucial when dating Hebrews. Even a cursory reading of the epistle suggests that it was composed while the Jewish worship and sacrificial system was still operational (see Heb. 7:27–28; 8:3–5; 9:7–8, 25; 10:1–3; 13:10–11). This scenario would be improbable if the Jerusalem temple—the core of the Jewish Levitical and sacrificial system—had already been destroyed at the time of writing. Another compelling piece of evidence comes from the overarching theme of the epistle, which underscores the superiority of Jesus as the initiator of the "new covenant" and all that he introduced, including the superiority of his sacrifice, priesthood, and promises. Had the temple already been destroyed, the author would have undoubtedly used its destruction to highlight

theca Edition, published by Writ Press and designed by Adam Lewis Greene. Owning this set has transformed the way I personally read and experience Scripture.

the transient and inferior nature of the old system, particularly since the temple was central to the sacrifices, priesthood, and all related ordinances of the "old covenant." Yet Hebrews makes no mention of the temple's destruction, which strongly suggests that the temple was still intact when the epistle was written.

However, knowing that Hebrews was written before AD 70 does not precisely pinpoint its date of composition. As with most biblical texts, the best we can do is establish a likely date range. For Hebrews, this range is probably between AD 68 and AD 70. The rationale for AD 70 as the latest possible date has already been discussed. But why consider AD 68 as the earliest?

The content of the epistle itself suggests that it was intended to bolster the faith of Jewish Christians who might have been faltering after some time had elapsed since their conversion. In Hebrews 13:7, the author notes that the individuals who first brought the gospel to the original recipients had passed away (possibly through martyrdom), likely including key church figures like James, Peter, and Paul, who were martyred before AD 68. Additionally, Hebrews 13:23 mentions that Timothy had been released from prison, a likely event following Emperor Nero's death in AD 68. The absence of any mention of Paul alongside Timothy implies that Paul might have already been martyred when the letter was written. Therefore, the epistle must have been composed sometime after AD 68 but before AD 70.

Outline of Hebrews

In our modern Bibles, Hebrews consists of thirteen chapters. However, when the letter was originally written, such divisions did not exist (this is true for all books of the Bible). Chapter-and-verse divisions were introduced starting in the 13th century, making them a relatively recent addition. Often, these divisions disrupt the reading experience and hinder our understanding of the text's coherence and unity. (Imagine reading any book—this one included—in which every few lines or paragraphs were arbitrarily assigned a chapter label!) Addressing this issue is one of the primary motivations behind the creation of this book.

To fully grasp the content of Hebrews' thirteen chapters, it is essential to recognize how the thoughts and ideas within the epistle are organized. This understanding is facilitated by an outline of the letter, such as the one presented below. It is important to note that the transitions between ideas do not always align with the chapter divisions found in modern Bibles. In other words, chapter divisions do not necessarily coincide with shifts in the author's thoughts or thematic breaks. Consequently, a complete unit of thought might commence in one chapter and conclude in another, or several thematic elements might begin and end within a single chapter.

The outline below offers a two-tiered depiction of the concepts and themes in Hebrews (that is, a general title followed by one or more subheadings). A detailed outline has been deliberately avoided here as it can sometimes be counterproductive. The presented outline reflects my interpretation of the divisions within Hebrews. Creating an outline for a biblical book is more an art than a science, subject to individual interpretation. It is not uncommon for readers and scholars to develop different outlines for the same text, and such diversity of perspectives is expected. In fact, as you read through the epistle, I encourage you to create your own outline. Consider penciling in your thoughts and interpretations next to each paragraph in your Bible, identifying the key ideas or themes you discern. The primary aim here is to aid your comprehension and appreciation of the text. The outline provided is intended merely as a visual tool to help organize the epistle's content in your mind as you read. This outline corresponds to—but does not exactly match—the chapter titles and subheadings used in this book. For convenience, chapter-and-verse references are included for each section of the outline.

I. The Superiority of the Son (1:1–14)
   a. The Son as the Radiance of God's Glory (1:1–4)
   b. Jesus versus the Angels (1:5–14)
II. Jesus Redeems His Brethren (2:1–18)
   a. So Great a Salvation (2:1–4)
   b. Jesus as a Brother among Many (2:5–18)
III. Greater Apostle, Greater Loss (3:1–19)
   a. Moses a Servant, Jesus a Son (3:1–6)
   b. Warning against Lack of Faith (3:7–19)
IV. Entering God's Rest (4:1–16)
   a. The Promise of Rest (4:1–13)
   b. The Tempted High Priest (4:14–16)
V. The Ultimate High Priest (5:1–14)
   a. A High Priest Called by God (5:1–10)
   b. Milk for Infants, Solid Food for Adults (5:11–14)
VI. Faith, Patience, and Attaining Promises (6:1–20)
   a. The Consequence of Apostasy (6:1–12)
   b. The Truthful Promises of God (6:13–20)
VII. The True Melchizedek (7:1–28)
   a. Melchizedek the High Priest (7:1–10)
   b. Jesus as the High Priest after the Order of Melchizedek (7:11–28)
VIII. Christ as the Minister of the New Covenant (8:1–13)
   a. The Old Covenant as a Shadow (8:1–6)
   b. A New Covenant Inaugurated (8:7–13)
IX. A Sacrifice through the Spirit (9:1–28)
   a. Worship in the Earthly Tabernacle (9:1–10)
   b. Christ as the Mediator of the New Covenant (9:11–28)
X. The First Abolished, the Second Established (10:1–39)
   a. The Single Sacrifice That God Desired (10:1–18)
   b. Exhortation to Persevere (10:19–39)
XI. The Miracles and Tribulations of Faith (11:1–40)
   a. Faith Defined (11:1–3)

b. The Miracles of Faith (11:4–34)
   c. The Tribulations of Faith (11:35–40)
XII. A New and Precious Covenant (12:1–29)
   a. God's Chastisement of His Children (12:1–13)
   b. Rejecting the Grace of God (12:14–29)
XIII. Conclusion (13:1–25)
   a. Final Exhortations (13:1–19)
   b. Prayer (13:20–21)
   c. Greetings (13:22–25)

CHAPTER ONE

Hebrews 1:1–14

"For to which of the angels did God ever say, 'You are my Son, today I have begotten you?'"

—Hebrews 1:5

The Superiority of the Son

The letter to the Hebrews begins with a rather unusual opening. When we read the first few sentences of Hebrews, we feel a sense of urgency and concern for the original audience, which compels the author to spend no time or writing space on greetings and introductions. For instance, the author does not identify himself or his audience, as discussed previously. Typically, letters begin with some form of opening in which the writer states his reasons for writing. If the author personally knows his audience (as is the case with Hebrews), he typically includes a greeting with a few regards to his audience. This is true of all other New Testament letters except for 1 John. But we find none of that here. From the opening line of this epistle, the writer immediately moves to introducing his argument.

His concern for his audience was the writer's main reason for skipping any introductory remarks, especially when we consider that he does the same thing again in the unusually short greeting at the end of the epistle. He remarks on his brevity at the end of the letter by saying, "Through few words I have written to you" (Heb. 13:22, YLT). We see something similar in Jude's letter, in which he states that he had planned to write about the common salvation he shares with his readers, but instead was later compelled to write to them about the false teachers who had infiltrated the church (Jude 3).

That the author of Hebrews starts immediately by comparing Jesus's superiority to that of angels tells us that this topic had occupied the forefront of his mind as he began writing. It should be noted that he spends more time comparing Jesus to angels than to Moses, Aaron, or anyone else. Later in the epistle, we will see that his comparisons to Moses and Aaron come as an afterthought. If Jesus is shown to be superior to all angels, he will be shown superior to all Old Testament prophets and priests. Thus, by comparing Jesus's glory to that of the angels, the author begins to build his argument from the ground up.

The Son as the Radiance of God's Glory (1:1–4)

The first paragraph of the epistle puts Jesus in his rightful place as the Son of God. The writer separates Jesus from all prophets by contrasting how God had spoken to mankind through them and how he spoke through Jesus as his only Son. Through the prophets God spoke "in many and various ways," but in Jesus he spoke directly and without mediation. As the Son of God, Jesus truly *is* the very image of God. Later in the epistle, the author shows how all that had been set in the law and spoken through the prophets was but a shadow of the real image that would be later revealed in Jesus. The expression the author uses to state this is profound. Most English translations struggle to accurately capture the depth and the beauty of Hebrews 1:3. The King James translation renders it best when it states that Jesus is the Son of God *"being* the brightness of [God's] glory, and the express image of his person" (Heb. 1:3, KJV).

Some translations use the word *reflect* to render this verse, but this is inaccurate. Jesus does not merely "reflect" the glory of God or his image. Moses did that when he had to cover his face with a veil, because the glory of God had been so imprinted on his face that the Israelites could not look directly at him (Exod. 34:33–35; see also 2 Cor. 3:13). In 2 Corinthians 3, Paul speaks of the literal veil that covered Moses's face and of the metaphorical veil that still covers the hearts and minds of the Jews when they read the books of the Old Testament (or the "old covenant"). That veil, says Paul, is taken away, set aside, or made obsolete in Christ alone (2 Cor. 3:13–14). Recall how the veil of the temple was torn from top to bottom after Jesus gave up his spirit on the cross (Matt. 27:51). Moses reflected the glory of God; but Jesus *is* the glory of God! Not only that, but he is the *brightness* of that glory. We can see the light of the sun from behind the clouds on an overcast day, but that is vastly different than looking straight at the bright disk of the sun on a clear, sunny day. In other words, in him we see the *fullness* of that glory manifested. Jesus does not simply carry a part of God's glory—he embodies it in its fullness. Paul puts it like this in Colossians: "For in him dwells all the *fullness* of the Godhead bodily" (Col. 2:9).

In the latter part of verse 3 the author of Hebrews makes an equally profound assertion of who Jesus is. Jesus is said to be "the express image of [God's] person" (KJV). I like how Young's Literal Translation renders this phrase: "the impress of His subsistence" (YLT). Jesus himself said it this way when Philip asked to see the Father: "He who has seen me has seen the Father" (John 14:9, RSV). It is important to note the immense difference between *bearing* the image of God and *being* the image of God. This difference goes much further than pure semantics. Merely bearing God's image means that one becomes a copy or an imprint of the *original*. But *being* God's image means that one *is* the original from which a copy or an imprint can be made. Paul affirms this reality when he says that Jesus is the Son of God's love, "who is the image of the invisible God, first-born of all creation" (Col. 1:15, YLT). What could not be beheld of God's being and glory was fully manifested in Jesus.

"Who being the brightness of his glory, and the express image of his person, and upholding all things by the word of his power, when he had by himself purged our sins, sat down on the right hand of the Majesty on high" (Heb. 1:3, KJV).

Photo Credit: Mithi Creation/Shutterstock.com

Man was created in God's own image and after his likeness (Gen. 1:26; 5:1). But man only *bore* the image of God; he never *was* the image of God. We later learn that sin caused man to lose that original image after which he had been created. It is quite telling that Genesis 5 begins by reiterating that man was created after God's likeness (Gen. 5:1) but a few verses later we read that Adam "begat a son in his *own likeness, after his image*, and called his name Seth" (Gen. 5:3, KJV). Having been deceived by the serpent and fallen into sin and disobedience, man lost the image and likeness he originally had—that of God himself. Jesus, being the true and full image of God, came so that those who believe in him can take on *his* image and thus regain the image of God they once had and lost. This is what Paul tries to capture when he writes, "For those whom he foreknew he also predestined to be conformed *to the image of his Son*, in order that he might be the first-born among many brethren" (Rom. 8:29, RSV).

In the second half verse 3 we find a bold claim regarding Jesus's divinity. Jesus is said to be upholding (sustaining) all things by the word of his power (literally, "by the word of his might"). There is no stronger claim of Jesus's deity than this. In Revelation, John saw the twenty-four elders casting down their crowns before him who is seated upon the throne, "who lives forever and ever" saying, "You are worthy, our Lord and God, to receive glory and honor and power, for you created all things, and by your will they existed and were created" (Rev. 4:11, NRSV). In speaking of how the LORD created the earth and all the inhabitants of the world, the psalmist says:

> By the word of the LORD the heavens were made, and all their host by the breath of his mouth. He gathered the waters of the sea as in a bottle; he put the deeps in storehouses. Let all the earth fear the LORD, let all the inhabitants of the world stand

in awe of him! For he spoke, and it came to be; he commanded, and it stood forth. (Ps. 33:6–9, RSV)

Thus, to say that Jesus sustains and upholds all things by the word of his power means that Jesus's word is equal to that of God's. This is an unequivocal claim of Jesus's divinity in this opening chapter of Hebrews. Through this early assertion of Jesus's deity, the author of Hebrews lays the foundation for all the subsequent affirmations he is about to make about the Son of God as high priest and the initiator and finisher of his faith and ours.

The following couple of verses employ rich rhetoric and vivid imagery. The author here uses colorful and vibrant language to depict Jesus's ascension and his sitting at the right hand of the Majesty in heaven:

When he had by himself purged our sins, sat down on the right hand of the Majesty on high. (Heb. 1:3, KJV)

Notice the rich imagery and the majestic phraseology used here compared to how Paul states it in plain, almost flat language:

That power is the same as the mighty strength he exerted when he raised Christ from the dead and seated him at his right hand in the heavenly realms. (Eph. 1:19–20, NIV)

Writing to the Colossians, Paul uses similar language that is far less poetic than that of Hebrews:

Since, then, you have been raised with Christ, set your hearts on things above, where Christ is, seated at the right hand of God. (Col. 3:1, NIV)[6]

---

[6] These are examples of how the language and phrases used in Hebrews differ significantly from that of Paul's, suggesting that he did not write this epistle. See the chapter on the authorship of Hebrews.

In language like Paul's, Peter writes something similar when speaking of water baptism:

> It saves you by the resurrection of Jesus Christ, who has gone into heaven and is at God's right hand—with angels, authorities and powers in submission to him. (1 Peter 3:21–22, NIV)

We will return to the significance of Jesus's sitting at the right hand of the Father in later chapters. But for our purposes here, suffice it to say that the priests in the Old Testament never performed any service or duty inside the tabernacle (or the temple) while seated. They always *stood* in the presence of the LORD. Sitting down signifies that one's work has been completed. The work in the Old Testament (atoning for sins) was never completed. This is why when Jesus presented the true sacrifice that truly atones for sins, he was able to enter the presence of his Father and *sit* at his right hand, for he said on the cross, "It is finished" (John 19:30). The writer of Hebrews uses this language later to signify our entering the LORD's "rest." He rested when he finished his work; we rest when we enter his presence to find salvation by the work that he has finished for us.

The phrase used here by the author of Hebrews is intended to show how much more superior Jesus's ascending to heaven is, compared to the angels who are also in heaven. Jesus occupies a far greater position than that of any angel or heavenly being. With passion and eloquence, the writer immediately proceeds to quote from the Old Testament scriptures to prove exactly that.

Jesus versus the Angels (1:5–14)

The next section of the letter begins with a direct quotation from Psalm 2, one of the most Messianic passages in all the Old Testament. In fact, this psalm contains one of two *explicit* mentions of the divine Son of God in the entire Old Testament (Ps. 2:12).[7] A few other passages in the Old Testament speak of *a* son (such as Isa. 7:14; 9:6), but these two are the only passages that contain *express* mention of *the* Son of God.

Here Psalm 2:7 is quoted: "You are my Son; today I have begotten you." Besides Hebrews, this verse is quoted one other time, in Acts 13:33. In that passage, Paul is preaching (with Barnabas) in a Jewish synagogue in Antioch of Pisidia. As Paul preaches the core message of the gospel to the Jews there, he quotes Psalm 2:7 in reference to the resurrection of Jesus from the dead. In his mind, Jesus was confirmed to be the Son of God when the Father raised him from the dead. Though Jesus is the eternal Son of God, it was at his resurrection from the dead that he was so "designated" to *us* beyond doubt. In Romans, Paul writes that Jesus "was descended from David according to the flesh and *designated* Son of God in power according to the Spirit of holiness *by his resurrection from the dead*" (Rom. 1:3–4, RSV). This is an appointment, a designation that no one else (man or angel) has received. This revelation (among many others) is what the author of Hebrews uses to show Jesus's superiority to every other earthy or heavenly being. Having established Jesus's status, the writer shifts his focus, in turn, to the angels of heaven to establish their rank. He proceeds to quote other Scriptures, but this time to show the position of angels.

Quoting directly from Psalm 104, the author asserts that the angels of heaven are but mere ministers (servants) of the LORD (Ps. 104:4). Though not directly quoted here, other Old Testament references come to illustrate this same concept, the most significant of which is Daniel 7. In that chapter, we are told of the Ancient of Days, who took his seat where "a thousand thousands served him, and ten thousand times ten thousand stood before him" (Dan. 7:10). This imagery is identical to what John the Seer beholds and describes later in Revelation, saying, "Then I looked, and I heard around the throne

---

[7] The only other direct reference to the Son of God is in Proverbs 30:4.

and the living creatures and the elders the voice of many angels, numbering myriads of myriads and thousands of thousands" (Rev. 5:11).

At this pivotal point, the skillful writer of Hebrews makes a significant shift by quoting a key verse from Psalm 45: "Your throne, O God, is forever and ever. The scepter of your kingdom is a scepter of uprightness" (Ps. 45:6). But notice that before he quotes that verse, he writes, "But of the Son he says" (Heb. 1:8). Though the psalm itself does not explicitly state that this was spoken of the Son, it is self-evident from the context, for later in that psalm we read, "Therefore God, your God, has anointed you with the oil of gladness above your fellows" (Ps. 45:7, RSV). For this reason, the author of Hebrews is careful to include this latter part of the verse in his quotation. Thus, the author here is solidifying his argument that the Son is equal to God.

The divinity of the Son is further proven by yet another Old Testament quote, also from the Psalter, but this time from Psalm 102. It reads,

> Of old you laid the foundation of the earth, and the heavens are the work of your hands. They will perish, but you will remain; they will all wear out like a garment. You will change them like a robe, and they will pass away, but you are the same, and your years have no end. (Ps. 102:25–27)

The significance of this quotation here is that it proves—through Scripture—that God is the creator of all and is everlasting. But the author of Hebrews has already asserted that the Son was himself partaker of creating with God, for he says that *through* the Son "[God] also created the worlds" (Heb. 1:2, NRSV). It becomes now evident that the Son is equal with God the creator!

In his gospel, John uses the same reasoning to prove the deity of the Word, for in the first verse of his gospel he says,

"In the beginning was the Word, and the Word was with God, *and the Word was God*" (John 1:1). Then, as in Hebrews, he supports his assertion by stating that through the Word the world itself came into being: "*All* things were made by him; and without him was not any thing made that was made" (John 1:3).

It is important to note that the author of Hebrews quotes from Psalm 102 not simply to prove that the Son is equal to God by being a creator himself. He intends to prove more than that. Here he quotes not one but three full verses from Psalm 102 (vv. 25–27). But for what purpose? The latter half of his quotation affirms the *everlasting nature of God* (Ps. 102:26–27). Recall that just a couple of verses earlier (Heb. 1:8), he quotes from Psalm 45:6—"Your throne, O God, is forever and ever" and applies it to the Son. By doing so, the author here asserts the *Son's* everlasting nature. Thus, the Son here is shown to be co-eternal with God. The author leaves no room for doubt that the Son is *fully* equal with the Father in both the creative work *and* eternality.

In these verses (Heb. 1:10–12), it is crucial to notice the literary shift in the writer's argument. Notice the beauty and the mastery of what he does here! When he speaks of God's creating the heavens and the earth, he is building more than just a convincing argument for the divinity of the Son and his equality with God, and he is asserting more than the superiority of Jesus to angels by being equal to God. *Having established that the Son is far more superior to angels and that they are the servants of God, he is now establishing that, since the Son is equal to God, not only is the Son far greater than angels but the angels themselves are also servants to the Son.* In other words, he is affirming the angels' *servitude* to the Son.

Finally, to conclude this beautifully crafted passage, the author closes with yet another quote from another richly Messianic psalm, and that is Psalm 110, which opens with one of the most theologically rich verses in the entire Bible: "The

LORD says to my Lord: 'Sit at my right hand, till I make your enemies your footstool'" (Ps. 110:1). This psalm, almost in its entirety, is spoken by God the Father and was quite known in the Jewish circles to be exclusively Messianic (meaning that it applies to the awaited Messiah only, not to any of the kings of Israel). Thus, when our Lord Jesus challenged the Jews regarding this psalm and asked them how David, by the Spirit, spoke of the Messiah, the Son of David, as his Lord, none of them could return an answer:

> Now while the Pharisees were gathered together, Jesus asked them a question, saying, "What do you think of the Christ? Whose son is he?" They said to him, "The son of David." He said to them, "How is it then that David, inspired by the Spirit, calls him Lord, saying, 'The LORD said to my Lord, Sit at my right hand, till I put thy enemies under thy feet'? If David thus calls him Lord, how is he his son?" And no one was able to answer him a word, nor from that day did any one dare to ask him any more questions. (Matt. 22:41–46)

Notice here that not one of them dared refute what Jesus said by claiming that this psalm was not Messianic, for that was beyond debate.

Knowing that David here spoke of the Messiah, the writer of Hebrews settles his argument by reaffirming that this too was never spoken to any of the angels of God. To demonstrate the exclusivity of God's promises to his Son, the author here uses the same phrase he used in verse 5: "For to which of the angels did [God] ever say...?" (Heb. 1:5, 13). The glory and honor that God the Father has bestowed upon his Son, Jesus, has never been conferred upon any of the angels. This clearly differentiates Jesus from the angels of heaven and affirms his exclusive and unique sonship to the Father. This dismantles any claims that Jesus—at some point of his existence—was an angel (or an archangel), later exalted by the Father to a higher rank, as adopted by some sects who nevertheless claim adherence to the Bible as Scripture. Christ's preincarnate identity as the second person of the Trinity who is co-eternal, co-creator, and co-enthroned with the Father is hereby established beyond doubt. This brings the writer's argument to a powerful conclusion: Jesus, as the Son of God, is equal to God and is infinitely superior to all angels.

Now, after making a compelling case for the superiority of Jesus from Scripture, the writer begins unpacking what that signifies to the New Testament believers—especially to his original readers who come from Jewish descent. For that discussion we now turn to chapter 2 of this epistle.

Questions on This Chapter

At the end of each chapter I will offer you a few questions related to the content of that chapter. The purpose of these questions is to encourage you to engage with this book—but more importantly, with the Scriptures. I realize that most readers tend to skip these sections altogether, but I hope and pray that in this case you do not. I urge you to read the questions and meditate on them the next time you open your Bible to spend time in God's presence.

Some of the questions that will be asked may be viewed as "prompts" or "motivators" to help you approach Scripture differently and with a fresh perspective, instead of "questions" to be answered. To get the most out of these questions, pray about them, think about them, and meditate on them. They are not questions or prompts that I expect you to address immediately as you read them. But I am confident that if you pray about them, the Lord will open your eyes to see how they may change the way you read his word. When the Holy Spirit guides you to find answers to these questions, write down the questions and the answers in a journal or a small notebook. Over the months and years, you will have a wealth of Holy Spirit-inspired revelations for Scripture reading. Here are the questions on this chapter:

1. Do you believe that Jesus is the Son of God who is equal to his Father? Why or why not?

2. What does it mean to you that Jesus is the Son of God? Is Jesus someone you have only heard of, or is he someone you know personally?

3. If challenged, can you provide evidence from the Scriptures to support your beliefs regarding who Jesus is?

Chapter Two

Hebrews 2:1–18

"But we see him who for a little while was made lower than the angels, namely Jesus, crowned with glory and honor because of the suffering of death, so that by the grace of God he might taste death for everyone."

—Hebrews 2:9

Jesus Redeems His Brethren

In contrast to exalting Jesus as the Son of God above all the angels of heaven, in this second chapter the author emphasizes Jesus's humbling himself to be counted among his brethren—those who believe in him. In the new state that Jesus took for himself through his incarnation, he now—for his time on earth—has become lower than the angels, who are his servants, as the author has just explained in the previous chapter.

The author here provides us with a rich theological treatise that echoes Paul's theological arguments elsewhere in the New Testament. What we are about to read in this second chapter of the epistle is one of the richest passages in the entire Bible in terms of its eloquence and depth.

So Great a Salvation (2:1–4)

In the first few verses of this chapter, we read one of several admonitions to the original audience. Concerned for their salvation and for the possibility of their rejecting their Christian faith, the writer warns his readers to take heed lest they be found guilty of rejecting the salvation wrought by the Son of God. Attempting to get his audience to recognize the gravity of rejecting Jesus's salvific work, the author speaks of the value of the salvation Jesus offered. The greater the work, the greater the sin of rejecting it! This warning is especially important, coming on the heels of the author's previous argument, showing the majesty and exaltation of the Son of God—Jesus—who died to secure such redemption.

In his usual style, the first building block the writer uses here to construct his argument points back to the Old Testament. In verse 2 he speaks of "the message declared by angels" (RSV). This allusion points to the receiving of the Old Testament law by the hand of angels. Speaking of the law, Paul says, "It was ordained by angels through an intermediary" (Gal. 3:19, RSV). We also read in Acts that before he was stoned to death, Stephen rebuked the Jews, saying, "You who received the law as delivered by angels and did not keep it" (Acts 7:53, RSV). But how was the law delivered to Moses by angels?

Earlier in Stephen's extended speech he speaks of how God appeared to Moses in the burning bush. Stephen says, "Now when forty years had passed, an *angel* appeared to him in the wilderness of Mount Sinai, in the flame of a burning bush" (Acts 7:30, RSV). Stephen uses the same expression again in Acts 7:35. The term *angel* in Hebrew (*malakh*) simply means a "messenger" (whether a literal angel that the LORD sends to perform an action or convey a message, or the appearance of the LORD himself manifested). This term is used frequently in the Old Testament to signify God's appearance and manifestation in a visible form. It was the "angel" of the

Jesus Redeems His Brethren

LORD who stayed Abraham's hand from sacrificing his son, Isaac, and who swore by himself that he would bless him and multiply his seed (see Gen. 22:11–18). It was also the "angel" of the LORD who appeared to the Israelites in Bochim to remind them of his promise to give the land to their fathers and to rebuke them for not killing all the inhabitants of the land of Canaan as he had commanded them (Judges 2:1–5). From the context, the speaker in both cases was none other than the LORD himself. (For other references see also Gen. 16:10; Judges 6:22; and others.)

An illustration showing God handing Moses the two tablets of the Ten Commandments. According to the Bible, this event was accompanied by angels, as portrayed here.

Photo Credit: Morphart/shutterstock.com

43

We also find an intriguing account of God appearing specifically to Moses when he received the law. In his farewell blessing of the Israelites, Moses says, "The LORD came from Sinai, and dawned from Seir upon us; he shone forth from Mount Paran. With him were myriads of holy ones; at his right, a host of his own" (Deut. 33:2, NRSV). This reference shows how the law was given to Moses and to the Israelites by the LORD himself in the presence of his angels (see Ps. 68:17). Thus, the author of Hebrews here describes how the law was given by the LORD in the presence of his heavenly host, with the fullness of his glory visibly manifested.

With all that glory, those who disobeyed the law were held guilty in the eyes of the LORD. The examples are many in the Old Testament. The book of Numbers tells us how a man who had been found gathering sticks on the Sabbath was stoned to death (Num. 15:32–36; see also Deut. 17:2–5, 12). The point here is that though abiding by the Old Testament law could not provide atonement for sins or justification, none of those who dared to violate it were held blameless before the LORD (see Rom. 3:20; Gal. 2:16; 3:11).

In this context, it is important to observe the significance of the mention of angels. Whereas the old covenant was delivered by brief and occasional appearances of the LORD among his angels—who, as the author just asserted in the previous chapter, are far lower than Jesus—the new covenant was inaugurated by Jesus himself, who, being the Word of God, tabernacled among us in the flesh, and now permanently dwells in us:

> And the Word became flesh and dwelt among us, and we have seen his glory, glory as of the only Son from the Father, full of grace and truth. (John 1:14)

> I have been crucified with Christ. It is no longer I who live, but Christ who lives in me. (Gal. 2:20)

Both Jesus's greatness above angels and the permanency of his dwelling among us make the new covenant far more valuable than the old!

Note that the author points out the significance of how the Mosaic covenant was inaugurated compared to that of Jesus's. Though the old covenant was ratified by the visible appearance of God in all his glory with his angels, it was not confirmed through signs and mighty deeds by the hand of eyewitnesses. Except for Joshua and Caleb, who died a short time later, all who witnessed the institution of the covenant perished in the wilderness. Though the LORD had performed mighty deeds by the hand of Moses, after the giving of the law, we do not see the sick healed, the dead raised, or demons cast out as we see under the new covenant by the very eyewitnesses who observed Jesus's crucifixion and his resurrection from the dead. In the old covenant the subsequent generations were able only to hear of what God had done for their fathers, but did not get to witness similar signs and wonders performed in their own generation. Under the new covenant, believers in Christ are still able to perform—in his name—the same kind of signs and wonders as those early eyewitnesses did. Unlike the old covenant, the new covenant was, and continues to be, confirmed by God's mighty works to this day.

The author here proceeds to explain how much greater is the salvation given under the new covenant through Jesus! For one, it was openly declared by the words uttered by the Lord Jesus (v. 3). It was also confirmed by the testimony of those who heard it directly from him. In the opening prologue of his gospel, Luke speaks of the accounts of the events that surrounded Jesus's earthly ministry. He describes how he verified and documented those events "just as they were handed on to us by those who from the beginning were eyewitnesses and servants of the word" (Luke 1:2, NRSV). God through his Holy Spirit authenticated the testimonies of those eyewitnesses through signs, wonders, and gifts. Last, unlike the Old

Testament law, which could not atone for or justify those who abided by it, the new covenant, ratified by Jesus's redemptive blood, atones for sins, justifies sinners, and sanctifies believers. Having captured how far greater the salvation provided by Jesus is compared to the old covenant, the author exclaims, "How shall we escape if we neglect such a great salvation?" if those who violated the Old Testament law could not escape death!

But how great is this "great salvation"? We will see in the next section that the value of Jesus's salvific work is not only based on how it came or on what it offers *us*, but it is deeply rooted in what *he* had to give up so that he can offer it. This is precisely what the writer explains in the remainder of this chapter.

Jesus as a Brother among Many (2:5–18)

Long before Jesus died on the cross, he humbled himself in taking our human nature. This, in and of itself, was a significant act of humility by the Son of God. In Ephesians, Paul explains this mystery referring to Jesus's sacrifice, not in his crucifixion but in the mere act of incarnation: "But emptied himself, taking the form of a slave, being born in human likeness. And being found in human form, he humbled himself and became obedient to the point of death—even death on a cross" (Phil. 2:7–8, NRSV).

In this section of Hebrews 2 the author of Hebrews quotes from Psalm 8. In these verses there is a bit of a paradox. On the one hand it is said of "man" that he is lower than angels; on the other hand, we read that he was given dominion over all the works of God's hands and that all things have been placed under his feet. This passage (Ps. 8:4–8) has an immediate meaning that applies to the first Adam and all his offspring, and a future meaning that applies to Jesus (the second Adam) and his offspring. Applying it to Adam and his offspring, they were placed on the earth, "lower than angels" who were in heaven. In their original state in the Garden of Eden, when God created the first human couple, he gave them dominion over all the earth and commanded them to subdue it. Though chronologically it was not the first commandment given to man, the first commandment written in the Bible was to multiply and to rule over creation: "Be fruitful and multiply, and fill the earth and subdue it; and have dominion over the fish of the sea and over the birds of the air and over every living thing that moves upon the earth" (Gen. 1:28, NRSV).[8] Applying this psalm to Adam, he was given authority over all God's *material* creation. This is evident from Psalm 8 itself, for it says that man was given dominion over "all sheep and oxen, and also the beasts of the field, the birds of the air, and the fish of the sea, whatever passes along the paths of the seas" (Ps. 8:7–8, NRSV). Therefore, the phrases "the works of [God's] hands" and "all things"—in Adam's case—mean God's *earthly* creation (see Ps. 8:6). Remember that as a result of sin, mankind fell from their first glory and lost the dominion that God had given them over the earth. Thus, God's earthly creation is no longer *fully* subjected to mankind.

Applying that same passage to Jesus and his offspring (those who believe in him as the Son of God), the writer of Hebrews shows us that there is another, deeper meaning to these verses. Jesus willingly chose to take our human nature, being born of a woman under the law (Gal. 4:4). Thus, he also became lower than the angels of heaven. The angels who are his servants—as discussed in the previous chapter—have now become superior to him! As spoken of the first human couple that "all things" were subjected to them, so will "all things" be

---

[8] Note that in the narratives of Genesis 1 and 2, not all of their contents are in chronological order. God had given the commandment to Adam forbidding him to eat from the Tree of the Knowledge of Good and Evil *before* Eve was created (Gen. 2:16–17). The commandment of Genesis 1:28 likely came afterward.

placed under Jesus's feet. The author exposits the broader, future meaning of these verses.

Though Jesus in his incarnate state and *before* he was glorified through the cross was lower than the angels of heaven, in his glorified state and *after* his resurrection he was exalted above all angels, powers, and principalities (1 Peter 3:22). It is important to note that the glory spoken of here in Hebrews—glory that Jesus received through his suffering—is *not* the same glory he referred to when he prayed to the Father, saying, "Glorify me in your presence with the glory I had with you before the world began" (John 17:5, NIV). This is an important theological distinction. The glory the Son—the second person in the Godhead—had with the Father and the Holy Spirit is different from that which the *man* Jesus received as a result of his obedience and suffering. The latter glory is what we will share with him as his brethren who accepted to themselves his suffering, death, and resurrection. Paul clearly describes this process of dying with Christ and then being resurrected with him: "For if we have been united with him in a death like his, we will certainly also be united with him in a resurrection like his" (Rom. 6:5, NIV). Receiving this final glory as a reward for suffering is what Jesus means by this promise we find in Revelation: "To the one who is victorious, I will give the right to sit with me on my throne, just as I was victorious and sat down with my Father on his throne" (Rev. 3:21, NIV). We will indeed share the glory of the one who was "perfected" through obedience, but will most certainly not share the glory of the Godhead.

While God's first creation was subjected to the first Adam, who lost that privilege through disobedience and sin, God's new creation will be subjected to Jesus through submission and righteousness. But note that, unlike Adam, who was given dominion over God's earthly, material creation, Jesus will be given dominion over God's heavenly, spiritual creation! The creation that will be subjected to Jesus cannot be the material creation we now see, for Peter tells us that everything we see today will be consumed with fire before a new earth and a new heaven will be created:

> But the day of the Lord will come like a thief, in which the heavens will pass away with a roar and the elements will be destroyed with intense heat, and the earth and its works will be burned up... But according to His promise we are looking for new heavens and a new earth, in which righteousness dwells. (2 Peter 3:10, 13, NASB)

In Jesus's case, this dominion over God's new creation has a deeper spiritual meaning. The writer of Hebrews tells us that "putting everything in subjection to him" means that nothing will be outside his control (Heb. 2:8). In this new state, the "everything" that will be subjected to Jesus includes not only God's new creation but also all spiritual powers and principalities—and most significant of all, Jesus's last enemy—death itself! David, writing in the Spirit, describes this mystery in Psalm 110: "The LORD says to my Lord: 'Sit at my right hand, until I make your enemies your footstool'" (Ps. 110:1). God's archenemy called "death"—the consequence of sin—is what has reigned over mankind since Adam (Rom. 5:12–17). It is *this* enemy that Jesus came to abolish. This is precisely what the author of Hebrews means when he writes that Jesus shared our flesh and blood to "deliver all those who through fear of death were subject to lifelong slavery" (Heb. 2:15).

It is evident, however, that even after Jesus died and rose from the dead, death has not been destroyed and overcome. This is precisely what the writer of Hebrews articulates about Jesus as he writes, "But now we see not yet all things put under him" (Heb. 2:8, KJV). Thus, we can see that this promise still has not been fulfilled and that not "everything" has yet been placed under Jesus's feet and made subject to him.

Jesus	Adam
• Lower than angels through his incarnation	• Lower than angels in the Garden of Eden
• Dominion and authority over the new, spiritual world	• Dominion and authority over the old, material world
• Acquired his dominion through obedience and submission to the Father	• Lost his dominion due to sin and disobedience
• Reigning over death	• Reigned over by death
• Future, full, and everlasting dominion	• Past, full dominion; present, partial and temporary dominion
• "All things" signifies all God's heavenly, spiritual creation and all God's enemies, including death.	• "All things" refers only to God's earthly, material creation.

A Comparison between Jesus and Adam according to Psalm 8

Thankfully, we have a significant reference in Paul's first letter to the Corinthians to help us understand how this promise will be finally fulfilled. Paul expounds this for us, capturing the essence of this mystery this way:

> Then comes the end, when he hands over the kingdom to God the Father, after he has destroyed every ruler and every authority and power. For he must reign until he has put all his enemies under his feet. The last enemy to be destroyed is death... When all things are subjected to him, then the Son himself will also be subjected to the one who put all things in subjection under him, so that God may be all in all. (1 Cor. 15:25–26, 28, NRSV)

It is apparent from Paul's teaching in this passage that this does not happen until the end comes. To be sure, Paul here is speaking of the end of the present world. As Paul reveals to us in the Holy Spirit, in that day, after the Father has put death—Jesus's last and fiercest enemy—under his feet, Jesus himself will be subjected to the Father and will turn over all dominion to him, that the Father himself becomes king of all and ruler of all.

Intriguingly, Jesus's victory over death is not "news" revealed only in the "New" Testament. Going back to Isaiah the prophet, we find the same phrase nearly verbatim. In speaking of the salvation and exoneration that God has in store for those who love him, Isaiah writes, "[God] will *swallow up death forever*; and the LORD God will wipe away tears from all faces, and the reproach of his people he will take away from all the earth, for the LORD has spoken" (Isa. 25:8). Thus, the promise that all things will be subjected under Jesus's feet does not become completely fulfilled until Jesus has conquered all his enemies, the last of which is death.

In the remainder of this chapter of Hebrews, the author explains that it was necessary for Jesus to take to himself our human nature so that he can be "perfected" through suffering and death. This "perfection through death" was necessary so that he might bring other, "perfected" brethren to the Father as children. (It is important to note that the author is speaking here strictly of Jesus's human nature, not his divine nature, which was, is, and will always be perfect—without any need of further "perfecting.") In this perfecting process, Jesus submitted to the suffering of death so that he might receive honor and glory. Such a lowly state was the prerequisite to achieving that exalted state. In this imagery, exaltation and glory are *paralleled* and *preceded* by lowliness and sacrifice. Before he was to be exalted, Jesus had to humble himself before his Father and put on the garment of a created being. His exaltation is the result of his humility and lowliness. This is what the writer of Hebrews expresses here: "But we do see Jesus, who for a little while was made lower than the angels, now crowned with glory and honor because of the suffering of death, so that by the grace of God he might taste death for everyone" (Heb. 2:9, NRSV).

Thus, Jesus had to take our nature to share in our suffering that we may be able to take his nature and share in his glory. Through his humiliation and descent to our lowly human state, Jesus is able to represent and act on behalf of all the believers in his name and bring them to God as his own brethren. As their representative before the Father, those who accept to share in his suffering will also share in his glory and honor (Rom. 8:17). Being the first such person to undergo this process of "perfection" through suffering and death followed by glory, honor, and resurrection to life in the new creation, Jesus is rightfully called "the founder of [our] salvation [made] perfect through suffering" (Heb. 2:10). As partakers in his death and resurrection, we too undergo the same process of perfection. Paul expounds this point by stating that we "were buried therefore with him by baptism into death, so that as Christ was raised from the dead by the glory of the Father, we too might walk in newness of life" (Rom. 6:4, RSV). As participants in this perfection, we are rightfully called, "his brethren." This happens when believers die and rise with Christ, being united with him in his suffering that they may be united with him in his glory. *The greatness of the "great salvation" that Jesus came to offer is that those who receive it will be made "brethren" of the Son of God.*

That Jesus precedes the believers to receiving glory in God's new creation is why Paul calls Jesus the head (the firstborn) of God's creation. Much has been made of this verse to show that Jesus is a created being and to disprove his eternality and equality to the Father. But in fact Jesus's being the head of the Father's *new* creation *is* what Paul means when he calls Jesus "the firstborn of all creation" (Col. 1:15). Many interpret this verse as referring to Jesus's being the first of God's present creation. However, just a couple of verses later Paul calls Jesus "the beginning, the firstborn from the dead" (Col. 1:18). Everywhere else in the New Testament, Jesus is called the firstborn of God's creation *in the context of his resurrection from the dead and his ushering in the new creation!* In Revelation, John calls Jesus "the firstborn of the dead" (Rev. 1:5). The writer of Hebrews calls Jesus "the firstborn" in Hebrews 1:6, immediately after he quotes Psalm 2:7, which is a direct reference to Jesus's resurrection from the dead (see discussion in the previous chapter). Therefore, it is evident that Jesus is the head (the beginning) of God's *new* creation by his being the firstborn among his brethren to receive glory and honor in the new creation.

In the Old Testament, the seven major feasts of Israel are summarized in Leviticus 23. The first, and probably the most well-known among Christians today, is the Passover, which always falls on the fourteenth day of the first month, Abib (later renamed Nissan). At the end of the Passover another feast starts immediately: The Feast of the Unleavened Bread, which lasts for seven days. A much lesser-known feast falls during these seven days: The Feast of the Firstfruits. To celebrate this feast, the Israelites were to bring to the priest a sheaf of the firstfruits of the harvest of the land. Significantly, we read that the priest was to wave it before the LORD "on the morrow after the Sabbath" (Lev. 23:11, RSV)—that is, the Sunday morning *immediately* following the first Sabbath after the Passover feast. If we cross-reference this chronological sequence with the events of the four gospels, we will readily see that Jesus was raised from the dead by the power of the Holy Spirit on the Feast of the Firstfruits, which was the Sunday morning following the first Sabbath after the Passover Feast. *Thus, Jesus was appointed and declared the Son of God, the firstfruit of God's new creation, by his resurrection from the dead that Sunday morning!*[9]

The writer of Hebrews closes this chapter with a statement that sums up the whole chapter. Here, and for the first time in Hebrews, Jesus is called "high priest." (Jesus is called "high priest" nowhere else in the New Testament besides Hebrews.) As the high priest in the Old Testament appeared before the LORD on behalf of the congregation, Jesus appears before the Father on behalf of his brethren. Since no one can represent those whose nature he does not have, to be regarded as high priest—a representative of his brethren—Jesus had to share the same nature with them so that he may be able to present himself as an acceptable sacrifice to his Father on their behalf. Having been "perfected" through suffering and temptation, he is also able to help those who are tempted (Heb. 2:18). Through his humility and lowliness, Jesus has become equal to us in our human nature and thus is not ashamed to call us his brethren. But through the glory and honor he received as a result of his suffering and death, Jesus has ascended above angels and all heavenly beings and trampled, in victory, all his enemies—especially death. It must now be demonstrated that he has also ascended above venerated biblical figures such as Moses, who was the harbinger of the Old Testament law.

---

[9] Our Lord Jesus has fulfilled four out of the seven feasts outlined in Leviticus 23: the Passover (his crucifixion), the Feast of Unleavened Bread (the complete removal of sin, symbolized by leaven and the number 7), the Feast of Firstfruits (his resurrection), and Pentecost (the descent of the Holy Spirit upon the church). Three feasts remain to be fulfilled. The first of these is the Feast of Trumpets, which will be fulfilled when our Lord returns to the earth "with the sound of the trumpet of God" (1 Thess. 4:16). The second is the Day of Atonement, signifying the final redemption of believers on the last day through the blood of our Lord, ushering them into his kingdom for an everlasting communion with the Father—symbolized by the high priest's entry into the Holy of Holies on the Day of Atonement. The last is the Feast of Tabernacles—symbolic of our permanent abiding in the LORD's presence as we receive our inheritance in his new kingdom.

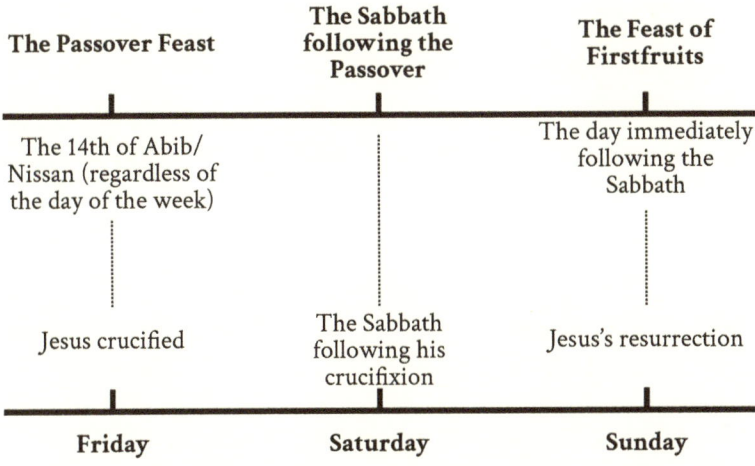

A timeline showing the events surrounding Jesus's death and resurrection and how they coincide with the first three major feasts outlined in Leviticus 23.

With this in mind, the author of Hebrews begins the next section of the epistle.

Questions on This Chapter

1. You now recognize that if you want to be glorified with Jesus in the life to come, you must share in his suffering in this life. Are you willing to do that? If yes, what does that mean to you in practice?

2. Write down a couple of things that you are not currently willing to give up so you can follow Jesus and partake in his suffering. Family? Relationships? Career?

3. Over the remainder of this book, be in prayer, placing these hinderances before the LORD and asking him to help you "sacrifice Isaac" in your life.

Chapter Three

Hebrews 3:1–19

"Therefore, holy brethren, who share in a heavenly call, consider Jesus, the apostle and high priest of our confession."

—Hebrews 3:1, RSV

Greater Apostle, Greater Loss

The author begins this chapter with a brief comparison between Jesus and Moses. Since the original readers were former adherents to the Mosaic law, it was important to warn them against sliding back from the faith they had embraced in Christ to their Jewish traditions, which they had abandoned. The author proceeds to assure his audience that if they rejected their faith in Jesus, as the Israelites had rejected God and tempted him of old in the wilderness, they too would be rejected and denied entry to God's promised land, as the Israelites had been. To lay the groundwork for this impactful declaration, the author affirms Jesus's greatness compared to Moses, calling the former "a son," and the latter "a servant." Before we proceed with our discussion of the contents of this section of the letter, I must make an important observation regarding the literary structure of the first three chapters of this letter, which usually gets lost in the distraction of chapter divisions.

The author began the first chapter by comparing Jesus to angels (Heb. 1:5–14). After he had asserted how much greater Jesus is, he gave his audience a strong admonition against neglecting "such a great salvation" at the opening of the second chapter (Heb. 2:3). Having explained what makes this great salvation "great" (Jesus's exaltation through suffering), he now begins the third chapter by comparing Jesus to Moses. Later in this chapter he issues yet another warning to his readers against rejecting the salvation that Jesus offers. Note a pattern here: comparison to show greatness, followed by an admonition, and back to comparison again. As we delve more deeply into the letter, we will see how the author uses every cycle of comparison-admonition as a building block to build his strong argument that no salvation can be attained either apart from faith in Christ or by adhering to the Old Testament ordinances, which were nothing more than a shadow and a resemblance of Jesus's true salvific work. In other words, our author compares so he can admonish! This pattern will become quite clear as we progress through the epistle. (Note that in some of these comparison cycles, the author shifts from admonition to encouragement and exhortations. His aim is not to discourage his audience but to encourage them to hold fast to their faith.)

Moses a Servant, Jesus a Son (3:1–6)

Having discerned this literary flow in the author's argument begs the question: After comparing Jesus to the angels of heaven, why did he choose Moses specifically for this second comparison? Why did he not choose Abraham, Joshua, or Isaiah? What is the significance of Moses to the author's argument?

Moses was—without question—the greatest prophet of the Old Testament. In fact, he is the only prophet in the Bible to whom the Bible itself assigns such a title. In the closing chapter of Deuteronomy we read this unique testimony about Moses:

> And there has not arisen a prophet since in Israel like Moses, whom the LORD knew face to face, none like him for all the signs and the wonders which the LORD sent him to do in the land of Egypt, to Pharaoh and to all his servants and to all his land, and for all the mighty power and all the great and terrible deeds which Moses wrought in the sight of all Israel. (Deut. 34:10–12, RSV)

For generations King David was the standard by which God measured how righteous—or unrighteous—a king in Israel was. Likewise, Moses was considered the standard to which prophets were compared. The LORD himself uses this language in his instruction to the Israelites regarding "the prophet" who would rise in Israel after Moses dies: "I will raise up for them a prophet *like you* from among their brothers. And I will put my words in his mouth, and he shall speak to them all that I command him" (Deut. 18:18). Being the sons of Abraham and having the law of Moses were the two foundational claims that represented a source of pride to the Israelites (see Matt. 3:9; John 8:39). Moses was so esteemed in Judaism that in the threefold division of the Hebrew Tanakh (the equivalent of the Christian Old Testament), the law of Moses was set apart from the rest of the prophets and the writings. In one of his many arguments with the Jews, Jesus makes this eye-opening declaration to them: "Do not think that I will accuse you before the Father; your accuser is Moses, *on whom you have set your hope*" (John 5:45, NRSV). The Jews had set their hope on Moses for their salvation and justification in God's eyes.

The LORD himself had elevated Moses above all other prophets or seers in the Old Testament. Describing how he communicates with Moses, the LORD says,

> If there is a prophet among you, I the LORD make myself known to him in a vision; I speak with him in a dream. Not so with my servant Moses. He is faithful in all my house. With him I speak mouth to mouth, clearly, and not in riddles, and he beholds the form of the LORD. Why then were you not afraid to speak against my servant Moses? (Num. 12:6–8)

Thus, unless Jesus were divine, for the author of Hebrews to elevate him above Moses would be a blatant blasphemy in the eyes of first-century Jews. Such elevation constituted an honor that no other prophet or king had ever attained in Israel. In the author's mind, illustrating the superiority of Jesus to Moses and showing that he is the more excellent figure would only mean affirming Jesus's divine nature and his equality to God.

The author starts by reminding his readers that Jesus, as the high priest of their confession of faith, proved faithful in all that the Father had given him, as Moses was faithful in God's house. As mentioned above, one of the remarkable descriptors that the LORD himself assigns to Moses is that "he is faithful in all my house" (Num. 12:7). However, what does it mean to be "faithful" in this context?

In the entire Bible there are three individuals who are said to have fulfilled all the work that the LORD had given them—Noah, Moses, and Jesus. Of Noah, this testimony is recorded twice in Genesis. The first occurs before he enters the ark: "Thus did Noah; according to all that God commanded him, so did he" (Gen. 6:22, KJV). The second follows his entry into the ark with all the animals that the LORD had commanded to take with him: "And Noah did according unto all that the

LORD commanded him" (Gen. 7:5, KJV). Of Moses, this testimony appears once, upon completing the tabernacle: "Thus did Moses: according to all that the LORD commanded him, so did he" (Exod. 40:16, KJV). In Jesus's final recorded prayer to God the Father before his crucifixion, he testifies of himself, saying, "I glorified you on earth, having accomplished the work that you gave me to do" (John 17:4). Moreover, lest his audience think that Jesus is simply equal to Moses, the writer of Hebrews continues further to illustrate how far greater Jesus is compared to Moses, as he is to the angels of heaven.

It is well known that the builder of a house is worthy of more honor than the house he or she builds; the creator is greater than his or her creation; the potter is worth more than the vessels he or she creates. The author uses this analogy to demonstrate that Jesus is infinitely greater than Moses. In verse 3 our author states that Jesus is above Moses as much as the builder of the house is greater than the house itself. That begs the question: How much greater is that? That depends on what is meant by "house" and who is meant by "the builder." Though it seems that every house is built by a man, the real builder of all things is God (v. 4). In other words, while it appears that there may be many builders, in fact, there is only one—God. But we know that God (the one and only builder) is infinitely above every "house" that has ever been (or will ever be) built. Then, if Jesus is greater than Moses to the extent that the builder (God) is greater than the house he builds, it follows that Jesus is *infinitely* greater than Moses! That he does not become misunderstood for being anti-Jewish is why our author constructs his argument in this oblique fashion. His goal is to show the true identity of Jesus, not to disparage his Jewish audience.

To strengthen his argument even further, the author reminds his readers that Moses was but a mere "servant" while Jesus is a Son. Moses served in God's house to testify to the things that would come later. These things are what Moses spoke of concerning the advent of Jesus (see Deut. 18:15, 18–19, and the discussion above). Though Moses was a faithful servant, he was a servant nonetheless. Since the writer uses the term "house" in verse 6 to refer to the New Testament believers, it follows that the "house" Moses oversaw as a servant was the people of God in the Old Testament, meaning God's household. But Moses *served* in that "house," while Jesus *built* the church of God as a Son and called it his own (verses 5–6). This cannot be more evident than in Jesus's own testimony that "on this rock I will build my church, and the gates of hell shall not prevail against it" (Matt. 16:18). This declaration came out of Jesus's mouth immediately after Peter confessed that Jesus is "the Christ, the Son of the living God" (Matt. 16:16). Thus, not only is Jesus greater than Moses as God is greater than his creation, but Jesus built God's house as the Son of God while Moses only served in it.

The difference between a servant and a son in this passage is manifest. A servant follows instructions from the builder (God), but the Son knows his Father's will and thus shares his vision of how the house is to be built. As the servant of God, Moses *received* commandments from the LORD concerning everything the Israelites were commanded to do. Jesus, on the other hand, *gave* commandments: "You have heard that it was said to those of old, 'You shall not murder; and whoever murders will be liable to judgment.' But *I* say to you that everyone who is angry with his brother will be liable to judgment" (Matt. 5:21–22). A servant would never own the house, but a son inherits the house of his father. As the Son of God, Jesus will inherit all nations: "I will tell of the decree of the LORD: He said to me, 'You are my son, today I have begotten you. Ask of me, and I will make the nations your heritage, and the ends of the earth your possession'" (Ps. 2:7–8, RSV). Thus, the Son speaks with the authority of one who owns, while the servant receives and carries out instructions.

Following his comparison-admonition pattern, in the next section, our author moves on to admonition now that he has finished comparing Jesus to Moses, illustrating Jesus's superiority.

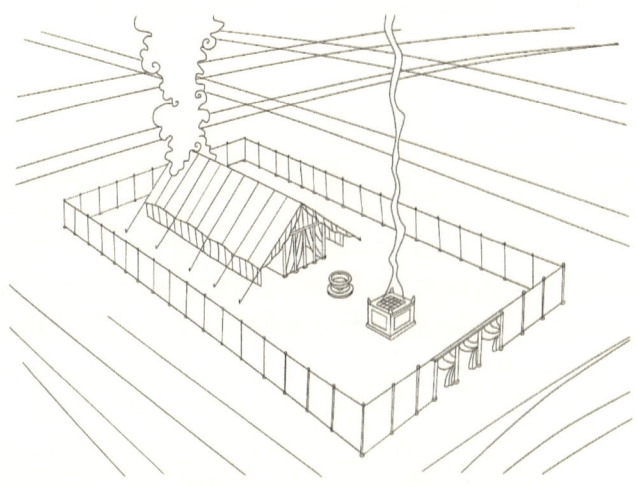

"And Moses verily was faithful in all his house, as a servant, for a testimony of those things which were to be spoken after; But Christ as a son over his own house; whose house are we, if we hold fast the confidence and the rejoicing of the hope firm unto the end" (Heb. 3:5–6, KJV).

This illustration shows the Old Testament tabernacle, where the LORD met with Moses and the Israelites.

Photo Credit: askib/Shutterstock.com

Warning against Lack of Faith (3:7–19)

In the next section of the letter, the author articulates his reason for comparing Jesus to Moses. By illustrating the greatness of Jesus compared to Moses, he can now express to his readers how much greater their loss would be if they rejected faith in Christ. The greater the value of what they reject, the higher the stakes, and the greater the loss! For this reason, the writer establishes in verse 1 that Jesus is the author of the faith they are at risk of rejecting.

The author connects this notion with the identity of Jesus as the exalted Son of God, as has been shown in the first chapter of the letter. Thus, if his audience rejected the Christian faith that they had confessed, they would be rejecting a faith preached—as the preaching of an "apostle"—by none other than the Son of God himself (Heb. 3:1). This notion is central to the author's argument. Though the faith they received was confirmed to them by those who were eyewitnesses of the Lord, it was inaugurated by none other than the Lord himself (see Heb. 2:3). Jesus's own parable helps us understand why that is so fundamental to the author's argument.

In Mark 12:1–12 Jesus narrates to the Jews the parable of the wicked tenants, who were entrusted with the master's vineyard to keep it and to harvest it. When the time came to collect his portion of the harvest proceeds, the master sent a few "messengers," all of whom the wicked tenants insulted, beat, and killed. Thinking they would have more respect for his one and only son, the master sent him to collect his share from those wicked tenants. Yet they conspired against his son and killed him too. It was only at *this* point of the narrative that the master decided to "come and destroy the tenants and give the vineyard to others" (Mark 12:9). It is noteworthy that the master did not send to destroy the tenants when they killed his messengers. Only when they killed his son did he move to destroy them and give the vineyard to others!

By stating that Jesus is the "apostle" of their confession, the author of Hebrews aims to remind his readers that they would not be rejecting a mere servant (as Moses was) but would be equating themselves to the wicked tenants who rejected the master's only son! I should add that the Greek word used to signify *apostle* in Hebrews 3:1 is *apostolos*. The Greek word translated as *sent* in this parable in Mark 12:6 (and in the other gospels) is *apesteilen*. Both words come from the same root, literally signifying "sending," "sent" (both verb and noun), or "to send." Jesus, therefore, is the "apostle" ("the one sent" or "messenger") sent to usher in the faith they received. From this point onward, the author begins outlining the consequences they would face if they rejected that faith.

In this passage the author uses a couple of quotations from the Psalter and from the book of Numbers. In the first quotation from Psalm 95, the LORD recalls how displeased he was with the very people he had brought up out of Egypt because they "go astray in their heart, and they have not known [his] ways" (Ps. 95:10). In his wrath, says the LORD in this psalm, he swore that they would not enter his rest (*rest* here signifies the promised land of Canaan). Though they had seen his mighty works in Egypt and in the wilderness for forty years, they were found unworthy to receive the blessings of entering the land he had promised to their fathers. As he quotes this psalm, the author's main point is that the same Israelites who received the promise to enter the land were denied entry due to their lack of faith (vv. 12, 19).

The Greek conjunction *dio* at the beginning of verse 10 is rendered "therefore" in the ESV, but more precisely in the NIV as "for this reason." It gives reason as to why the LORD "loathed that generation." The reason is given in verse 9: because they put the LORD to the test and saw his works for forty years. Though seeing the works of the LORD is usually considered a blessing, here it is accounted against them as an indictment. Seeing the LORD's works and believing is a blessing; seeing them and refusing to believe is a condemnation. Those who see and believe shall be blessed, but those who see and disbelieve, what they saw shall be a cause for judgment against them. This is what Jesus meant when he—on a few occasions—instructed those whom he had healed to go and show themselves to the priests in the temple "as a testimony to them" (see Matt. 8:4; Mark 1:44; Luke 9:5, NIV).

The second direct quotation in this passage comes in verse 18 and is taken from Numbers 14 (and also from Deuteronomy 1). In this narrative, which begins in Numbers 13, Moses sends one man from each of the twelve tribes of Israel to spy out the land of Canaan, which the LORD had promised their fathers to give to their descendants.[10] Numbers 13 enumerates the names of all twelve spies, among whom were two notable men, Joshua the son of Nun and Caleb the son of Jephunneh (Num. 13:4–15). After spying out the land for forty days, they returned, bringing back a branch with a single cluster of grapes. They also brought back an ill report of the land and its inhabitants, saying, "We seemed to ourselves like grasshoppers, and so we seemed to them" (Num. 13:33).

Hearing the reports of the spies, the Israelites began grumbling against the LORD, saying that they wished they had died in Egypt or in the wilderness instead of falling by the sword in Canaan and their wives and children becoming prey to the inhabitants of the land. Joshua and Caleb, who had a "different spirit," rent their clothes when they heard the Israelites grumbling against the LORD, for they believed that he would give the land into their hands. This is the "spirit of faith" that Paul refers to in 2 Corinthians when he writes, "Since we have the same spirit of faith according to what has been written, 'I believed, and so I spoke,' we also believe, and so we also speak" (2 Cor. 4:13). Though all of the twelve spies went to the same land and saw the same inhabitants, it was only Joshua and Caleb who believed and therefore spoke.

The narrative takes a different turn, however, when the Israelites begin grumbling against the LORD. Hearing their murmuring against him, the LORD decreed that those who refused to believe him—twenty years and older, except

---

[10] This is yet another sad example of the literary unity of Scripture becoming disjointed due to the chapter division between Numbers 13 and 14.

Joshua and Caleb—would not enter his land. The children about whom they grumbled and said would fall prey to their enemies would enter in their stead!

To understand the severity of this punishment, we should remember that the Israelites were supposed to possess the land of Canaan shortly after their departure from Mount Sinai. Instead, due to their disobedience, they wandered in the desert for forty years (one year for every day of spying). Their corpses would fall one by one until "the last of [their corpses] lies in the wilderness" (Num. 14:32–33). This is literally the same expression the author of Hebrews borrows centuries later to depict this grief-filled conclusion to this sad episode of doubt and unbelief. Building his argument on events from the Old Testament, the author shows his readers that although Israel received the blessings of being delivered from Egypt and led miraculously through the wilderness, most of them were not pleasing to the LORD and ended up perishing in the wilderness of Sinai.

Moving to the more specific point he desires to address—warning his audience against having the same lack of faith—the author exhorts them to watch lest they too have the same unbelieving hearts. When the Israelites disobeyed, they were destroyed; so would his readers be if they disobeyed. Therefore, they must keep watch and remain vigilant lest they also share the same fate. The overarching theme of his argument is thus summed up, "Take care, brethren, lest there be in any of you an evil, unbelieving heart, leading you to fall away from the living God. But exhort one another every day, as long as it is called 'today,' that none of you may be hardened by the deceitfulness of sin" (Heb. 3:12–13, RSV). So dire he believes the consequences would be that he instructs them to exhort one another (or each person himself) every day that none of them hardens his or her heart by sin, refusing to heed his warning. As the Old Testament scriptures reveal, the author forewarns his readers not to presume that they are in some way exempt from God's judgment or that they are somehow better than the Israelites. He illustrates to his readers that as the Israelites saw God's glory and experienced his outstretched arm but rejected the faith and perished, they too would face a similar fate if they rejected faith in Christ. The same way God exacted punishment on the Israelites for disobedience, he would not hold them guiltless if they likewise disobeyed. No privilege would cause the LORD to turn a blind eye to their transgression if they rejected his Son. He also gives them this stark reminder that the bodies (literally *corpses*) of those who dared to test the LORD fell in the wilderness (verse 17).

This entire passage is reminiscent of Paul's powerful argument in 1 Corinthians where he builds a similar case from other Old Testament events, stating that "these things happened to them as an example, but they were written down for our instruction, on whom the end of the ages has come" (1 Cor. 10:11). We too, twenty-first-century believers, must never be deceived that we will be spared or exempted from the LORD's judgment if we try to test him or if we are found disobedient in his eyes. This warning is not just for first-century Christians; it is for us today.

Questions on This Chapter

1. Do you think the Israelites had a good reason to grumble against the LORD in the wilderness? Why or why not?

2. If you were in their shoes, would you grumble against God?

3. We often criticize and fault the Israelites for murmuring against God as if we are better than they were. Do you remember a time when you disobeyed or grumbled against the LORD?

4. Moses instructed the spies to be "of good courage and bring some of the fruit of the land" (Num. 13:20). Why do you think it was important for them to bring of the fruit of the promised land back to their camp?

5. Building on the previous question, have you ever felt that you could stretch forth your hand by faith and "touch" something the LORD had promised you, even though you still do not have it?

Chapter Four

Hebrews 4:1–16

"Therefore, since we have a great high priest who has ascended into heaven, Jesus the Son of God, let us hold firmly to the faith we profess."

—Hebrews 4:14, NIV

Entering God's Rest

As the writer of Hebrews continues his previous admonition to his readers, he begins this chapter by distinguishing between the rest promised to the Israelites—but not received due to their lack of faith—and the rest promised to the New Testament believers, which still stands. He does this by showing his readers that the first rest was instituted when the LORD was finished with creating the present, visible world. The second rest, our author explains, was instituted through the promise of a second world that is yet to become visible and manifest in the life to come.

As is his habit, the author uses a series of Old Testament quotations followed by an exposition. The writer deliberately mixes promises with warnings and encouragement as he continues to admonish his readers against backsliding from their faith in Christ, explaining the potential dangers.

It is critical to note that the writer of Hebrews continues his theme of comparison-admonition-encouragement in this chapter as well. This time, however, he does not compare Jesus to others; he compares the Israelites of the Old Testament to the followers of Jesus in the New Testament. He highlights the similarities in the promises given to both groups and the differences in the faith that each group possessed. He continues with the theme that if we make choices similar to theirs, we will also face a similar fate.

The Promise of Rest (4:1-13)

Most modern English translations omit the stark warning that opens this chapter or render it much later in the verse (except the NASB and the much older KJV and YLT). The opening phrase in this chapter is, "let us fear." Though the closing of the previous chapter carried some harsh admonitions for his readers, the author still feels the need to go even deeper in this precautionary message. For this reason, he proceeds to quote the same Scripture verses from the previous section and states the unadulterated truth that, as precious as the promise is, they must fear losing it.

Though he states that the promise of entering God's rest still stands, he warns his readers against failing to achieve it. A few chapters later he repeats the same warning: "See to it that no one fails to obtain the grace of God" (Heb. 12:15). Notice here that he does not neglect to give a reason for this warning but provides evidence for it. In the next verse he tells his audience that the "good news" was preached to them as it had been proclaimed to the Israelites in the wilderness. He adds that although the Israelites had heard this good news, it did not profit them because it was not united by faith with those who listened (Heb. 4:2; but more literally, "[it] not being mixed with faith in them that heard it"). While this good news had been proclaimed to them, they could not obtain the promise it offered because they refused to believe.

Reflecting back on the narrative from Numbers that the author alluded to in the previous chapter, there is a small but important detail that shows how receiving the word must be "mixed" with faith so that it can produce fruit in the hearts and minds of those who receive it.

Before sending off the spies to spy out the land, Moses instructed them saying, "*Be of good courage* and bring some of the fruit of the land" (Num. 13:20). While some may attribute this odd directive to Moses's desire that the rest of the Israelites could see the fruit of the land and its beauty before they entered it, the first part of the command suggests otherwise. Moses instructed the spies to be of good courage when they would enter the land and to bring back its fruit. The LORD, through Moses, desired that his people would take from the fruit of the land and bring it back to the camp because he wanted them to act as if the land were already theirs. God wanted to instill faith in their hearts. As the author of Hebrews explains later in the epistle, *only by faith* were God's promises received by those to whom the promises were made. This episode in Numbers is just another example of how, by faith, those spies were instructed to stretch forth their hands and take from what was not yet theirs as if it were.

In his epistle to the Galatians, Paul shows the importance and the results of receiving the word by faith. By posing the same rhetorical question twice, he explains to his audience that receiving the Holy Spirit and his miraculous work among them came, first and foremost, by receiving the word and believing it. On one occasion he poses this question to his readers: "Let me ask you only this: Did you receive the Spirit by works of the law or by hearing with faith?" (Gal. 3:2). This is a rhetorical question to which Paul expects no answer. Two verses later he repeats the same question: "Does he who supplies the Spirit to you and works miracles among you do so by works of the law, or by hearing with faith?" (Gal. 3:5). Again, not expecting an answer to his rhetorical question, Paul makes the point that the obvious choice is the latter option: hearing with faith. Thus, receiving the word of the "good news" must be done in faith if it is to produce the desired fruit in the lives of the recipients.

We see a practical example of this in Acts. While Peter was preaching and proclaiming the good news to Cornelius and to his relatives and close friends, because they received the word that Peter had been speaking to them with faith, the Holy Spirit fell upon "all who heard the word" without Peter laying hands on them, and they immediately began to speak in tongues (Acts 10:44–46). This was the direct result of the simple act of believing the word preached to them. This is precisely what the writer of Hebrews means when he speaks of receiving the message of the good news "mixed" with faith.

We must also recognize that although the recipients of Hebrews initially received the good news with faith, the author warns them once more of falling away and abandoning their faith. In the parable of the sower, we read an important remark from our Lord that explains this concern, which the author of Hebrews has for his readers.

While there were three kinds of ground that failed to produce fruit, the second is particularly noteworthy. It is the kind of ground that produces fruit for a short season, but when tribulations or persecutions "on account of the word" arise, any fruit it may have produced fades away (Matt. 13:21). Jesus explains that "this is the one who hears the word and *immediately* receives it with joy" but does not endure for long (Matt. 13:20, NRSV). Though the word was indeed received with joy and produced *some* fruit, it quickly withered away. Although some may be true believers—or have the appearance of being so—being weak and rootless, their faith quickly withers away when tested by trials, as gold is tried in the fire of a furnace. The author warns his readers against having such a faith.

"For we also have had the good news proclaimed to us, just as those also did, but the message they heard did not benefit them, because they were not united with those who heard it in faith" (Heb. 4:2, LEB).

Due to their murmuring and lack of faith, the LORD sent fiery serpents to kill the disobedient Israelites in the wilderness. Moses is here seen as he erects the bronze serpent so that whoever is bitten by a serpent may look on it and live (Num. 21:4–9).

Photo Credit: Morphart Creation/Shutterstock.com

The author also differentiates between the rest instituted upon the creation of the world, which was denied to those who did not believe in the Old Testament, and the rest promised to the New Testament believers, which he says in the first verse "still stands" (Heb. 4:1).

We know that the LORD rested from all his works on the Sabbath day. In Genesis we read that "on the seventh day God finished the work that he had done, and he rested on the seventh day from all the work that he had done" (Gen. 2:2, NRSV).

To understand the significance of "rest" in God's mind in the Genesis narrative, it is critical to observe that the LORD's *original* plan was to cease from work forever and simply enjoy his fellowship with man. God had planned to fully rest from all his work after he created the world and everything in it. A careful reading of the first three chapters of Genesis reveals that, in the Garden of Eden, there was no work involved of any kind for either the LORD or mankind except spending time in fellowship and communion together. Though Adam was to till the ground in Eden (Gen. 2:15), it was not for food but for keeping and preserving the garden that the LORD had given him (compare Gen. 3:17–19). Nonetheless, through man's disobedience, the LORD had to return to work and develop a plan of salvation for mankind. However, this was not God's original plan of rest and enjoyment. God's return to work and his salvific plan was first announced to the serpent after the fall: "I will put enmity between you and the woman, and between your seed and her seed; he shall bruise your head, and you shall bruise his heel" (Gen. 3:15, RSV).

Because this state of rest became reflective of God's original plan of enjoying his fellowship with sinless mankind, the Sabbath—as a day of rest—later became a sanctified day in the mind of God. Breaking it was punishable by death since violating that state of holiness resulted in certain death, as it did in Eden. The Sabbath signified mankind's original state of holiness and sinlessness in which the LORD created them for communion with him. This day of rest later became a manifestation of the covenant between God and his holy people.

Though keeping the Sabbath was one of the Ten Commandments, the LORD gave the Israelites a separate ordinance concerning the Sabbath. We encounter this intriguing commandment later in Exodus:

> Therefore the Israelites shall keep the sabbath, observing the sabbath throughout their generations, as a perpetual *covenant*. It is a sign forever between me and the people of Israel that in six days the LORD made heaven and earth, and on the seventh day he rested, and was refreshed. (Exod. 31:16–17, RSV)

It is significant that the LORD associated the Sabbath with the covenant he had established with his people. The author of Hebrews helps us understand the implications of this association as he expounds to his readers the significance of the Sabbath to the LORD.

To the Israelites, observing the Sabbath was a visible sign and an outward expression of their belief in God's promise to bring them to the promised land—their rest and his. When God created the world, he instituted the promise of rest with it. This can be readily observed since the Sabbath was mentioned at the conclusion of the creation narrative in Genesis. In the creation account, the Sabbath was a *state* that God entered after completing his creative work, including the creation of man.[11] Entering God's rest was a gift bestowed on mankind. This is where the LORD finds his own rest. In both the Old and the New Testaments we learn that God finds his rest in man. In Proverbs the wisdom of God rejoices with God "in his inhabited world and [delights] in the sons of men" (Prov. 8:31, RSV).[12] When Jesus was born in the flesh, Luke tells us that hosts of angels appeared to the shepherds in the fields, praising God, saying, "Glory to God in the highest,

---

[11] The Hebrew word *shabbat* literally means *rest*. It is where the English word Sabbath gets its origin.

[12] Note that in the Old Testament the wisdom of God is a pre-incarnational manifestation of our Lord Jesus, whom the New Testament plainly calls "the wisdom of God" (1 Cor. 1:24).

and on earth peace among people *with whom he is pleased*" (Luke 2:14, LEB). Thus, the LORD instituted his rest so that man may enter it and that God may find his own rest in him.

It is noteworthy that the commandment to observe and keep the Sabbath was not given until the Israelites came out of Egypt. This was a foreshadowing of the rest that God's people would find in the promised land and eventually in God's eternal presence. God put forth his promise of the land where his people would find rest. That his covenant people believed God's promise is the reason they had to observe his Sabbath day and keep it holy. The Sabbath was one way the LORD reminded his covenant people on a weekly basis that they would enter his rest. This is the reason that, though the writer of Hebrews insists that many did not receive the promise due to their lack of faith, there remain some who will receive it if they believe. To the author, this was and still is a standing, irrevocable promise.

The writer then reconciles two separate scriptures that seem at odds with one another. Psalm 95, speaking of the Israelites who disobeyed and tempted God, states that the LORD swore in his wrath that they would not enter his rest (Ps. 95:11). Conversely, it is evident from God's repeated instructions regarding the Sabbath that he had instituted rest for his covenant people and promised them entry. The author reconciles these two ideas together by asserting that the LORD has promised *another* day of rest—another Sabbath to those who would come later, receiving and believing his promises. As quoted earlier, their unbelief never annulled God's promise, as is evident by the commandment that the Sabbath must be a "perpetual covenant" (Exod. 31:16).

A generation after the unbelievers perished in the wilderness, the LORD still instructed those who entered the land to keep his Sabbath. Quoting Psalm 95 once again, the author shows that a few generations after Joshua had led the Israelites into the promised land, the LORD still appointed yet *another* "day" in which he encouraged his people not to harden their hearts when they hear his voice. In other words, after their "day" of disobedience in the wilderness, another "day" of obedience was expected. Summing up the main point of this section, the author concludes that we know that *another* rest awaits (Heb. 4:9). The writer then promises his audience that, as God himself rested after he had completed his work, total rest awaits them if they endeavor to obey him. Shifting from warning and admonition to encouragement, the author bids his readers to make every effort (more literally, "endeavor" or "labor") to enter God's rest without falling into the same example of disobedience (Heb. 4:11).

In verse 12 the writer of Hebrews makes an unexpected leap in his argument to exclaim one of the most famous verses in the Bible concerning the word of God. As these accounts were written for our learning and instruction, the word of God has become the standard by which all man's intentions and actions are measured and judged. It is well capable of discerning man's inner secrets and desires. The living word of God is the beam of light that the Holy Spirit shines in one's heart to reveal his or her innermost thoughts! Verse 13 reveals that the intended meaning is that nothing can be hidden from God's eyes since his word is his instrument of such discernment. Whether they endeavor in truth and abide in faith to the end, or believe at first and then go astray, in all cases the intents of their hearts and minds are revealed before the LORD, "with whom is our reckoning" (Heb. 4:13, YLT).

The Tempted High Priest (4:14–16)

Despite the chapter division in our modern Bibles, this unit of thought begins in the last few verses of this chapter and continues nearly uninterrupted through the tenth verse of the next chapter. For the sake of consistency and for the purpose of our discussion, I will adhere to the chapter division as shown in our Bibles.

It is worth noting that the exact expression "Jesus the Son of God" appears only here in the entire New Testament and the entire Bible. Similar to calling Jesus "high priest," this expression is unique to Hebrews.[13] These expressions (especially, "high priest") are significant to the author's argument and are used a number of times throughout the epistle.

Following his affirmation in the preceding section that God's "rest" *still* awaits his people, the writer continues encouraging his audience instead of admonishing them. One way he does this is by reminding them in whom they have confessed. This should recall to your mind the author's earlier declaration that Jesus is the "apostle" of their confession of faith (Heb. 3:1). The author revisits this motif later in the epistle with an even stronger affirmation that Jesus is the author and finisher of our faith (Heb. 12:2).

Priesthood in the Old Testament was inherited through biological descent, and the high priest had to be a Levite from the offspring of Aaron. Although the high priest represented the people of Israel before God, he himself had to offer sacrifices to atone for his own sins. This is stated more than once in the Old Testament. To begin their priestly duties for the first time before the LORD, Moses instructed Aaron, saying, "Come to the altar and sacrifice your sin offering and your burnt offering and make atonement for yourself and the people; sacrifice the offering that is for the people and make atonement for them, as the LORD has commanded" (Lev. 9:7, NIV). Later in the institution of the Day of Atonement, Aaron was reminded to offer a sacrifice for himself *first* before he could sacrifice on behalf of the Israelites. As he brought a young bull and a ram for himself and his household, and two

---

[13] Such unique phraseology is yet another strong reason that Paul could not have penned this epistle. See the introductory chapter on the authorship of Hebrews.

male goats and a ram for the rest of the congregation, the first step in the process of offering atonement was that "Aaron shall offer the bull as a sin offering for himself, and shall make atonement for himself and for his house" (Lev. 16:6, NRSV). After he had gone into the Holy of Holies to offer atonement for himself and for his household, he entered the Holy of Holies once more to offer atonement for all Israel (see Lev. 16:11–16). The book of Leviticus remarks that "there shall be no man in the tent of meeting when he enters to make atonement in the holy place until he comes out and has made atonement for himself and for his house and for all the assembly of Israel" (Lev. 16:17, RSV). This signifies Jesus's redemptive sacrifice for our sins as an atonement that he—and he alone—offered on our behalf.

The high priest in the Old Testament shared the same nature as those whom he represented. Therefore, he was able to empathize with those who were overcome by the sinfulness of their nature, since his own nature was sinful. The author of Hebrews makes use of this theological consideration in the next chapter. At this point in his treatise, he briefly touches upon it to remind his audience that though they confessed Jesus, who is the heavenly high priest, he is still able to share in their weaknesses and temptations, for he willingly took to himself their very nature while without sin. Unlike the earthly high priest, who shared their nature and their sins, Jesus was and is without sin (see 1 Peter 2:22; 1 John 3:5). He shares their weakness not through sharing in their sin but by sharing in their nature. They did not confess their faith in a sinful earthly high priest; they confessed in a sinless heavenly high priest, Christ.

Jesus, sharing the same nature as his brethren, also shares their weaknesses and is able to sympathize with them. Yet because he is the pure Lamb of God, who is without the blemish of sin, he is able to help and intercede for the weaknesses of those whom he represents. Isaiah prophesied of God's Servant, calling him "a man of suffering and acquainted with infirmity" (Isa. 53:3, NRSV). He also prophesied that he would do no violence and that there would be no deceit in his mouth (Isa. 53:9).[14] Having affirmed these two facts about Jesus, the writer reassures his readers that because Jesus represents them before God the Father, they too can obtain mercy and grace if they boldly approach his throne, holding fast to "the faith [they] profess" (Heb. 4:14, NIV). This theme repeats a number of times in the remainder of the epistle, as we will see later (see Heb. 10:19–22).

The notion of approaching the throne of God in boldness (or with confidence) is not unique to Hebrews. In speaking of "Christ Jesus our Lord," Paul tells the Ephesians that in him "we have access to God in boldness and confidence through faith in him" (Eph. 3:12, NRSV).[15] To the Jewish community of the first century, this concept would have been unfathomable. Coming before the throne of God in the Old Testament would have resulted in certain death. When instituting the ordinance concerning the Day of Atonement, despite coming into the presence of the LORD with the blood of sacrifice, Aaron was instructed to burn incense before the mercy seat (the cover of the ark of the covenant), so that the cloud of the burned incense comes between him and the presence of God, that he may not die (Lev. 16:13). This is scarcely more evident anywhere in the Bible than in the case of Nadab and Abihu,

---

[14] To refute that Isaiah 53 applies to Jesus of Nazareth, modern-day Jews assert that it applies to the nation of Israel. They claim that the Servant of the LORD is the Jewish nation and not who Christians call the Christ. Howbeit, under this interpretation, it would be nearly impossible to explain how the Servant in Isaiah 53 is said to be sinless with no deceit in his mouth.

[15] Though the use of unique phraseology likely rules out Paul as a potential author of Hebrews, here we find a striking similarity to some of Paul's epistles. As stated in the introductory chapter concerning the authorship of this epistle, such similarities with Paul's letters suggest that Paul may have supplied the ideas contained in Hebrews but did not compose it himself.

Aaron's own sons, who offered "strange" (unauthorized) incense before the LORD. A fire came out from the presence of the LORD and consumed them (Lev. 10:1–2).

To show the gravity of coming into his presence, the LORD later gives Moses this instruction: "Tell Aaron your brother not to come at all times into the holy place within the veil, before the mercy seat which is upon the ark, lest he die; for I will appear in the cloud upon the mercy seat" (Lev. 16:2, RSV). Thus, when the Jews of the New Testament heard that they could now come into the presence of the LORD at any time they chose—with no incense, no animal sacrifice, and without being priests themselves—in their eyes this must have been a heretical doctrine that would result in their certain deaths. In fact, the Greek word rendered here as *boldness* literally signifies "the trait of being willing to undertake activities that involve risk or danger."[16]

In the following chapter, the author continues with the theme of Jesus as God's high priest, expounding further on what it signifies for us as New Testament believers. As one of the most beautifully written sections in the epistle—and maybe of all the New Testament—the author weaves this motif with two other significant theological themes: priesthood in the Old Testament and Jesus's sonship to God the Father.

Questions on This Chapter

1. In light of this chapter of Hebrews, do you believe that Christians today can backslide from their faith and "lose their salvation?" Why or why not?

2. Reflecting back on the last couple of years or so of your life, has your relationship with God's word grown, stayed the same, or declined?

---

[16] Bible Sense Lexicon. Logos Software.

3. What plans would you put in place to make sure that your relationship with the word of God continues to grow?

Chapter Five

Hebrews 5:1–14

"Who in the days of his flesh, when he had offered up prayers and supplications with strong crying and tears unto him that was able to save him from death, and was heard in that he feared."

—Hebrews 5:7, KJV

The Ultimate High Priest

Our author started expounding the theme of Jesus's high priesthood in the previous chapter for the first time in some detail. In chapter 5 he continues his exposition of this motif. He will return to this central topic in the subsequent chapters, especially chapters 7 and 8, where he develops it in depth. It must be noted that no other book in the entire Bible speaks of Jesus's priesthood directly besides Hebrews. This theme is unique to this rich epistle.

In addition, nowhere else in the New Testament (or in the whole Bible, for that matter) do we find such a refined theological treatise as we find here in this chapter and the subsequent chapters of Hebrews. We would have to turn to Romans to find another book of the Bible that comes close to matching Hebrews. Though it is a close second, Romans still does not quite measure up to Hebrews in its refined Greek, eloquence,

Reading Hebrews | Chapter 5

"Therefore he had to be made like his brethren in every respect, so that he might become a merciful and faithful high priest in the service of God, to make expiation for the sins of the people. For because he himself has suffered and been tempted, he is able to help those who are tempted"
(Heb. 2:17–18, RSV).

As the high priest in the Old Testament sacrificed the blood of animals to atone for the sins of the people, to fulfill the Scriptures, Jesus, who is the true Lamb of God, needed to be sacrificed at the hands of Israel's high priest. In this illustration Jesus is being tried and condemned to death at the hands of Caiaphas, Israel's high priest during Jesus's earthly ministry (John 18:12–24). Even during his trial, Jesus was fulfilling the Old Testament scriptures!

Photo Credit: Morphart Creation/Shutterstock.com

and the intertwining of major theological themes to weave an extraordinarily beautiful discourse.

The writer of Hebrews—as we have already seen in previous sections and as we will see in the first section of this fifth chapter—is like a weaver who is weaving a fine garment with multiple threads, each of which has a different color. Each of these different-color threads is an extraordinarily rich theological doctrine of its own. The author intertwines them all together into one.

A High Priest Called by God (5:1–10)

Since this chapter is a continuation of the last few verses of the previous chapter, it begins with the Greek conjunction *gar*, which literally means "for" (untranslated in many English translations). Defining the role of the high priest in the Old Testament, the writer asserts that the high priest was chosen from among the people to represent them in the "things pertaining to God on their behalf" (Heb. 5:1, NRSV). The role of the priest, and of the high priest in particular, was to be a representative or an agent, acting on the people's behalf in matters related to worship, such as offering sacrifices, offering atonement, burning incense, and the like. Apart from his priestly duties, the high priest, being human, is subject to human weaknesses. He is reminded of this every time he offers a sacrifice on behalf of his congregation because he must first offer a sacrifice for his own sins (Heb. 5:2–3).

This was a well-known fact among the original recipients of Hebrews. When instituting the ordinance of the sin offering for unintentional sins, the LORD instructed Moses, saying, "If it is the anointed priest who sins, thus bringing guilt on the people, he shall offer for the sin that he has committed a bull of the herd without blemish as a sin offering to the LORD" (Lev. 4:3, NRSV). Insofar as the high priest has to offer a sacrifice for his personal sins, he is subject to the same weaknesses as the people. Thus, he is able to act gently toward those who behave ignorantly or those of his congregation who are lost, knowing that he is nowise above temptation.

Notice the contrast in verse 2, however. Observe the indirect but effective comparison—the favorite writing style of the author—that undergirds this section as he weaves together two of the three themes presented in this chapter.

In the previous chapter when the author speaks of Jesus as the high priest, who is able to empathize with our weaknesses, he described him as "one who in every respect has been *tempted* as we are, yet without sin" (Heb. 4:15, RSV). In this chapter when he now speaks of the earthly high priest, he captures the same idea using a different term that is sadly glossed over in most English translations: "being able to deal gently with those who are ignorant and led astray, since he himself also is *surrounded* by weakness" (Heb. 5:2, LEB; this is a literal rendering of the original Greek). Owing to the extraordinary writing skills of the author, the use of the term *surrounded* is both deliberate and significant.

Jesus, who shared our sinful nature on earth but is the sinless Son of God, could only be *tempted* by weakness. Being *fully* man and *fully* God, temptations were not inherent to his nature. They came not from within but from without and were defeated and overcome, as in the temptation account in the wilderness (Matt. 4:1–11). An earthly high priest, however, who is not fully God, is *surrounded* by weakness (beautifully rendered *compassed* in the KJV or *beset* in other translations). For this earthly high priest, temptations compass him about inside and out. In this case weakness is inherent, integral, and inseparable from his nature. It *surrounds* him on every side. Because of this weakness, which causes him to sin, the earthly high priest must offer sacrifices to atone for his own sins. By emphasizing the sinful nature of the earthly high priest and its intrinsic weakness, the author underscores the sinlessness, perfection, and righteousness of the heavenly high priest, Jesus.

Moving from this indirect comparison to a direct one, the writer mentions Aaron by name for the first time—one of the revered figures of the Old Testament, Judaism's first high priest, and the older brother of Moses. Aaron, however, is now mentioned not to highlight dissimilarities between him and Jesus, but similarities. As Aaron was called or invited (literally "officially summoned to duty"), so too was Jesus.

The narrative of Aaron's direct calling or invitation to the priesthood is found in the Old Testament. In Exodus the LORD sets Aaron and his sons apart for his exclusive service: "Then bring near to you Aaron your brother, and his sons with him, from among the people of Israel, to serve me as priests—Aaron and Aaron's sons, Nadab and Abihu, Eleazar and Ithamar" (Exod. 28:1, RSV). It is evident that Aaron was invited by none other than the LORD himself. This calling is affirmed in later Old Testament books, such as the Chronicles: "Aaron was set apart to consecrate the most holy things, that he and his sons for ever should burn incense before the LORD, and minister to him and pronounce blessings in his name for ever" (1 Chr. 23:13, RSV). Thus, the fact that Aaron and all his sons were separated for the service of the "things pertaining to God" was well established with the recipients of Hebrews. Likewise, Jesus did not exalt himself as the high priest but was called by God (Heb. 5:5).

Having quoted Psalm 2 in the opening chapter of the epistle, the author returns to it once more to substantiate his claim that Jesus was called by God the Father to receive the honor of priesthood. He then quotes Psalm 110, which he quotes two other times in chapter 7 for a total of three direct quotations from this psalm alone. We will discuss this psalm at length when we come to chapter 7. For our purposes here, the author desires to establish that Jesus was *ordained* as the ultimate high priest of God by a divine calling and not by unlawful or dishonest usurping of that office.

To show the legitimacy of his ministry and to give validity to his works, Jesus himself used a similar strategy with the Jews of his day (or at least tried to). In one instance Jesus said to the Jews, "If I testify about myself, my testimony is not true. There is another who testifies about me, and I know that the testimony which he testifies about me is true" (John 5:31–32, NIV). When the Jews were astonished by the power of his teaching, "Jesus answered them and said, 'My teaching is not mine, but is from the one who sent me'" (John 7:16, LEB). Every invitee needs someone to invite him or her, and every person called requires someone to call him or her. Such invitation or calling gets its legitimacy from the one who initiates it. If the person is authorized to extend such an invitation, this becomes an endorsement of the invitation and of the invitee. The Jews of the first century fully understood this concept.

In Mark we read that they came and asked Jesus, saying, "By what authority are you doing these things, or *who* gave you this authority that you do these things?" (Mark 11:28, LEB). They understood that no one could exalt himself to do and teach the things that Jesus had been doing and teaching unless someone else—higher than him—had called him to such ministry. For this reason our writer goes to great lengths to authenticate the ministry of Jesus as the ultimate high priest by showing that it was God the Father who had called him. There is no one greater, higher, or more authorized to endorse such a calling than the Father himself. He calls whom he wishes to be *his* high priest. In the last few verses of this section, the writer intertwines the last of the three strands he weaves together in this chapter—Jesus's sonship to the Father.

In an intriguing move, after the writer has spared no effort to show Jesus's superiority to the angels, Moses, and Aaron as the one and only Son of the Father, he here appears to set aside his deity, almost entirely, to highlight his humanity. The closing verses of this section speak of the *man* Jesus in such a lowly manner, unmatched anywhere else in the New Testament. One passage in the Old Testament comes close to being a match, albeit indirectly, and that is Isaiah 53—the suffering servant discourse.

The author uses yet another phrase that is entirely unique to Hebrews: "the days of his flesh" (Heb. 5:7). This is a clear reference to Jesus in his incarnate state and is the author's distinctive style of referring to the mystery of Jesus's emptying himself. Paul describes that same mystery in Philippians, writing of Jesus that he took "the *form* of a slave, being born in human *likeness*. And being found in human *form*, he humbled himself and became obedient to the point of death—even death on a cross" (Phil. 2:7-8, NRSV). Words like *form* and *likeness* indicate that these lowly states are statuses that Christ *acquired* for himself, but they are not the *essence* of who he is. This is quite unlike all other humans, whose essence of being is defined by their human nature.

With unparalleled writing skills, our author goes on to emphasize Jesus's apparent weakness during the days of his flesh. Some of what the writer of Hebrews conveys here may be awkward at first, considering that it is written about the Son of God, who is equal to his Father. The author knows—and so does his audience—that he is writing this regarding the *man* Jesus in his humanity and not regarding the eternal Son of God in his deity. He describes him as offering up "prayers and supplications, with loud cries and tears, to the one who was able to save him from death" (Heb. 5:7, NRSV). This ingenious literary device serves as evidence of the author's earlier assertion that Jesus, as a high priest, is able to sympathize with our weaknesses since he himself has experienced injustice, hardship, and trials (Heb. 4:15).

It may be puzzling at first that our author speaks of Jesus offering up prayers with loud cries and tears. Almost definitely writing after the three synoptic gospels, the writer of

Hebrews was quite likely familiar with the gospel accounts of Jesus praying in the Garden of Gethsemane. Matthew tells us that Jesus "began to be distressed and troubled" (Matt. 26:37, LEB). In this passage we read that Jesus went and prayed three times to the Father with a similar petition: "My Father, if it is possible, let this cup pass from me; yet not what I want but what you want" (Matt. 26:39, NRSV). Luke documents a detail that many find uncomfortable reading about concerning our Lord Jesus while he was praying in Gethsemane: "An angel from heaven appeared to him and strengthened him. And being in anguish, he prayed more earnestly, and his sweat was like drops of blood falling to the ground" (Luke 22:43–44, NIV). So uncomfortable in fact were these words that some ancient manuscripts omit them, apparently due to the scribes' reluctance to document such a detail of the suffering of our Lord.[17] As some do today, many in the early church found in such statements about Jesus's humanity reasons to doubt his divinity. It is not so, however. Statements like this, found throughout the Bible (both the Old and New Testaments), only show the *fullness* of Jesus's humanity. When he took to himself our human nature, he did not take it in part; he took it in its fullness: body, soul, and spirit. This means that he ex-

---

[17] It is disheartening that some modern English Bible translations do not contain these verses and, in some cases, do not even note that some verses were omitted in their translation, except in the footnotes (as in the RSV). In the world of textual criticism, verses that are theologically challenging are almost always deemed authentic. If these verses were not authentic, one must ask the obvious question: Which scribe would add such verses to Luke, challenging the divinity of our Lord Jesus? Because the more theologically challenging reading is usually thought to be authentic, it is far more likely that these verses were indeed written by Luke and later found problematic and thus omitted in later manuscripts. Additionally, those who question the reliability of the gospel accounts struggle to explain such references. If the gospel narratives were fabricated, one would expect the deity of Jesus to be embellished and references to his human weakness to be omitted. Yet we observe the opposite throughout the New Testament.

perienced everything all other human beings experience, apart from sin, including the full spectrum of human emotions.

In the narrative of Hebrews the humble and submissive state that Jesus assumed *follows* (instead of precedes) the Father's *calling* him as the ultimate high priest after the order of Melchizedek (Heb. 5:6). The *fulfillment* of that calling, however, did not take place until Jesus was "perfected" through obedience and suffering (Heb. 5:9). To be more precise, it was *through* this obedience and suffering that God's calling of Jesus to become the great high priest was fulfilled.

When our author speaks of Jesus "learning obedience," he is *not* referring to the second person of the Godhead, who is fully God and who was with the Father before the foundation of the world (John 1:1; 17:5, 24). On the surface it may appear that our writer is suggesting that Jesus had not been initially obedient to the Father and then, through suffering, "learned obedience." However, a more complete understanding of New Testament theology shows otherwise.

The very act of incarnation, which preceded his crucifixion, was done in obedience to the will of the Father. We also have witness from God the Father that Jesus is his obedient Son. Immediately after Jesus's baptism, the Holy Spirit descended upon him and the voice of the Father was heard from heaven saying, "You are my beloved Son; with you I am well pleased" (Mark 1:11, LEB). Matthew bears the same witness concerning Jesus's baptism: "And when Jesus had been baptized, just as he came up from the water, suddenly the heavens were opened to him and he saw the Spirit of God descending like a dove and alighting on him. And a voice from heaven said, 'This is my Son, the Beloved, with whom I am well pleased'" (Matt. 3:16–17, NRSV).

Moreover, during his transfiguration, we find an equally strong testimony from the Father concerning his Son, Jesus. As Jesus was transfigured in his glory and as Moses and Elijah were seen and heard speaking with him, Peter asked Jesus that three tents be made because "it is good that we are here" (Luke 9:33). As Peter spoke these very words, Luke tells us that a cloud came and covered them all, and a voice was heard out of the cloud saying, "This is my Son, my Chosen One. Listen to him" (Luke 9:35, LEB). In all these occasions it is evident that the speaker was none other than God the Father, since he always referred to Jesus as "my Son." It is equally true that these heavenly testimonies show that Jesus had been obedient and submitted to his Father *before* his crucifixion, as he did during and after it. Thus, when the writer of Hebrews states that Jesus learned obedience, he intends to relay that *Jesus's obedience was gradually* revealed *to us through one act of obedience after another until it was fully shown in his crucifixion.* In other words, Jesus's obedience was *fully* manifested at the cross. To describe this idea, our writer uses an eloquent term in verse 9—"perfected."

Therefore, there is nothing new in Hebrews about Jesus's obedience. The writer is here speaking of Jesus the *man*, who was born in the flesh, learned how to talk and walk, and matured as all men do. Luke uses a very similar language on more than one occasion in his gospel. At the conclusion of Mary's purification according to the law and after baby Jesus's encounter with Simeon the elder and their return to Nazareth, Luke writes, "And the child *grew* and *became strong,* filled with wisdom; and the favor of God was upon him" (Luke 2:40, NRSV). In the same chapter, Jesus, at the age of twelve, was left behind in the temple and later found by his parents. Once again we read something similar by Luke: "And [Jesus] went down with them and came to Nazareth, and was *obedient* to them; and his mother kept all these things in her heart. And Jesus increased in wisdom and in stature, and in favor with God and man" (Luke 2:51–52, RSV). Luke highlights Jesus's obedience to his earthly parents. At the same time, the writer of Hebrews emphasizes his obedience to God the Father, culminating in his sacrificial death on the cross, as Paul notes in

Philippians 2:8. Through his obedience to his earthly parents, Jesus increased in favor with God and people; yet through his obedience to the point of death on the cross he became the *means* by which those who believe in him can obey, gain favor with, and please the Father.

In verse 9 our writer once more demonstrates his skill as a talented theologian. Though Jesus obeyed the Father, accepted death on the cross in his body, and thus "learned obedience," he has now become the cause for (or more literally, "source of") eternal salvation to all who obey *him.* It is significant how the writer shows that Jesus attained perfection and glory by obeying the Father; but we obtain eternal salvation by obeying Jesus himself.

Milk for Infants, Solid Food for Adults (5:11–14)

Following this theologically rich section, the author gives a gentle rebuke to his original recipients. This is the first such instance in the letter but not the last. He rebukes them for being needful of teaching instead of being teachers themselves. As explained in our discussion concerning the audience of Hebrews, this is one of the indirect references suggesting that the original audience was well-versed in the Old Testament scriptures. These Jewish Christians should have understood and should have taught others that Jesus of Nazareth is the Messiah, who fulfills all that Moses and the prophets have written of him. The two disciples on the road to Emmaus could not understand how the Messiah needed to suffer and "enter into his glory" even after having been informed that his tomb was empty and that his body could not be found. Jesus's rebuke to them echoes the one found here in Hebrews when he says to the two disciples, "O foolish and slow in heart to believe in all that the prophets have spoken!" (Luke 24:25, LEB). These basic truths of the faith are what the writer of Hebrews refers to as "the basic principles of the oracles of God" (Heb. 5:12).

To relay basic spiritual principles, the author uses basic life practices well known to his readers. The notion that infants need milk and cannot digest solid food is self-evident. Paul uses the same basic analogy in 1 Corinthians. Describing how he first preached the gospel to them, Paul reminds the Corinthians how at first he fed them milk as infants, hoping he could feed them solid food later. His hopes had not come to fruition at the time of his writing:

> And so, brothers and sisters, I could not speak to you as spiritual people, but rather as people of the flesh, as infants in Christ. I fed you with milk, not solid food, for you were not ready for solid food. Even now you are still not ready, for you are still of the flesh. For as long as there is jealousy and quarreling among you, are you not of the flesh, and behaving according to human inclinations? (1 Cor. 3:1–3, NRSV)

Notice that both in 1 Corinthians and Hebrews the term *infant* (or *child* in some translations) means one who is spiritually immature, while the term *mature* refers to one who is spiritually mature in Christ. This is evident from the context and the intended meaning in both cases.

To Paul, harboring jealousy and engaging in quarrels (being of the flesh) were manifestations of being spiritual infants. In Hebrews, not being able to discern good from evil is likewise a sign of being spiritually immature. This can be inferred from the way that the author of Hebrews uses the term *mature* to refer to "those who have their powers of discernment trained by constant practice to distinguish good from evil" (Heb. 5:14). By contrast, we can infer that *infant* in this case means those who cannot distinguish good from evil. In other words, those who are infants or immature in this context experience a sort of spiritual blindness that hinders their ability to distinguish right from wrong or good from evil. In Hebrews this is an underlying rebuke for doubting that Jesus is the awaited Messiah and for considering a return to Judaism.

The writer of Hebrews dedicates the first section of the following chapter to further expound the notion of discerning good from evil, giving a practical explanation of its significance.

Questions on This Chapter

1. Most Christians understand the importance of obedience in their walk with God. Looking at Jesus as the ultimate example of submission to the Father and being fully truthful with yourself—are you submitted to God in the same manner?

2. Do you consider yourself an "infant" or an "adult" spiritually? What criteria do you use for your self-assessment?

3. Write down a couple of Bible verses that you find challenging to understand regarding the deity of Christ. What was your previous understanding of these verses before you started reading this book? What is your current understanding of these verses?

4. Make yourself a note to revisit these verses once again after you have finished this book in its entirety to see how your understanding has changed.

Chapter Six

Hebrews 6:1–20

"And we desire that every one of you do shew the same diligence to the full assurance of hope unto the end"

—Hebrews 6:11, KJV

Faith, Patience, and Attaining Promises

In the last chapter our author gave a gentle rebuke to his audience, calling them "infants" in matters of faith, who cannot digest solid food (deeper teaching). He begins this section by illustrating the fate of those infants who have once embraced the truth of the gospel but later reverted to their old beliefs, rejecting the Son of God and falling into apostasy. As we have come to learn about our author, he never gives an illustration frivolously. He has both a literary and a theological purpose behind every illustration he provides.

Here he aims to show his readers by way of demonstration an example of what he hopes they are not and will never become. He does not hesitate to make his intentions known. Later in the section he forthrightly tells his readers that he is certain they will not become another illustration of such apostasy, as a way of encouraging his audience by imparting his confidence in them. This is consistent with the pattern we have observed thus far: comparison followed by warning, admonition, or encouragement.

In the closing verses of the previous chapter, we observed that he compared infants and the mature in faith, identifying them as the former. Now he begins this chapter with a similar comparison: the good land that receives the rain and produces good fruit versus that which produces thorns and thistles. He immediately follows by encouraging them to be the former. After his previous gentle rebuke, he now moves on to encouragement.

The Consequences of Apostasy (6:1–12)

The first few verses in this chapter are confusing in some translations. In some older translations, it appears as though the author is saying that we should *not* lay again the foundation of repentance from dead works, faith in God, and the like. Of course, this is not a correct rendering of the Greek or something the author could have meant. Most modern translations render it more accurately: "Therefore let us go on toward perfection, leaving behind the basic teaching about Christ, and not laying again the foundation: repentance from dead works and faith toward God, instruction about baptisms, laying on of hands, resurrection of the dead, and eternal judgment" (Heb. 6:1–3, NRSV). We should keep in mind that punctuation marks were not available in the first century and, therefore, were not used in any ancient manuscripts. They were implied and could be discerned only from the context. In this case the colon (":") after the word "foundation" in this rendering makes the meaning clearer to the modern reader.

The author does not desire to once again lay the foundation, which is repentance from dead works and so on; he wants to move beyond that foundation. Hence, not laying the foundation *again* simply means that he hopes his readers will "leave behind" these elementary tenets—what he refers to as "milk"—and embrace the deeper truths of the faith (see Heb. 5:13). This "leaving behind" does not mean abandoning but rather moving beyond the basic and simple to the advanced and refined—what he terms "solid food" (see Heb. 5:14). Not abandoning these basic principles of faith is evident since in verse 3 he expresses his wish to return to these topics at some point in the future, likely during his face-to-face encounter with the original recipients—which he expresses later in the epistle (Heb. 13:19, 23). He hopes that his original readers move from being infants to being mature adults in the faith. He proceeds to enumerate what those fundamental tenets of the faith are.

Repenting from dead works can refer either to works that produce death (sin) or to trusting in works that are dead in the eyes of God (the works of the law that are deemed dead before God apart from faith). Because of how this same phrase is used again in 9:14, most interpreters tend to understand it as referring to sin. I believe it is better understood as the works of the law in this context. We will visit what this phrase means in the context of chapter 9 when we discuss that chapter. Here we will address how it is used in this sixth chapter of Hebrews.

In the present context the author seems to use the phrase "dead works" to refer to the dead works of the law. For one, it is the works of the law that his audience relied on for righteousness and justification before the LORD. This is especially true with his original readers, who came from a Jewish background. Second, the term "dead works" is never used anywhere else in the New Testament to refer to sin (but see the discussion in chapter 9). It is also the works of the law that are said elsewhere to be the cause of curse—and thus death—for those who rely on them: "For all who rely on works of the law are under a curse; for it is written, 'Cursed be every one who does not abide by all things written in the book of the law, and do them'" (Gal. 3:10, NRSV). Furthermore, in the New Testament, it is the Gentiles—not the Jews—who are said to have lived in sin before accepting the Christian faith. The "sin" of the Gentiles generally refers to fornication, idolatry, homosexuality, and greed. The emphasis for the Jews, however, has been on the works of the law by which they believed they gained justification before the LORD. For the Gentiles it was their attachment to sinful practices that hindered them from accepting the faith; for the Jews it was their presumed righteousness through the works of the law that hampered their repentance. This is evident from how the Jews always took pride in being righteous before God because of their works. Therefore, for the author's original Jewish readers, if they were to apostatize and return to "dead works," that would mean returning to the works of the law.

The following verses give a stern warning against apostasy, likening those who apostatize from their faith in Christ to the ground that has "drunk the rain" but instead of producing good fruit, it produced thorns and thistles. Our writer uses the reference to the rain to signify tasting the heavenly gift, partaking of the Holy Spirit, and having tasted the word of God and the power of the age to come (Heb. 6:4–5). Those who have experienced all these precious gifts are expected to produce good fruit, in which case they would receive a blessing from God (Heb. 6:7). However, if these same people backslided and fell away from the faith, the consequences would be so dire that, as the author warns, it would be impossible to renew them again to repentance (Heb. 6:4). This metaphor of the ground that produces fruit versus that which produces thorns and thistles is all but a direct allusion to the imagery used in Isaiah, which Jesus used to rebuke the Jews, who were offended, since they were sure that he had been speaking of their apostasy and rejection of God.

In the song of the unfruitful vineyard, the LORD spoke through Isaiah of how Israel in the Old Testament was a cause for his wrath, disappointment, and pain (Isa. 5:1–7). This poignant song illustrates how the LORD planted for himself a choice vineyard on a fertile hill—Israel in the land of Canaan, which was known for its abundance as the land of milk and honey. Using typical farmers' language, the LORD depicts how he cleared all the stones from the ground around his new vineyard, symbolizing the removal of enemy nations surrounding Israel (see Ps. 44:1–3). The LORD built a watchtower around his new vineyard—his protection and shield around his beloved Israel, the apple of his eye (Deut. 32:10). He hewed a wine vat (receptacles), expecting his vineyard to flow with wine produced from good grapes. Instead, it produced wild ("sour" or "unpalatable") grapes. The song goes on to portray how the LORD, in his hurt and frustration, resolved to destroy his vineyard, removing the tower he had placed around it and allowing it to be trodden down. He would no longer prune it or command the rain to fall upon it, leaving it prey to thorns and thistles. The song concludes with this startling remark that identifies who the vineyard is: "For the vineyard of the LORD of hosts is the house of Israel, and the people of Judah are his pleasant planting; he expected justice, but saw bloodshed; righteousness, but heard a cry" (Isa. 5:7, NRSV).

This is nearly identical imagery to that which our Lord Jesus used to express his dismay with the Jews of his day (Matt. 21:33–46). Rebuking them for refusing to believe the message of repentance of John the Baptist, Jesus reminded his audience of how this song from Isaiah rightly spoke of the hardness of their hearts. The Jewish leaders of the time well understood that he had spoken of them, as Matthew gives us this editorial note: "When the chief priests and the Pharisees heard his parables, they perceived that he was speaking about them. But when they tried to arrest him, they feared the multitudes, because they held him to be a prophet" (Matt. 21:45–46, RSV).

The author of Hebrews uses the same imagery to refer to those who reject the Son of God. As the LORD in Isaiah refused to prune that rejected vineyard, our author maintains that it is impossible to restore those backsliders again to repentance (Heb. 6:4). Whereas Isaiah describes the LORD's vineyard as the object of his wrath, represented by the lack of rain, our writer emphasizes that those who fall away resemble the ground that "drinks up the rain falling on it repeatedly" (Heb. 6:7, NRSV). Hebrews uses the same language found in Isaiah to depict God's judgment and rejection of those who have rejected his Son, leaving them to produce thorns and thistles (Heb. 6:8). The time for repentance endures for a while, but it is always limited.

Esau was an example of that. He sought the blessing of his father, Isaac, but despised his birthright and sold it to his brother Jacob for a meal. Later he went on to marry two Hittite women, who "made life bitter for Isaac and Rebekah" (Gen. 26:35). Still, not realizing his own sin and refusing to accept any responsibility for his actions, he hated his brother Jacob and sought to kill him (Gen. 27:41). Refusing to accept any correction, it was impossible to redeem Esau, as the writer of Hebrews tells us later: "He found no chance to repent" (Heb. 12:17).

But perhaps there is no worse example of this than Judas Iscariot, who was one of the Twelve. He drank from the fountain of our Lord Jesus for more than three years, as did all the other disciples. He cast out demons in the name of Jesus; he healed the sick; he was promised a seat to judge the twelve tribes or Israel; and he partook of the body and blood of the Lord (see Matt. 19:28; Luke 9:1–2; 22:14–23). Yet despite the Lord's repeated warnings, it was impossible to bring him to repentance even after he had betrayed and surrendered his Master over to his enemies. The author of Hebrews tells us that the end of those who have crossed the point of no return is to be burned (Heb. 6:8).

It may be shocking to some of us to hear the author of Hebrews speak of those who cannot be renewed once more to repentance (or through repentance). This sort of language is foreign to many twenty-first-century Christians, since most churches today teach that "the door of repentance is always open." This teaching cannot be farther from biblical truth. The Bible teaches—as you can see in this chapter of Hebrews—that the opportunity for repentance may be available for a long time, but that time eventually comes to an end. God is longsuffering, slow to anger, and quick to forgive (Exod. 34:6; Joel 2:13; Jonah 4:2); nonetheless, his patience is not infinite. The Bible promises that true repentance is *always* accepted by the LORD *whenever* it is offered, but it *never* promises that there will be *another* chance for repentance. In fact, listen to what Paul says: "Behold, *now* is the acceptable time; behold, *now* is the day of salvation" (2 Cor. 6:2, RSV). If you are reading these words and have not repented and surrendered your life to Christ, do it *now*—because tomorrow may not come for you. You are never promised a tomorrow, but you are promised that if you repent *now*, your repentance will be accepted. If you hear his voice, do not harden your heart (Heb. 3:7–8).

Although many modern-day Christians may not accept it, this is precisely aligned with what Jesus himself taught and preached. Our Lord Jesus taught that "the gate is wide and the way is easy, that leads to destruction, and those who enter by it are many. For the gate is narrow and the way is hard, that leads to life, and those who *find* it are few" (Matt. 7:13–14, RSV). Notice that of the wide gate and the easy way that leads to destruction, Jesus says, "Enter by it." Yet of the narrow gate and the way that leads to life, Jesus did not say, "Enter by it," but said, "Find it." *Many will find the narrow gate but shall in nowise enter therein.* Those who enter it shall be even fewer! Many will know the way that leads to life but will not have the strength to walk therein. Many will desire to repent and inherit eternal life but will not be willing to pay the cost. Many will start their walk with the LORD but will not be able to endure to the end and finish the race. Many will receive the message of the gospel with joy but will then turn away from it under tribulations or persecutions (Matt. 13:21).

We find another sobering testimony from Peter in his second epistle to this effect:

> For if, after they have escaped the defilements of the world through the knowledge of our Lord and Savior Jesus Christ, they are again entangled in them and overcome, the last state has become worse for them than the first. For it would have been better for them never to have known the way of righteousness than after knowing it to turn back from the holy commandment delivered to them. What the true proverb says has happened to them: "The dog returns to its own vomit, and the sow, after washing herself, returns to wallow in the mire." (2 Peter 2:20–22)

The language that Peter and the author of Hebrews use may be difficult to reconcile with doctrines echoed in many churches today that a Christian who is "once saved is always saved." The Bible, on the other hand, teaches that many will come to the knowledge of the way of righteousness but will turn back from the faith and perish. It is evident that Peter is not speaking of "fake" believers who pretend to be Christians. He is certainly speaking of some who will repent, forsake their sinful ways, and come to the knowledge of our Lord Jesus Christ but will eventually get entangled again in the same labyrinth of sin and iniquity. As Peter clearly states it, their latter end will be worse than their beginning. Rightly says the Preacher in Ecclesiastes, "Better is the end of a thing than the beginning thereof" (Eccl. 7:8).

The writer of Hebrews equates those who have fallen away from the faith after having known the truth with the Jews who crucified the Son of God. Those who reject Christ, having known him as the Son of God, crucify him once again to themselves. They do this by "holding him up to contempt" (Heb. 6:6) in the same manner the Roman soldiers, the chief priests, the scribes, and the elders did when they mocked the crucified Christ, saying, "He saved others; he cannot save himself. He is the King of Israel; let him come down now from the cross, and we will believe in him" (Matt. 27:42). Since Jesus bore the shame and mockery of rejection by those who crucified him, those who now reject him as Lord and Savior crucify him once again.

Following this somber image, our author expresses his hope and confidence that his audience will not be just another example of falling away and receiving judgment. This is apparent in the way he phrases verse 9: "Even though we speak in this way, beloved, we are confident of better things in your case, things that belong to salvation" (Heb. 6:9, NRSV). This is his way to draw a distinction between what precedes and what follows.

He then articulates the good news to his audience: the same way God does not hold the guilty blameless, he would never overlook the work and faithfulness of those who love him and others (Heb. 6:9–10). It is noteworthy that in Revelation, Jesus invariably uses the phrase "I know your works," in every message he asks John to relay to the seven churches (see Rev. 2:2, 9, 13, 19; 3:1, 8, 15, KJV). Our Lord never overlooks sin or allows it to go unpunished. Likewise, he never overlooks the works of love and faithfulness, allowing them to go unrewarded. Jesus also emphasized the importance of producing such fruits. In the Parable of the Sower, for example, he mentions that the good ground produces in one case a hundredfold, in another sixty, and in another thirty. They all bore fruit in some measure. John the Baptist, through the Holy Spirit, had this rebuke to the Jews: "Bear fruits worthy of repentance" (Luke 3:8). Works of love are the outward sign of inner transformation by faith, wrought by the work of the Holy Spirit in one's heart.

Likely not everyone among the original readers of Hebrews had the same level of commitment and perseverance in righteousness. Some had fallen away and thus deserved the writer's previous rebuke and admonition. Hence, he proceeds to express his desire that *all* would show the same diligence. Notice how he does not neglect to emphasize that they must remain steadfast and endure *to the end* (Heb. 6:11). Enduring to the end in faith and patience is how the promises of God are attained.

The Truthful Promises of God (6:13–20)

In the next few verses of this chapter, the author demonstrates to his readers how enduring hardships and trials, in faith and patience, is the means by which one receives God's promises. As has been his strategy to construct his arguments, he uses Old Testament examples to illustrate his point and provide evidence for it from Scripture. Here he uses Abraham as an example of faith and patience. The direct Old Testament reference in this case is the episode of God's testing Abraham's faith by asking him to sacrifice his only son, Isaac, on Mount Moriah (Gen. 22:1–19). While this is a well-known biblical story, it merits a short summary of its main theological implications for our purposes here, especially since the author of Hebrews returns to it again in chapter 11.

Having been given a son despite his old age and his wife's barrenness, God wanted to test Abraham's faith by asking him to sacrifice his one and only son, whom he loved. God's own words emphasize his knowledge of Abraham's love for Isaac: "Take your son, your *only* son Isaac, *whom you love*, and go to the land of Moriah, and offer him there as a burnt offering on one of the mountains that I shall show you" (Gen. 22:2, NRSV). Obeying God's command, Abraham walked for three days to reach the mountain designated for the sacrifice, as most sacrifices back then in the ancient Near East were offered on a mountain or a high place. Not wanting anyone to witness this painful and personal act, Abraham departed with his son alone, leaving behind the two young servants whom he had taken with him to assist on the journey. He ascended the mountain with the fire torch and the knife in his hand, while Isaac carried the wood on which the sacrifice was to be offered. Noticing the absence of one crucial element of sacrifice offering, Isaac wondered to his father where the lamb of the sacrifice was. Honest with himself and with his son, Abraham told Isaac that God would provide a lamb for himself. When they reached the top of the mountain, Abraham built an altar and stacked the wood on it. He then bound his own son Isaac, placing him on the altar, and grabbed the knife, ready to slay his son on the altar of God. At this pivotal moment, the angel of the LORD—whom we discover a moment later was the LORD himself—called Abraham to stop him from sacrificing his son. After sacrificing the lamb provided by the LORD, which was caught by its horns in the thicket, the LORD spoke once again to Abraham, but this time blessing him with both a promise and an oath—the "two unchangeable things" that the author of Hebrews refers to in 6:18. The text in Genesis thus records one of the most important verses in the Bible:

> By myself have I sworn, saith the LORD, for because thou hast done this thing, and hast not withheld thy son, thine only son: That in blessing I will bless thee, and in multiplying I will multiply thy seed as the stars of the heaven, and as the sand which is upon the sea shore; and thy seed shall possess the gate of his enemies; And in thy seed shall all the nations of the earth be blessed; because thou hast obeyed my voice. (Gen. 22:16–18, KJV)[18]

---

[18] Though in Galatians 3:16 Paul underscores the significance of using

Though human sacrifice was quite common in the pagan cultures and worship practices of the ancient Near East, it was strictly prohibited and punishable by death according to the commandments of the God of the Bible. In fact, those who refused to exact the death penalty on anyone who engaged in child sacrifice would be subject to punishment by death themselves. Molech, the god of the Ammonites, was among the pagan gods most worshiped by child sacrifice. Thus, we find in Leviticus this strict prohibition against sacrificing one's "seed" or "offspring" to Molech:

> The LORD spoke to Moses, saying: Say further to the people of Israel: Any of the people of Israel, or of the aliens who reside in Israel, who give any of their offspring to Molech shall be put to death; the people of the land shall stone them to death. I myself will set my face against them, and will cut them off from the people, because they have given of their offspring to Molech, defiling my sanctuary and profaning my holy name. And if the people of the land should ever close their eyes to them, when they give of their offspring to Molech, and do not put them to death, I myself will set my face against them and against their family, and will cut them off from among their people, them and all who follow them in prostituting themselves to Molech. (Lev. 20:1–5, NRSV)

Hence, it is reasonable to understand how Abraham did not see God's command to sacrifice his son, Isaac, as odd or uncommon. Clearly, at the time the command was given to

the singular form *seed* and not the plural *seeds*, most modern English Bible translations render this singular Hebrew word in Genesis 22:18 in the plural form, using terms such as *descendants* (as in the RSV) or terms that can be both singular or plural such as *offspring* (as in the ESV, NIV, and NRSV). The original Hebrew *zera* is distinctively singular.

Abraham, there had been no prior commandment from the LORD prohibiting child sacrifice. Not having the written word of God through which he would know the character of God, Abraham would have thought that the LORD God was like all the other gods worshiped in the region who required human sacrifice. Doubtless, not only does the LORD God abhor child sacrifice and prohibit it, but this entire passage was a "type" of God the Father sacrificing his own beloved Son, Jesus, for us.

It must be noted that the Hebrew word *zera* used in the Leviticus passage above is the same word that appears in Genesis 22, signifying the "seed" of Abraham. This is a significant linguistic observation that usually goes unnoticed in most translations. While other pagan nations sacrificed their "seed" to their gods, the LORD not only prohibited sacrificing it but he blessed the "seed" of Abraham and made it a cause for blessings to all the nations of the earth. The very "seed" that others sacrificed, the LORD redeemed and blessed.

Commenting on the divine oath-promise given to Abraham at the end of the Genesis narrative, our author shows how that, since there is no one greater than him, when God wanted to swear to Abraham, he could swear only by himself. In the Near and Middle East, oaths are commonly used to settle disputes or to distinguish truths from lies. This is commonly practiced in those regions to this day. If one refuses to swear by an oath, his statement is usually thought to be either untrue or less reliable. In most other cultures today, it is commonplace to use oaths to confirm and uphold promises, statements, and covenants. Oaths are used to confirm one's commitment to the truthfulness of the statement made, whether it contains a promise or an assertion. To give authenticity to what is spoken, many resort to oaths. This is evident by the oaths witnesses must swear in courtrooms before giving their testimony to confirm their intention and commitment to giving factual statements, or the oaths most government officials must take before assuming office. Notably, one must swear by someone or something greater than himself or herself. In the case of a courtroom, that is usually the word of God—the Bible. In other forms of verbal communication, the name of God—or things related to him—are usually invoked as an oath, something the New Testament strictly prohibits (Matt. 5:33–37; James 5:12). But when God gives an oath, he swears by himself, for there is no one greater than him (Heb. 6:13). Thus, to show that his promise to Abraham cannot and will not be revoked, he affirms the promise by an oath.

The writer of Hebrews shows that with such an immutable oath-promise, it is impossible for God to lie. This surety of God's promise enables us to trust in the very promise that God gave to Abraham, which now has become ours to receive. With our being the children of Abraham through faith, it is evident that God's promise to Abraham has become fulfilled through Christ and through our faith in him.

In Galatians we find this assurance from Paul to the churches of Galatia and thus to all believers in Christ: "And if you are Christ's, then you are Abraham's offspring, heirs according to promise" (Gal. 3:29, RSV). More specifically, the original readers of Hebrews, who were the biological descendants of Abraham, are thus encouraged to trust that what God has spoken to their father Abraham will not be rescinded. In fact, not only is the promise not revoked—but it is irrevocable. The author of Hebrews emphasizes the permanent and irreversible nature of the promise. The significant point the author is making here is this: if the Gentile Christians of the New Testament are promised to receive Abraham's inheritance through faith in Christ, those who are the ethnic descendants of Israel and believers in Christ should be far more certain of inheriting God's promise to their father Abraham. He therefore seeks to encourage and strengthen them by using the example of their father Abraham, who, despite the trials and setbacks that he experienced, remained steadfast and unshakable in his faith, willing to sacrifice his only son to please his God. Abraham was confident—no matter the circumstances—that God would remain faithful to his promise. In like confidence, the recipients should find in this reassurance hope to keep their souls anchored like a ship, refusing to be carried away with the waves of doubt and unbelief.

It is noteworthy that the hope the author speaks of in these verses is both the *cause* and the *means* by which we enter the heavenly Holy of Holies of the Father. Through our hope of entering, we in fact enter. In other words, this hopeful confidence of entering is what allows us to enter. Because we hope in faith, we will receive the privilege of entering the Father's presence. In chapter 11 our author returns to the topic of faith and hope, where he draws an interconnected relationship between them, defining faith as the assurance of things hoped for (Heb. 11:1). Faith and hope are thus two sides of the same coin.

This chapter closes with the opening thought of the next one. Here the topic of Melchizedek is introduced once more. This theme was introduced for the first time in the epistle in chapter 5. In 5:10 the author introduced Jesus as the high priest, who is the cause and the source of our salvation. Here he introduces him as the high priest, who precedes us in entering behind the veil (curtain). Jesus is thus introduced as our forerunner whom we all follow. The reference to the curtain is a direct allusion to the veil in the tabernacle or, later, the temple. This curtain separated the Holy Place, where priests often went in for various kinds of service, and the Holy of Holies, where no one was allowed to enter—at the risk of death—except the high priest once a year on the Day of Atonement (Yom Kippur; see Lev. 16:12, 15). The imagery in view is that of our entering therein, following in the footsteps of Jesus, our high priest, who went in first as a forerunner on our behalf (more literally, "a forerunner for us"). The Greek word *prodromos* (rendered here *forerunner*) literally signifies someone who undergoes an experience in advance of someone else.[19] Jesus entered behind the curtain as our "forerunner" so that he might prepare a way for us to follow him into the heavenly Holy of Holies and behold the face of the Father. Our writer returns to this same theme in later chapters at greater lengths, and so will we.

The next chapter of this epistle (along with chapters 8 and 9) is considered the heart of Hebrews. As the midpoint of the epistle, this is where our author packs his most theologically dense arguments. None of what precedes or follows these chapters of Hebrews contains more theology.

Questions on This Chapter

1. The story of Abraham and Isaac in Genesis 22 is one of the most impactful in the Bible. It is a story full of obedience and love for God. In your devotional time, read this chapter of Genesis (preferably more than once) with a pen and paper nearby. Jot down what each element or key event in the story signifies to you, and then answer this question: How far would you be willing to go to demonstrate your love for God?

2. The divine promise to Abraham is mentioned multiple times before this passage in Genesis 22. So we know that this story is not necessarily about God's promise to Abraham. Why then do you think it was important to the Holy Spirit to document this story for us at this particular point of the Genesis narrative?

---

[19] James Swanson, *Dictionary of Biblical Languages with Semantic Domains: Greek (New Testament)*, electronic ed. (Oak Harbor, WA: Logos Research Systems, 1997), entry 4596.

CHAPTER SEVEN

Hebrews 7:1–28

"Accordingly Jesus has also become the guarantee of a better covenant."

—Hebrews 7:22, NRSV

The True Melchizedek

Chapter 7 of Hebrews is somewhat unique in that it is the first chapter we encounter that makes such studied use of the Old Testament scriptures and events to bring out specific theological implications. This particular chapter of Hebrews reads almost like a commentary on some Old Testament scriptures, synthesizing themes from Abraham's encounter with Melchizedek in Genesis, the Aaronic priesthood, and not surprisingly, God's oath to his Messiah in Psalm 110.

To appreciate its significance, one must carefully examine the Old Testament references contained in this chapter in their *original* context to become familiar with the Hebraic background against which this chapter was written. For this reason we must take a slightly different approach in our study of this chapter than what we have done thus far in this book. This will help us grasp the fullness of this seventh chapter of

Hebrews. Hence, the structure of this chapter will deviate from that of the previous six. We will not examine the text of Hebrews as it appears in your Bible (by paragraph or by verse). Instead, we will begin by examining the Old Testament context of Melchizedek's encounter with Abraham in Genesis 14. We will then briefly explore the significance of Psalm 110 in its original context. Finally, we will study the text of Hebrews 7 in light of this brief Old Testament study.

The Priesthood of Melchizedek

As discussed in the introductory chapters of this book, one of the major themes in Hebrews is the superiority of Jesus Christ in every aspect over any past prophet, hero, or even the angels of heaven. This superiority is invariably illustrated in the epistle using the word *better*. At the heart of this *better* theme is the priesthood of Jesus Christ. In the seventh chapter of Hebrews the author compares Jesus's priesthood to that of the Old Testament, showing that Jesus is a better priest.

Showing how Jesus—the promised Messiah—is the true and everlasting high priest after the order of Melchizedek, the author of Hebrews underscores Jesus's divine nature by using language that is uniquely divine, thus differentiating him from all other dignified kings or priests. Founded upon Jesus's better priesthood, the writer shows that Jesus has offered a better sacrifice and therefore offers a better hope, a better covenant, better promises, and thus a better salvation. To argue for the superiority of Jesus's priesthood, the author refers to Melchizedek's lone Old Testament appearance in Genesis 14. He also makes frequent use of Psalm 110, where David writes, "The LORD says to my Lord... you are a priest for ever after the order of Melchizedek" (Ps. 110:1, 4). The writer argues that the priesthood of Melchizedek is far superior to that of Aaron. As the promised Messiah, the son of David, Jesus's priesthood—after the order of Melchizedek—is therefore likewise superior to Aaron's.

Melchizedek in Genesis 14

To understand the significance of Melchizedek's reference in Hebrews, one must examine his appearance in Genesis in its original context. This encounter between Abram and Melchizedek appears quite briefly in no more than three verses in Genesis 14:18-20. Yet as we will see shortly, these three short verses carry tremendous theological implications in both the Old and the New Testaments.

After his return from rescuing his nephew Lot from the hands of the kings of the East, Abram (Abraham) is met by Melchizedek, king of Salem (Jerusalem's ancient name). Melchizedek had brought with him bread and wine as he is introduced in the narrative as "priest of God Most High" (Gen. 14:18). In this encounter Melchizedek blesses Abram and receives from him a tenth of all that Abram had. Although he is mentioned in Psalm 110 and in Hebrews, this is the sole *appearance* of Melchizedek in the Old Testament and in the entire Bible. The Bible is intriguingly silent about who Melchizedek is. The biblical account is devoid of any background information about him, such as his descent, how he became the LORD's priest, or what the nature of his priesthood was, given that he predates Aaron by at least a few centuries. He appears in a context in which the reader of Genesis is given the impression that Abram was the only person of his time who knew or worshiped the LORD, having been chosen by him. Melchizedek's appearance on the scene is sudden, with no background information. He is introduced into the narrative with the conjunction *and* as if the reader should already know who he is (Gen. 14:18). He disappears from the biblical narrative as suddenly as he appears.

One of the interpretive issues evident in this passage, of course, is the identity of Melchizedek. Was he a divine appearance in the Old Testament or a real, historical figure? There are different views on this issue in the context of Genesis 14.

One view maintains that since his name, Melchizedek, signifies "King of Righteousness," and since he was the king of Salem (that is, king of peace)—both of which are uniquely divine qualities—then Melchizedek was none other than God himself. Those who adopt this view understand Melchizedek as one of the many Old Testament pre-incarnational appearances of the Son of God. Supporting this view is the fact that these qualities are never applied to any other prophet, king, or priest in the Old Testament, nor are they applied to anyone else in the New Testament except Jesus. In some extrabiblical Jewish sources, Melchizedek is seen as a heavenly figure, perhaps an exalted angel. Under this view one can understand why Abram readily recognized Melchizedek and accepted his blessing, even though Melchizedek is never mentioned in Genesis prior to this encounter. As we read this Genesis narrative, it seems likely that Abram had prior knowledge of Melchizedek before meeting him when he returned from battle. This interpretative view explains why Abram gave him a tenth of all his possessions. Since giving tithes throughout the Old Testament is an act of worship, it is likely that Abram recognized Melchizedek not simply as an earthly king worthy of honor and respect but as a divine figure worthy of worship.

Another view of Melchizedek's identity argues that he was a real, historical king of Salem (Jerusalem) and not a heavenly figure in any way. This view, too, offers compelling reasons for why Melchizedek could not have been an appearance of Christ. These reasons mainly arise from Hebrews 7. In this chapter Melchizedek is said to be *resembling* the Son of God" (Heb. 7:3). This would be an odd use of language if he were truly Christ incarnate. Second, he is called a "man" in Hebrews 7:4 (as in the KJV, ESV, LEB, and others). Thus, the author of

The True Melchizedek

Hebrews clearly did not believe that Melchizedek was an Old Testament appearance of the Son of God. Third, though his genealogy is not mentioned anywhere in the Bible, in Hebrews 7:6 he is said to have a human descent: "But this man who does not have *his* descent from them received tithes from Abraham and blessed him who had the promises." While in 7:3 our author remarks that Melchizedek "is without father or mother or genealogy," it is plain that the author is referring to the lack of *recorded* genealogy in the Bible. This is clear from the remainder of the verse: "having neither beginning of days nor end of life, but resembling the Son of God he continues a priest forever" (Heb. 7:3). As man, Melchizedek must have had a beginning and an end of days. Likewise, he cannot continue as a priest forever in literal terms. Therefore, our writer could not have intended to speak in absolute or literal terms here but rather concerning what came down to us in the recorded biblical narrative. Fourth, Melchizedek seems to have been king of Salem for some time, whereas all other appearances of Christ in the Old Testament were brief, with no earthly office. From the Genesis narrative it is clear that Melchizedek was known as the king of a real, historical city, that is, Jerusalem. This is not something we find with any other appearance of a heavenly figure in the Bible, let alone the Son of God. Finally, Psalm 110 distinguishes between the Messiah and Melchizedek, suggesting that they are not the same person. Taking all these facts into account, it seems best to adopt the view that Melchizedek was indeed a real, historical figure, resembling Christ but not Christ himself.

I realize that this may not be at the heart of our present discussion, but before we continue our discussion on Hebrews 7, I feel compelled to make a few additional remarks on the topic of tithing as an act of worship.

While many in the Christian laity—and in numerous cases, even teachers and preachers—argue that tithing, as an Old Testament ordinance, does not apply to modern-day Christians, it is self-evident that tithing *as an act of worship* predates the advent of the Mosaic law, going back to the days of Abraham, Isaac, and Jacob. This act of worship, signified by giving one-tenth of all one's possessions, is unmistakably evident in the encounter between Melchizedek and Abraham. It is also present in the story of Jacob.

As he left his father Isaac's house in Beersheba and escaped to Padan-aram from the face of his brother, Esau, Jacob lay his head to rest for the night after a full day's journey. He then saw a dream of a ladder connecting heaven and earth, with angels ascending and descending on it. The LORD appeared to him in the dream, renewing the promise he had given to his father, Isaac, and to his grandfather Abraham. After Jacob woke up from his sleep, he acknowledged that "surely the LORD is in this place" (Gen. 28:16). The following morning, Jacob erected the stone that had been under his head and poured oil on it (as a sign of consecration or dedication to the LORD). He called that place "Bethel," signifying "the house of God." Intriguingly, he made a vow that if the LORD were to prosper his ways, keep him safe, and bring him back to his father's house, he would worship the LORD as his God and give him a tenth of all his possessions (Gen. 28:22). It is beyond debate that in speaking the words of his vow, Jacob was acknowledging that giving the LORD one-tenth of his substance was an act of worship toward the LORD his God. Thus, it is frivolous to argue that tithing was simply "an Old Testament law" since it predates the time of Moses by centuries. Having established that, we now return to our discussion.

Melchizedek in Psalm 110

Apart from Genesis 14, the only other mention of Melchizedek in the Old Testament is in Psalm 110. The header of this psalm indicates that it was written by King David. Its general theme is the victory of the LORD and his Messiah over their enemies. In the opening verse of the psalm, the LORD (God the Father) promises the Messiah (whom David calls "my Lord") that he will subdue his enemies and make them his footstool. From his discussion with the Jews, we know that Jesus and the Jews of his time understood the referent in this verse to be the Messiah, the Son of David. In his discussion Jesus asked the Pharisees, "'What do you think of the Messiah? Whose son is he?' They said to him, 'The son of David.'" (Matt. 22:42, NRSV). Immediately Jesus replied, saying, "How is it then that David by the Spirit calls him Lord, saying, 'The LORD said to my Lord, "Sit at my right hand, until I put your enemies under your feet"'? If David thus calls him Lord, how can he be his son?" (Matt. 22:43–45, NRSV). Therefore, it is beyond any doubt that the one David calls by the Spirit "my Lord" is the awaited Messiah, who would descend from David's own seed.

Then we read in Psalm 110:4 that God the Father speaks to his Messiah, swearing by an oath that he is a priest forever after the order of Melchizedek and will remain so forever: "The LORD has sworn and will not change his mind, 'You are a priest for ever after the order of Melchizedek'" (Ps. 110:4, RSV). It is noteworthy that the nature of the promise itself is what demands an oath. In the context of this psalm, it is evident that the recipient of this promise is a king, as it says, "The LORD sends forth from Zion your mighty scepter. Rule in the midst of your foes" (Ps. 110:2, RSV). Thus, verse 4 is essentially the priestly ordination of a king. With this rare oath and for the first time in the Old Testament, God unites the functions and the offices of priest and king in one person—the Messiah.

These offices were always separate in Israel. To unite them, an oath was necessary.

Thus, as a priest-king, Melchizedek foreshadowed Christ. Not only will Christ rule his people but he will also *represent* them before God. Yet again, up to this point in the biblical narrative, the text remains completely silent regarding who Melchizedek is or why his priesthood—rather than Aaron's—is chosen to foreshadow that of the Messiah. Although the Bible reader does not learn the full significance of Melchizedek until Hebrews 7, the reference to him in Psalm 110 is already remarkable. There, Melchizedek is revealed as a type of the promised Messiah. Whatever the nature of the Messiah's priesthood, it would follow the pattern of Melchizedek's. Yet for the Old Testament reader, the significance and superiority of Melchizedek's priesthood remain a mystery—one that is fully explained only in the New Testament. No book unpacks this typology more thoroughly than the letter to the Hebrews.

The Priesthood of Melchizedek in Hebrews

Of all the manifold occasions where Hebrews refers to Melchizedek, chapter 7 is of special significance; it is the longest and richest theologically. As mentioned earlier, in this passage, the author of Hebrews intertwines Genesis 14 and Psalm 110—the only two instances of Melchizedek's mention in the Old Testament—to draw theological inferences that are of utmost importance. This passage in chapter 7 makes clear use of *typology* as it refers to Melchizedek.

In the field of biblical interpretation, the term *typology* is used to denote instances where parallelism occurs between Old Testament and New Testament themes. In these instances the Old Testament figure (or event) foreshadows what would happen centuries later in the New Testament. The former is called a "type," while the latter is an "antitype." For example, there is parallelism between calling Israel out of Egypt and Jesus's descent to and return from Egypt. Israel was called God's firstborn son in the Old Testament (Exod. 4:22–23); so is Jesus in the New Testament (Luke 1:32). This parallelism caused Matthew to use Hosea 11:1—which had been written about Israel's deliverance from the bondage in Egypt—and apply it to Jesus's own return from Egypt to his homeland, Israel: "This was to fulfil what the LORD had spoken by the prophet, 'Out of Egypt have I called my son'" (Matt. 2:15, RSV). In this instance Israel is the type and Jesus is the antitype.

In Hebrews 7 the author highlights multiple parallelisms between Melchizedek as the type and Christ as the antitype. The author's use of typology in this case is one of the most detailed found in the New Testament. The parallels found between Melchizedek and Christ are so fundamental to the writer's argument that he dedicates nearly all of chapter 7 to outlining them for his readers.

The author begins by expounding Melchizedek's name, explaining that it signifies "king of righteousness" (Heb. 7:2). Then he explains that as king of Salem, Melchizedek was a type of the king of peace—Christ. All significant characters in the Bible who were relevant to the biblical storyline had known descent, if not detailed genealogies. Melchizedek is the lone exception to this rule. With no biblical genealogy, Melchizedek had no known descent and no beginning or end of days (but see discussion above). In all these parallels, explains the author, Melchizedek was a clear type of Jesus Christ. In fact, the author seems to indicate that the sole reason Melchizedek mysteriously appears and likewise disappears from the biblical narrative *is* to be a type of Christ, "resembling the Son of God" (Heb. 7:3).

The author's use of this typology is not without its own interpretive issues. One that arises is this: In the absence of his genealogy, how can Melchizedek be a type of Christ, given that Jesus has not one but two genealogies? (See Matt. 1:1–16;

Luke 3:23–38). To contend with this issue, it is important to bear in mind that, in typology, there are facets of similarities and others of dissimilarities. In other words, types and antitypes are *not* meant to be *identical* but similar in some respects and dissimilar in others. What is true about Melchizedek as a type of Christ is true in reality of the *divine* Son of God. That is to say, Melchizedek is a type of Christ in his *deity*, not in his humanity. Though in his human nature, Jesus had a mother and a presumed earthly father (Luke 3:23), in his divine nature, he has neither a descent nor a beginning or end of days (Heb. 7:3). In other words, Melchizedek is a man whose earthly life in certain of its elements represents a type of Jesus in his divine nature. This agrees with the aforementioned view that Melchizedek was a historical figure who only parallels Christ but is not Christ himself.

Another related question that may be asked is this: Was Melchizedek, *in fact*, without a father or a mother? Since the Bible does not contain any mention of his genealogy, one is led to believe that he was. Nonetheless, that would be a classic case of what is often called an "argument from silence." This, however, does not seem to agree with what the author of Hebrews is asserting or with how the New Testament writers interpret the Old Testament in general.

Under the view that Melchizedek was none other than God himself, it would be expected that he would not have a father or a mother. If one adopts the view that Melchizedek was a historical figure, the writer of Hebrews would not be arguing from silence that Melchizedek did not have a father or a mother. Instead, the argument would be valid if we confined it to what is mentioned in the Bible. The author of Hebrews is not saying that Melchizedek did not *actually* have a father or mother; he is simply emphasizing that he did not have a father or mother *that we know of*. This is noted in Hebrews 7:6, where the writer, regarding Melchizedek, states, "But this man who does not have *his descent from them* received tithes from Abraham and blessed him who had the promises." This verse seems to indicate that Melchizedek has a descent, but it is not from the sons of Levi (see Heb. 7:5). Thus, the writer is not using the literary silence of the Bible to claim that Melchizedek did not have biological descent. He is only pointing out the *deliberate* silence of the text of Genesis, with respect to his descent, to portray Melchizedek as resembling the Son of God.

In fact, the author suggests that Melchizedek had a biological descent, which the biblical text intentionally omits to show that he did not receive his priesthood through heredity. Since kingship in the Old Testament came from the tribe of Judah through the line of David (Gen. 49:10; 2 Sam. 7:12–16) and the priesthood came from the tribe of Levi through the line of Aaron (Deut. 10:8; 18:1–5), the same person could not be both king and priest. The exception to that rule is the person of the Messiah. As Jesus receives his right to the throne hereditarily through his descent from the line of David, the writer of Hebrews explains that he receives his priesthood—like Melchizedek—not by heredity but by divine promise.

Starting with verse 7:4, the author develops this theme even further. He underlines the significance of Melchizedek's blessing of Abraham and receiving tithes from him. It is without a doubt that blessings are bestowed by the superior upon the inferior (Heb. 7:7). Since Melchizedek is the one who blessed Abraham, it follows that he is greater than Abraham. Because Abraham is the father of all the tribes of Israel—including the Levites, who were later in charge of receiving tithes—it becomes evident that Melchizedek, being greater than Abraham, is far greater than Levi and all his descendants. This includes Aaron, who himself was a descendant of Levi, who "was still in the loins of [Abram] when Melchizedek met him" (Heb. 7:10, RSV). Our author uses this layered comparison to highlight Jesus's superiority to Abraham, to Aaron, and to the Levites at large. This comparison is summarized as follows:

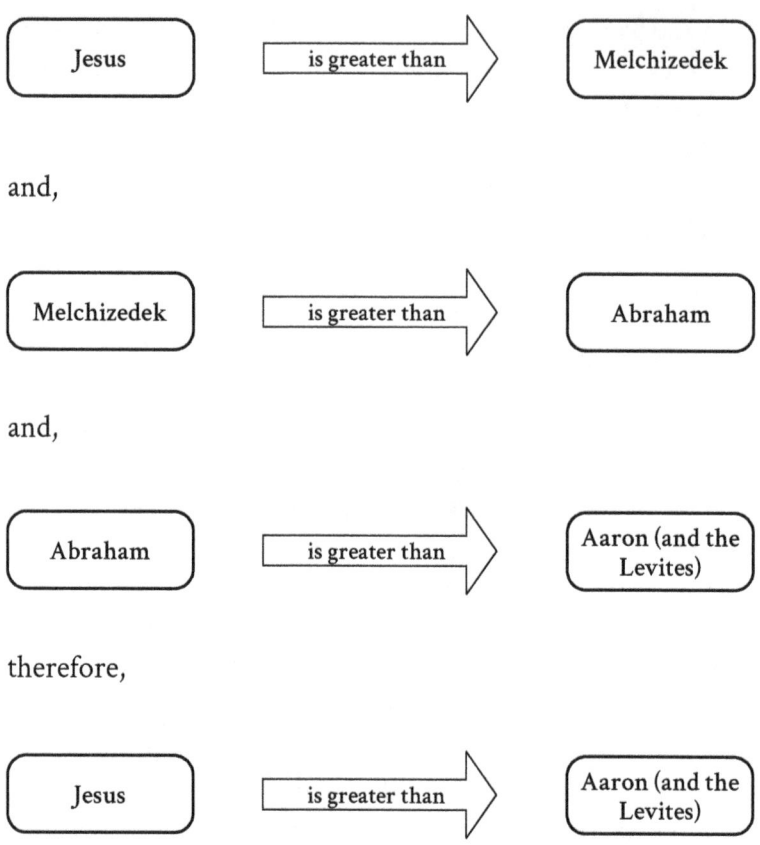

He who is called a priest after the order of Melchizedek must be a greater priest than Aaron and his children. This is where the writer of Hebrews makes masterful use of Psalm 110.

The Background of Psalm 110

Psalm 110 is almost exclusively uttered by the LORD God to his chosen Messiah. In verse 4 of this psalm the LORD swears to his Messiah that he will be a priest, not according to the Aaronic priesthood but after the order of Melchizedek. It is significant that this psalm was written by King David centuries after the institution of the Aaronic priesthood, which was still in effect at the time this psalm was composed. Founded upon the significance of Melchizedek's appearance in Genesis, this divine promise in Psalm 110 institutes the priesthood of the Messiah after an order that is far superior to that of Aaron's. Equally significant, this psalm establishes the notion that Melchizedek's priesthood (not Melchizedek himself) is one that will have no end.

Since God's promise to his Messiah comprises an everlasting priesthood, the order after which that priesthood is established must also be everlasting. In the absence of any mention in the Scriptures of Melchizedek's death, the author of Hebrews writes, "Resembling the Son of God he continues a priest forever" (Heb. 7:3). Those who view Melchizedek as a pre-incarnational appearance of Christ understand this verse to signify Melchizedek's everlasting priesthood. Others see this verse as a reference to the perpetuity of Melchizedek's priesthood, not of Melchizedek himself. The likely meaning here is not that Melchizedek lives forever, but rather that Scripture, by omitting mentions of his descent, birth, or death, presents him as a figure without beginning or end.

The Significance of Melchizedek in Chapter 7

The author of Hebrews creates a theological-literary masterpiece of the theme of Melchizedek's priesthood throughout this epistle, particularly in chapter 7. After detailing the clear parallels between Melchizedek and Jesus in the first half of the chapter, he connects this motif to the overarching theme of the epistle, which is, as explained above, the notion of "better." In the latter half of the chapter he makes a powerful argument that Jesus has ushered in a better covenant through a more superior sacrifice (Heb. 7:22, 27).

To advance his argument, the author of Hebrews points out that the priesthood of Melchizedek is distinct and separate from that of Aaron's (Heb. 7:11–14). The Levitical priesthood came through the tribe of Levi. The Messiah, on the other hand, came from the tribe of Judah, which was not connected with the priesthood in any way, for the Old Testament never authorized any form of priesthood for any tribe except the Levites. Thus, Jesus's priesthood is a completely different priesthood from Aaron's. Second, each priesthood comes with its own law (that is, ordinance). Since the priesthood of the Messiah is separate from that of Aaron, it cannot be founded upon the same Old Testament sacrificial law. Therefore, the old law, its sacrifices, and its priesthood have all been set aside, giving way to a new law, a new sacrifice, and a new everlasting priesthood. This new priesthood is inaugurated by Christ Jesus after the order of Melchizedek (Heb. 7:15–19). Of equal import, the old priesthood did not come with an oath. That of the Messiah comes with an everlasting, irrevocable oath for an everlasting, irrevocable priesthood (Heb. 7:20–21).

It is significant to observe the meaning of "order" in the context of Melchizedek's priesthood. Remarkably, Melchizedek presented bread and wine to Abram (Gen. 14:18). This echoes the sacrifice that Jesus himself offered on the night he was betrayed (see 1 Cor. 11:23–26). By breaking bread, Christ offered up his own body. By taking the cup and offering it to his disciples, he voluntarily shed his own blood. Melchizedek's offering of bread and wine foreshadowed Jesus's real sacrifice on the cross. Notice that there is a much deeper typology here. Not only was Melchizedek a type of Christ in the absence of his descent, the significance of his name, and the offices he held of both king and priest, but far more significantly, in the "type" of sacrifice he offered. Melchizedek was a type of Christ in his person and in his sacrifice and ministry. Thus, when Psalm 110:4 speaks of the Messiah being a priest after the *order* of Melchizedek, it is not only referring to the *perpetuity* of Christ's priesthood but it is also signifying the *nature* of his sacrifice and the *means* of his becoming the ultimate high priest—through offering his own body and blood represented by bread and wine. It is through this personal sacrifice that "[Jesus] is able for all time to save those who draw near to God through him, since he always lives to make intercession for them" (Heb. 7:25, RSV).

Two significant elements in this verse must be noted. The first is the perpetuity of Jesus's sacrifice, not only of his priesthood. That is, the efficacy of Jesus's sacrifice extends to "all time." This signifies that Christ's sacrifice has no successor. That is to say, it is the one and only sacrifice that was, is, or will ever be needed or sufficient to atone for sins. Meaning, it is not to be repeated or succeeded by any other sacrifice. (Our author returns to this topic in chapter 9.) Second, those who are *saved*, when they draw near to God, are those who would be otherwise worthy of death, for the Scripture says, "Man shall not see me and live" (Exod. 33:20, RSV). For this reason, when Isaiah beheld the glory of God, he exclaimed, "Woe is me, for I am ruined! Because I am a man of unclean lips, And I live among a people of unclean lips; For my eyes have seen the King, the LORD of hosts" (Isa. 6:5, NASB). No man can draw near to the LORD and live except those who are sinless and holy, for no evil or evildoer can abide in God's presence (Ps. 5:4). The sacrifice that Jesus offered on our behalf is the only sacrifice capable of saving those who draw near to God the Father from certain death by imputing Jesus's righteousness on them, thus making them sinless and holy in the eyes of God and therefore worthy of entering his terrifyingly holy presence, the Holy of Holies and not die (see Heb. 9:12; 10:19–22).

While this chapter of Hebrews was written centuries ago and speaks of historical figures who are long gone, the implications for our lives today as modern-day believers are manifold. Let us remember that the occasion for writing Hebrews was to encourage wavering Jewish Christians not to forsake their faith but to hold fast to their trust in Jesus in the face of all doubt and despite all trials. This passage in Hebrews powerfully relates that Jesus, whom we all believe in and worship, is the only path to God and is far superior to any other prophet, king, priest, or any other man who has ever lived. The faith that we have in him is greater and "better" than any other worldly wisdom. Acting on the encouragement, admonitions, and warnings that our writer gave to his original readers, and while we run our *own* race, let us remain intently focused on whom we believe in and who has died for us.

The doctrinal implications of this pericope are also significant, given that most traditional churches emphasize the need for Old Testament-style priesthood—the Eucharist—and other ritualistic practices to obtain, maintain, or be assured of one's salvation. In the context of discussing the necessity of human "priesthood" or other "works" for salvation, the theme of Christ's priesthood as discussed in Hebrews 7 proves central to New Testament theology. It reassures the believers that no human priesthood or works can either be necessary or sufficient for their salvation. This passage upholds the superiority of Christ's sacrifice to all Old Testament sacrifices. Since the superiority of priesthood is determined by the superiority of the sacrifice it offers, it follows that Jesus's priesthood is far superior to that of Aaron's, given that Christ offered a far more precious sacrifice than Aaron and his sons ever had (Heb. 7:11, 18–19). This is manifested by the fact that Christ's new priesthood came with an oath, while Aaron's did not (Heb. 7:20–22). Moreover, Jesus's priesthood is everlasting, while all other orders of priesthood are temporal (Heb. 7:23–24). Therefore, the sacrifice of Christ not only supersedes those of the Old Testament but it also abolishes them (see Col. 2:17; Heb. 8:5; 10:1) As the writer of Hebrews explains, the priesthood itself existed for the *sole* purpose of offering sacrifices *on behalf of* the people (Heb. 5:1; 8:3). *If there is no need to offer a sacrifice, there will be no need for a priest.* Abolishing the sacrifices abolishes the priestly system connected with them. Christ offered himself once for all, and that is sufficient to forgive sins. Thus, there is no need for any other sacrifice or for re-offering Jesus's body and blood to God the Father. His is the only necessary and acceptable sacrifice in the New Testament. As a result, all types of priesthood in the New Testament, except that of Christ's, have been entirely abrogated (Heb. 9:12).

New Testament believers can be certain of their eternal salvation by believing that the sacrificial work that Christ has done is all that is needed and all that would ever be acceptable before God to atone for their sins. Christians are not under the law of any human priesthood to perform works or offer up sacrifices to God the Father on their behalf. All ordinances of human priesthood are wholly insufficient for salvation since they never provided atonement in the Old Testament in the first place (Heb. 10:4). Salvation comes only by believing in the perfect sacrifice of Jesus. All throughout the Old Testament, sacrifices pointed to the one and only sacrifice who truly forgives sins, sanctifies, and makes perfect.

A Personal Note

When I studied this seventh chapter of Hebrews for the first time, I came face-to-face with the reality of what this signifies concerning the role of "priests" in the traditional churches (mainly the Catholic and the Orthodox churches).

One would be hard-pressed to read *and* comprehend what the letter to the Hebrews is asserting regarding priesthood and not conclude that all forms of *human* priesthood in the Old Testament were but a foreshadowing of Jesus's own priesthood in the New Testament. It *necessarily* follows that *no* human priesthood can still be claimed under the new covenant. It is evident that everything Aaron and his sons performed in the Old Testament signified—as a copy and a shadow—what Christ would come and perform himself on our behalf *in reality.* Starting with the patterns of the tabernacle itself and all its furniture, and ending with the *entire* Levitical priestly system, including the offering of sacrifices, all this was a figure and a representation of the person of Christ and his sacrifice. *When the real and true is revealed, the shadow and the figure must be done away with!*

I mentioned in the introduction of this book that I had a personal journey with Hebrews, and that it was what set the writing of this book in motion. It was when I finished my study of *this* seventh chapter of Hebrews that I realized that all forms of human priesthood in the New Testament have been abrogated. It was at that moment that I decided to finally exit the church I belonged to for forty-four years—the Coptic Orthodox Church.

Questions on This Chapter

1. In this chapter the author of Hebrews uses two Old Testament scriptures to provide compelling evidence for the priesthood of Jesus. What does that say about the relevance of the Old Testament books to our theology as Christians? How does that affirm or negate the notion that today's Christians do not need to study the Old Testament?

2. Had it not been for Hebrews, what would be our view of the priesthood of Jesus today? Would it have been lacking? If so, how?

Chapter Eight

Hebrews 8:1–13

"Now this is the main point in what has been said: we have a high priest such as this, who sat down at the right hand of the throne of the Majesty in heaven, a minister of the sanctuary and of the true tabernacle which the Lord set up, not man."

—Hebrews 8:1–2, LEB

The Minister of the New Covenant

Before we move on with our discussion of chapter 8 of this epistle, let us take a moment to assess the elements of the treatise that our author has covered thus far and why they are important to building his argument. Situating these chapters under discussion in their literary setting in relation to the preceding chapters of the epistle is critical to our ability to comprehend the overall picture that the author is so artistically attempting to paint for us.

Reading through this section of Hebrews, one may wonder: Why is it so important to the author to establish that Jesus is the true high priest, who has a priesthood superior to that of the Aaronic line? The answer becomes evident when we follow the author's reasoning from the opening chapter up to this point in the epistle.

Our author started by comparing Jesus to the angels of heaven (chapter 1). But if Jesus is not lower than angels, how are we to understand his lowly state while here on earth? The author addresses this question in the second chapter, showing that we should not mistake Jesus's humility for his being lower than angels. The writer was keen to show that this humility was temporary, and for our sake. Moving from comparing Jesus to the heavenly beings to comparing him with key earthly figures in the Jewish belief system, the writer compares Jesus, as a Son, to Moses as a servant in chapter 3, using language and comparison elements that set Jesus infinitely above Moses, the progenitor of the entire religious Jewish system. Having established that infinite superiority, the subsequent chapters are centered around warning the original readers against the dire consequences of apostasy and unbelief, using Old Testament motifs to establish that.

Arriving at chapter 7, the author begins establishing Jesus's superiority over another key figure in the Old Testament, Aaron and his descendants. He does this by showing that Jesus, as the promised Messiah, is set as an everlasting priest after the order of Melchizedek, which is distinct, separate, and above the entire Levitical priestly system. In this eighth chapter our gifted author sets Jesus as a more excellent high priest using a different approach. Here he shows that Jesus inaugurated not only a superior priesthood but a much more excellent *covenant*. While the Old Testament priests were the servants (ministers) of the old covenant, which was but a copy and a shadow of what was to come, Jesus is the servant (minister) of the new covenant, which is real and everlasting.

It is worth mentioning that Moses and Aaron are the only two central figures to whom our author compares Jesus in all of Hebrews (besides a brief comment on Abel's blood in 12:24). We note that Hebrews does not contain any comparison between Jesus and any other Old Testament prophet, king, or forefather. This begs the question: Why did our writer compare Jesus to these two characters and no one else? Why does he not compare Jesus to, say, David, Isaiah, or Elijah? The answer becomes clear when we examine what Moses and Aaron each signified in the Old Testament context and in mainstream Jewish thinking.

Moses represented the law of God, while Aaron was emblematic of the priesthood. It was by the hand of Moses that the law of the old covenant was given. As its inaugurator, Moses carried out the ratification of the Old Testament covenant between the LORD and his people. He was so associated with the law of God that the Bible uses the phrase "the law of Moses" some twenty-nine times! Aaron, on the other hand, as the first high priest of Israel, signified the priestly system by which the people of God were purified and sanctified to remain in compliance with the terms of the covenant. The phrases "the sons of Aaron" or "the descendants of Aaron" appear about thirty-six times in the Old Testament alone. In the eighteenth year of Josiah, king of Judah, centuries after the death of Aaron and his sons, the priests of the Old Testament were still referred to as the "Aaronic priests," as they prepared the first Passover since Samuel the prophet (see 2 Chr. 35:14, NIV).

On both Moses and Aaron the entire Jewish worship system of the Old Testament was founded. Therefore, by comparing Jesus to both Moses and Aaron, the author of Hebrews is comparing him to the two individuals who represent the very foundation of the religious Jewish system—the law and the priesthood. By showing Jesus's greatness above Moses and Aaron, the writer achieves an even higher purpose still. He thus sets Jesus, the covenant he has ratified, *and* the sacrifice with which he ratified it far above the old covenant and above all its practices, sacrifices, and glory! If our author aims to show that the new covenant *as a whole* is far greater than the old—which is certainly his main purpose—then he must dissect what the old covenant was founded upon and compare those individual elements to what Jesus came to offer. Chapter 8 of the epistle is central to his efforts in doing exactly that.

The Old Testament priestly system served as a copy and a shadow of both Jesus's true, future sacrifice and his everlasting priesthood. This depiction shows Aaron (middle), the first high priest of Israel, wearing the breastplate with the names of the twelve tribes of Israel. To his left, holding a censer, is Eleazar, his third oldest son, who became his heir after the death of Nadab and Abihu (Lev. 10:1–3). To his right is Ithamar, his youngest, holding one of the vessels used in the tabernacle.

Photo Credit: ArtMari/Shutterstock.com

The Old as a Shadow of the New (8:1-6)

The author begins this passage with what we can call the "thesis statement" of these chapters. In fact, it is his main proposition statement for setting Jesus as the high priest after the order of Melchizedek, higher than Aaron: "Now this is the main point in what has been said: we have a high priest such as this, who sat down at the right hand of the throne of the Majesty in heaven, a minister of the sanctuary and of the true tabernacle which the LORD set up, not man" (Heb. 8:1-2). That the author calls it "the main point" shows how, in his mind, it sums up his entire argument.

We find all the main elements of this statement elsewhere in the epistle. Jesus sitting at the right hand of Majesty in heaven appears in 1:3, 10:12, and 12:2. Verse 24 of chapter 12 tells us that Jesus is the mediator of the new covenant. In 9:11 the writer reiterates that Jesus serves, ministers, or mediates in a tabernacle that is greater and more perfect than its earthly counterpart.

As stated at the end of the previous chapter, offering a sacrifice was the central function of the ministry of every priest or high priest, to stand before the LORD *on behalf of* the people. This is nowhere more evident in the Bible than in God's commandment to Moses that the high priest must wear the breastplate bearing the names of the twelve tribes of Israel whenever he appears before the LORD to minister on their behalf:

> So Aaron shall bear the names of the sons of Israel in the breastpiece of judgment upon his heart, when he goes into the holy place, to bring them to continual remembrance before the LORD. And in the breastpiece of judgment you shall put the Urim and the Thummim, and they shall be upon Aaron's heart, when he goes in before the LORD; thus Aaron shall bear the judgment of the people

of Israel upon his heart before the LORD continually. (Exod. 28:29–30, RSV)

While giving instructions to Moses regarding the sin offerings, the LORD outlines the priest's other functions, which include acting on behalf of the congregation in presenting sacrifices and offering atonement for their sins: "He shall do with the bull just as is done with the bull of sin offering; he shall do the same with this. The priest shall make atonement for them, and they shall be forgiven" (Lev. 4:20, NRSV). Hence, the priest's primary role is to appear before God the Father on behalf of the congregation—a role that necessarily involves offering sacrifice.

In light of his prior argument that Jesus is a priest forever after the order of Melchizedek, the author of Hebrews affirms that Jesus is not—and cannot be—an earthly priest. Earthly priests adhere to certain ordinances regarding bodily purification and present animal sacrifices, all of which the author here terms "gifts according to the law" (Heb. 8:4). These ministerial duties are performed in a tent or in a tabernacle built by the hand of man. Notice that while the author does not offer us a direct comparison (yet) between the "tabernacle" in which Jesus ministers and that in which the Levitical priests ministered, there is definitely an implied notion of comparison and superiority.

Our writer finds it necessary not only to compare the person of Jesus to Moses and Aaron but also to bolster his argument by comparing Jesus's *mode of ministry* to that of the Levitical priests. His original audience not only revered Moses and Aaron as central characters in their Jewish religion but equally prided themselves on having the tabernacle or the temple of God while no other nation did. This can be readily observed in one of the major accusations brought against Jesus: that he had said he was "able to destroy the temple of God and to build it in three days" (Matt. 26:61, NRSV). John's editorial note provides clarity that Jesus "was speaking of the temple of his body" (John 2:21, NRSV). This charge was one of the derisions directed against Jesus while he was on the cross: "Those who passed by derided him, shaking their heads and saying, 'Aha! You who would destroy the temple and build it in three days, save yourself, and come down from the cross!'" (Mark 15:29–30, NRSV). This level of exasperation and fury against Jesus shows the extent of indignation that the Jews felt against anyone who was suspected of bringing the smallest offense against their sacred things, not the least of which was the temple. Therefore, it was of utmost importance to the author that he address the habitation in which Jesus's ministry takes place, demonstrating its superiority and greatness compared to any other earthly mode or place of worship.

In the author's mind it should be quite plain to his readers that whichever habitation or mode of ministry is heavenly, the service—and thus the servant—connected with it must be greater. It is understood that the heavenly is far better than the earthly. As Paul writes in another context, "What can be seen is temporary, but what cannot be seen is eternal" (2 Cor. 4:18, NRSV). (The author of Hebrews will return to this notion at the end of this chapter, showing that the visible vanishes away!) John the Baptist also asserts the same meaning during his exchange with his disciples, stating, "The one who comes from above is above all; the one who is of the earth belongs to the earth and speaks about earthly things. The one who comes from heaven is above all" (John 3:31, NRSV). The Jews of Jesus's time surely knew and believed that to be true as well. In their debate with Jesus they never refuted what he said when he confronted them, showing his superiority by saying, "You are from below, I am from above; you are of this world, I am not of this world" (John 8:23, NRSV). Thus, to the readers of Hebrews, it was self-evident that the heavenly ministry, which takes place in heaven and is unseen, must be far greater in God's eyes than that which is earthly and visible.

We are then taken back to the earliest stages of constructing the earthly tabernacle for the first time. The author's intended meaning here is to show that such a visible house of worship was constructed after a model of the heavenly and the invisible habitation, where Jesus is the minister and the high priest. As such, this earthly tabernacle was nothing but a copy and a shadow of the heavenly (real) one. Paul expands this notion for us to include the tabernacle and beyond, stating that all matters in connection with the law, such as "eating or drinking or participation in a feast or a new moon or a Sabbath ... are a shadow of what is to come, but the reality is Christ" (Col. 2:16–17, LEB).

During his forty days and forty nights on the mountain in the presence of God, Moses received numerous commandments, including a detailed plan of the tabernacle (or the tent of meeting). It is clear from the context that Moses was *literally* shown a model after which he was instructed to make the tabernacle and all its furniture, tools, and vessels. This is affirmed in both the Old and the New Testaments. Immediately after Moses entered the presence of God on the mountain, we read that the LORD began giving instruction to receive contributions from the Israelites of gold, silver, bronze, and other materials, such as animal skins, that would be needed to build a sanctuary to the LORD so that he may dwell among his people (Exod. 25:1–8). We then find this instruction: "Exactly as I show you concerning the pattern of the tabernacle, and of all its furniture, so you shall make it" (Exod. 25:9). The pattern that was shown to Moses included all the details of all the furniture and vessels that were to be made for the tabernacle. In the same chapter, we later read about the utensils of the tabernacle that Moses was to "make them after the pattern for them, which is being shown you on the mountain" (Exod. 25:40). We also find similar testimonies to the same effect multiple times in the Old Testament (see Exod. 26:30; Num. 8:4). This was common knowledge to any first-

The Minister of the New Covenant

century Jew, as we find Stephen—right before he was stoned to death—testifying that the forefathers of Israel "had the tent of witness in the wilderness, just as [the LORD] who spoke to Moses directed him to make it, according to the pattern that he had seen" (Acts 7:44). Undoubtedly the pattern Moses saw on the mountain was so detailed that it included every fine detail of what he was to construct. The model that was shown to Moses was the heavenly version of what he built on earth. Thus, when the author of Hebrews writes that Moses saw such a pattern, his original audience would have fully recognized the significance and the authenticity of that assertion (Heb. 8:5).

We find another powerful instance of a similar occurrence in the Old Testament when King David was preparing to build the temple of God centuries after Moses died. Shortly before his death, David gave his son Solomon all the plans of the vestibule of the temple, its treasuries, its upper rooms, and its outer and inner chambers (1 Chr. 28:11–12). We then read David's testimony to his son that all this had been given to him *directly* by the hand of the LORD. None of the modern English translations capture the power of this verse except the NASB (and the much older KJV): "'All this,' said David, 'the LORD made me understand *in writing by His hand upon me*, all the details of this pattern'" (1 Chr. 28:19, NASB). This is literally how the original Hebrew reads! Whereas Moses was shown a pattern on the mountain, the LORD's hand was *literally* upon David as he imparted to him the detailed plans of his temple.

The Jewish roots of this Old Testament context are essential to understanding the New Testament, including its last book—the book of Revelation. There we find not one but three indications not only that such a pattern exists in heaven but also that there is an actual temple (tabernacle) of God in heaven and that it was indeed seen by John. Not only did John see the temple of God in heaven but he also saw the ark of the covenant in it! After the seventh angel blew his trumpet, John heard the praise and singing of the twenty-four elders. Then he saw that "the temple of God in heaven was opened, and the ark of his covenant appeared in his temple, and there were lightnings and sounds and thunders and an earthquake and large hail" (Rev. 11:19, LEB). A few chapters later, John testifies two more times that he saw the temple of God (or the tent of the testimony) in heaven (Rev. 15:5, 8). That heavenly abode of God was filled with smoke because of the glory of God and his power, much as we repeatedly read in the Old Testament about the tabernacle in the wilderness and later in the Temple of Solomon (see Exod. 40:34; 1 Kings 8:10; Isa. 6:4).

As expected of the writer of Hebrews, this detail is fundamental to his argument. By showing that the earthly sanctuary was a mere copy of the heavenly original, he proceeds to assert that, therefore, the ministry that was given to Jesus, who serves in the heavenly tabernacle, is much greater than the ministry of the Aaronic priests who served in the earthly. Hence, not only is Jesus a greater high priest but also the ministry he administers is far greater, for it takes place in a superior habitation. The author then makes a strategic literary and theological shift by mentioning a key term, taking his readers back to one of the most important passages in the Old Testament: Jeremiah 31:31–34.

A New Covenant Ratified by Blood (8:7–13)

This second half of this chapter consists largely of a single quotation from the prophecy of Jeremiah bookended by a single comment from the author of Hebrews on either end of it. This verbatim quotation is the longest uninterrupted Old Testament quotation found in the entire New Testament. As he quotes other Old Testament passages that he feels are fundamental to his argument multiple times (for example, Psalm 110), our writer quotes an abridged version of this Jeremiah passage again in chapter 10. This time the notion of *covenant* is what occupies his mind! As in the previous chapter, to understand the meaning of this passage of Hebrews and appreciate its significance, we must return to and study the Old Testament passage quoted in its *original* context. Therefore, we must examine this passage of the new covenant in Jeremiah.

Before we dive into this Jeremiah passage, however, we should observe that our author is quoting that specific prophecy to demonstrate to his audience that going as far back in Israel's history as the time of Jeremiah, the LORD had already promised a new covenant between him and his people Israel—meaning that the new covenant through the advent of Jesus is nothing "new" that God has introduced into his plan of salvation but is something that was promised long before Jesus and has always been a part of God's plan for his people. The writer of Hebrews uses this promise to establish in the minds of his readers that a new covenant was promised *because* the old covenant had already become ineffective. This too is not a new theme but is part of God's own blueprint.

Jeremiah 31:31–34 in Its Old Testament Context

In its original context, Jeremiah 31:31–34 promises consolation and future restoration to the then-suffering Israel at the time Jeremiah penned these words. For easy reference I have included these verses from the book of Jeremiah, retaining their verse numbers, as they will be substantive to our discussion.

> [31] Behold, the days are coming, declares the LORD, when I will make a new covenant with the house of Israel and the house of Judah, [32] not like the covenant that I made with their fathers on the day when I took them by the hand to bring them out of the land of Egypt, my covenant that they broke, though I was their husband, declares

the LORD. ³³ For this is the covenant that I will make with the house of Israel after those days, declares the LORD: I will put my law within them, and I will write it on their hearts. And I will be their God, and they shall be my people. ³⁴ And no longer shall each one teach his neighbor and each his brother, saying, "Know the LORD," for they shall all know me, from the least of them to the greatest, declares the LORD. For I will forgive their iniquity, and I will remember their sin no more. (Jer. 31:31–34)

We must bear in mind that Jeremiah's prophetic office began shortly before the Babylonian exile of the southern kingdom of Judah. He later witnessed his own prophecy come true as he was an eyewitness to the exile and the events that unfolded shortly thereafter (see Jer. 39–41; 52). Therefore, the words of this promise of a new covenant were written to an Israel that was undergoing exile and persecution from their enemies as retribution for their sins against their God. Hence, the phrases "the days are coming" and "after those days" signify a period of time after the Israelites return from exile. It is worthy of mention that this promise was made to *all ethnic* Israel (see verse 31). This includes the house of Israel, the northern kingdom—which had already been exiled by Assyria by the time of Jeremiah—and the house of Judah, the southern kingdom, which was being actively ravished and taken captive by Nebuchadnezzar, king of Babylon.

Unlike other Old Testament promises, it must be noted that, in *this* promise, any mention of the Gentiles is conspicuously absent. (Compare, for example, God's promise in Isa. 2:2–4.) This promise in Jeremiah is exclusively to the twelve tribes of Israel. This element is significant in the context of Hebrews since it is an epistle written to a predominantly Jewish audience, hence the author's repetition of this passage from Jeremiah in chapter 10, which shows that Jesus of Nazareth is the *fulfillment* of this Old Testament promise made to Israel. *Therefore, by accepting and upholding their faith in Jesus, the original audience of Hebrews would not be adopting a new faith; instead, they would be only adhering to a continuation of the faith they had already inherited from their forefathers.* This is so fundamental in the mind of our author that he quotes four full verses from Jeremiah, adding little commentary to them, knowing that these verses alone are sufficient to show that Jesus is the Christ, the inaugurator of the new covenant promised by the LORD through Jeremiah.

Note that in this Jeremiah passage God promises a new *covenant*, not a new *law*, for he says, "I will put *my* law within them," *not* "my *new* law" (see verse 33). This indicates that the LORD would put an *already existing* law in the hearts of Israel. This new covenant is new only in the *manner* in which God's law would be written and in its *outcome*, as manifested by the unmediated knowledge of God.

It is quite common in today's mainstream Christendom to hear and read that the Old Testament law has been abolished, set aside, or was somehow flawed or incomplete since it produces judgment and condemnation, and since salvation comes through faith in Jesus alone. This doctrine of abolishing the law is taught every day by what I call "cultural Christianity."[20] It is a detrimentally distorted view of the Old Testament law as seen and communicated by the New Testament writers. Paul, for example, clearly asserts that "the law is holy, and the commandment is holy and righteous and good" (Rom. 7:12).

---

[20] In this context it is essential to distinguish between "cultural Christianity" and "biblical Christianity." The doctrines promoted from the pulpits of "cultural Christianity" do not always reflect sound biblical teaching. "Cultural Christianity" encompasses beliefs and doctrines that resonate within certain Christian communities but may lack accurate biblical interpretation. In contrast, "biblical Christianity" is grounded solely in Scripture, even if it may not align with the prevailing cultural norms. Every corrupt doctrine has used Scripture to support its views!

In the same chapter and a couple of verses later he writes, "We know that the law is spiritual, but I am of the flesh, sold under sin" (Rom. 7:14). Quoting from Leviticus, Paul upholds what is written about the commandments of God contained in the law, stating, "The one who does them shall live by them" (Gal. 3:12). Many in our modern-day Christendom teach and preach that the Old Testament law does not apply to Christians today. This teaching ignores Paul's rhetorical question, Do we then overthrow the law by this faith?, to which he immediately responds: "By no means! On the contrary, we uphold the law" (Rom. 3:31).

Not only does this teaching of abolishing the law of God go against what other New Testament writers believed but it also flies in the face of what Jesus himself taught. When asked by a teacher of the law what he should do to inherit eternal life, Jesus answered, "What is written in the *Law?* How do you *read* it?" (Luke 10:26). Knowledgeable in the law of God, that teacher was ready to recite by heart the main commandments of the law: one must love the LORD his God and must love his neighbor as oneself. Then Jesus gave him this unambiguous answer that should be sobering to many of us today: "You have answered correctly; *do this, and you will live*" (Luke 10:28). It is beyond debate that the "this" in Jesus's response squarely refers to the commandments of the law. It is equally beyond *any* doubt that our Savior was both truthful and intentional in his answer. In other words, he meant exactly what he said. On a different occasion our Lord Jesus famously said, "Do not think that I have come to abolish the law or the prophets; I have come not to abolish but to fulfill" (Matt. 5:17, NRSV).

We must also distinguish between the heart of the law contained in the commandments of God and the *practices* or ordinances of the law, set forth in the form of rituals, feasts, and the sacrificial and priestly system. These practices and ordinances are what Paul rightly refers to as "the works of the law," by which there can be no justification (Gal. 2:16). This is a vitally important distinction that is often ignored. These two elements of the law are usually and wrongfully conflated. As the author of Hebrews makes clear on numerous occasions, the ritual *practices* of the Old Testament were a copy and a shadow of what was to come through Jesus. They were meant to serve as a "type" of his sacrifice and ministry. Thus, it was appropriate that they be abolished by the advent of the Son of God. Nonetheless, the divine *commandments* contained in the law were never a shadow or a "type." They are the eternal statutes of God that constitute the heart of his law and therefore will never be replaced or made obsolete. This is yet another reason why Old Testament statutes that were *not* a shadow or type of Christ's life and works must be upheld by New Testament believers. An example of that is the statute of tithing (though there are other reasons for upholding tithing in the New Testament; see the previous chapter for the fuller discussion).

Therefore, as New Testament believers we *are* commanded and required to fulfill God's law as outlined in the Old Testament. How can we do that? We cannot! That is precisely why the Son of God was incarnate: "But when the time had fully come, God sent forth his Son, born of woman, born under the law, to redeem those who were under the law, so that we might receive adoption as sons" (Gal. 4:4–5; see also Gal. 3:13). *Jesus came to fulfill the law of God on our behalf so that through him we can fulfill it as well!* Hence, we must recognize that, as with all other things given by God, the Old Testament law was complete and perfect. There is no need to give *another* law under this new covenant.

The author of Hebrews, quoting from Jeremiah, articulates that the need for a new covenant is not because God's law was deficient or imperfect but "because they did not remain faithful to my covenant, and I turned away from them, declares the LORD" (Heb. 8:9, NIV; see Jer. 31:32). Thus, the law itself was not lacking, nor was the covenant associated with it.

That Israel failed to keep God's law is what necessitated a new covenant written in a new way. Hence, the fault lies squarely with Israel and not with the perfect law of God.

This new covenant will also be *preserved* differently than that of the Old Testament. The covenant given at Sinai was written on stone tablets, as we see in Exodus: "The LORD said to Moses, 'Cut for yourself two tablets of stone like the first, and I will write on the tablets the words that were on the first tablets, which you broke'" (Exod. 34:1; see also Exod. 32:15–16; 34:28; Deut. 4:13; 5:22; 9:10). A generation later, Moses wrote all the commandments of the law that he had received from the LORD and entrusted the Levites to keep them by the side of the ark of the covenant of God:

> When Moses had finished writing the words of this law in a book to the very end, Moses commanded the Levites who carried the ark of the covenant of the LORD, "Take this Book of the Law and put it by the side of the ark of the covenant of the LORD your God, that it may be there for a witness against you." (Deut. 31:24–26)

In contrast, under this new covenant God's law will be put *within* the people of Israel and will be written upon their hearts (Jer. 31:33). Therefore, this new covenant will be "internalized," as it were, within the Israel of the new covenant. As a result of internalizing the law within them, the LORD will be their God and Israel will be his people; the knowledge of the LORD will be prevalent in Israel from the least to the greatest. The law will be *directly* accessible to and understood by *all* of Israel (see discussion below). Through this new covenant God would forgive the sins of Israel and will no longer remember them (Jer. 31:34).

Having established what this Jeremiah prophecy signifies, the next logical question one must ask is, Has this prophecy been fulfilled, and if not, how and when will it be fulfilled?

Fulfillment in the Old Testament

In its original Old Testament context, the fulfillment *began* with the return of the Jews from the Babylonian exile. This led to the reunification of Israel and made viable the possibility of complete fulfillment. Nonetheless, this promise contains multiple elements. First, it is a promise made to *one* united Israel. Second, God's law will be written on their hearts and not on stone tablets or books for safekeeping. Third, and more significantly, *all* of Israel will know the LORD. Last, the LORD will forgive their sins and will not remember them any longer. The return from the exile represents only a *partial* fulfillment of this promise since it fulfills only *one* of these four components. But God's promises are not completely fulfilled until *all* elements have been satisfied. Therefore, the majority of this promise was not fulfilled in the Old Testament.

As the return from exile laid the foundation for the first component to be fulfilled by reuniting Israel, other essential elements must also pave the way for the remainder of the promise to be realized. There must be a way for God's law to be inscribed on people's hearts. There must also be a means by which total forgiveness of sins is attained. The sacrifice of Jesus provides exactly that.

Fulfillment in the New Testament

The author of Hebrews returns to this topic in chapter 9 and much of chapter 10. We are told elsewhere that at the Passover meal Jesus instituted a new covenant by voluntarily shedding his own blood: "And likewise the cup after they had eaten, saying, 'This cup that is poured out for you is the *new* covenant in my blood'" (Luke 22:20; see also Matt. 26:28 and 1 Cor. 11:25). This was to emphasize the *inauguration* of the new covenant through the blood of Jesus, in a manner similar to what had been performed at the initiation of the Sinaitic covenant.

In that Sinaitic ceremony, Moses took half the blood of the sacrifice and put it into bowls. Then he took the other half and poured it onto the altar before the LORD. After he had read all the words of the Book of the Covenant in the hearing of all Israel, they agreed to the terms of the covenant, saying that they would obey all the words written in it. In a revelatory act signifying the "cutting" of the covenant between the LORD and his people, "Moses then took the blood, *sprinkled it* on the people and said, '*This is* the *blood of the covenant* that the LORD has made with you in accordance with all these words'" (Exod. 24:8, NIV). In both the Old Testament and the New Testament accounts, we read that a covenant is established through the shedding of blood. At Sinai it was inaugurated by shedding the blood of animals; at the Passover meal it was formed by shedding Jesus's blood. Thus, we can see that with every "new" covenant comes the shedding of blood; or more accurately, by the shedding of blood, covenants are established (or "cut," to use the authentic language of the Old Testament. See Gen. 15:7–21).

As a required element of establishing a new covenant, Jesus had to shed his blood. Connecting the Exodus scene with the Jeremiah promise, Jesus in the New Testament "cut" a new covenant with his followers by shedding his blood. Therefore, the blood of Jesus marked the *beginning* of a new era, in which the Jeremiah promise would be *completely* fulfilled. Since the forgiveness of sins is an essential element of that promise, the blood of Jesus provides the *means* by which it would be *ultimately* fulfilled.

Recognizing this significance, the author of Hebrews builds upon the LORD's promise in Jeremiah to show that it was necessary for God to institute a new covenant since the old covenant had become obsolete and no longer useful for the purpose that God had intended. Hence, the obsolescence of the old demands the advent of the new. Conversely, the introduction of the new confirms God's desire to replace the old.

This is precisely what the writer of Hebrews refers to, stating, "In speaking of 'a new covenant,' he has made the first one obsolete. And what is obsolete and growing old will soon disappear" (Heb. 8:13, NRSV).

Notice how the author of Hebrews masterfully structures his argument by comparing the foundations of each covenant. The old covenant was founded upon an image and a shadow set up by the hand of man (Heb. 8:2–5). The new covenant, however, is established upon a much more excellent ministry enacted on "better promises" (Heb. 8:6), characterized by the writing of God's law on the hearts of Israel, thus leading to true forgiveness of sins (Heb. 8:12). In Hebrews 10 the author explains that by offering a far more excellent sacrifice, Christ established a superior covenant. This new sacrifice provides forgiveness of sins—something the animal sacrifices of the old covenant could not. Whereas in chapter 8 the author illustrates the superiority of the ministry, in chapter 10 he emphasizes the superiority of Christ's sacrifice, which forgives sins.

As a promise made to ethnic Israel, it is self-evident that this Jeremiah promise has not been fully realized. It has been *partially* fulfilled in the Old Testament, and the foundation of its complete fulfillment has been laid in the New Testament. The Old Testament fulfillment of this promise took place in the return of the exiled Jews to their homeland from the Babylonian exile. This was the historical, immediate, but partial fulfillment. This *initial* fulfillment provided the reunion of the Israelites into one people to whom this promise was given. The *second* phase of the fulfillment took place through the redemptive work of Christ. This second phase provided the *means* by which the sins of Israel (and of all nations) could be forgiven—the blood of Jesus. The *third* and final stage of this fulfillment has not occurred yet. This ultimate fulfillment will be accomplished when "the times of the Gentiles are fulfilled" (Luke 21:24) and "all Israel [is] saved" through their faith in Christ (Rom. 11:26). This will take place once "the full number of the Gentiles come in" the faith (Rom. 11:25). In this final phase of fulfillment the promise will be completely realized and the law of God will be written on Israel's heart, and he will be their God and they will be his people. Only then will Israel—from the least to the greatest—enjoy unmediated access to the LORD forever (Jer. 31:34).

Questions on This Chapter

1. What does the blood of Jesus mean to you? Why was it necessary for your salvation (if you so believe)? What does that say about your state as a member of the fallen human race? Meditate on your answers.

2. Many critics and skeptics claim that God did not need to send his own Son to die for our sins and that he could have simply forgiven our sins and restored us to himself. After all, as a sovereign God, he should be able to do whatever he pleases. What is your view concerning this claim, given the contents of this eighth chapter of Hebrews?

CHAPTER NINE

Hebrews 9:1–28

"And as it is appointed unto men once to die, but after this the judgment: So Christ was once offered to bear the sins of many; and unto them that look for him shall he appear the second time without sin unto salvation."

—Hebrews 9:27–28, KJV

A Sacrifice through the Eternal Spirit

This chapter contains the most detailed discussion of the Old Testament worship system found in Hebrews. Despite the editorial note in verse 5 stating that the author does not wish to speak in detail of such matters, he spends the first half of this chapter recounting specific features of the tabernacle and the Old Testament Levitical system. As we will see later, he does not do this superfluously. The author points out these components of the tabernacle and the sacrificial system of the Old Testament not because he doubts his readers' awareness of their details but because, as it should be clear to us by now, he will immediately use them to support his reasoning. In his mind these elements are meaningful in how they apply to and signify Jesus's sacrifice. After a brief recounting of the design of the tabernacle in the Old Testament, our writer swiftly moves to identify how these rituals were perfected—that is, fulfilled and replaced—through the sacrifice of the Son of God.

Worship in the Earthly Tabernacle (9:1–10)

The first ten verses of this chapter include the author's succinct description of the tabernacle in the days of Moses, not the least of which is its division into two chambers: the Holy Place and the Holy of Holies. Before we move to discussing the design of the tabernacle, it would be helpful to understand what the tabernacle is and why it was constructed in the first place.

The God of Israel never instructed any of his people to build him a "house to dwell in" prior to the time of the exodus. Though for centuries (not years) the LORD communed with those who believed in him, such as Enoch, Noah, Abraham, Isaac, and Jacob, nowhere in the Old Testament do we find any indication that the LORD desired that a house be built for his name. Places such as Bethel (which literally means "the house of God") were denoted only by an altar erected in the name of the LORD. However, no building was ever constructed in the name of the LORD before the time of Moses, let alone a complete system of worship including rituals, purifications, sacrifices, and priesthood.

After the exodus from Egypt, we read the LORD's command to the Israelites to give offerings of precious metals, linens, animal skins, and other materials, each according to his desire and ability, to "make me a sanctuary, that I may dwell in their midst" (Exod. 25:8, RSV). This is the first time the Scriptures speak of God's desire to dwell among his people by their constructing a sanctuary for him for that purpose. A few generations later the tabernacle was replaced by Solomon's Temple, which was destroyed by the Babylonians and subsequently rebuilt in the days of Zerubbabel, Ezra, and Nehemiah after their return from the Babylonian exile.

To best understand the significance of the theme of the tabernacle in Hebrews, it is fitting to briefly recount some of the details of the layout of the tabernacle of the Old Testament, starting with the innermost chamber—the Holy of Holies—and working our way outward.

The Holy of Holies

The Holy of Holies is the innermost chamber of the tabernacle and its holiest chamber. This inner chamber contained nothing else except the ark of the covenant. A curtain (or a veil) between the Holy of Holies and the Holy Place separated the two chambers. As we will soon find out, no one was permitted to enter behind that veil except the high priest, and only once a year, on the Day of Atonement.

The ark of the covenant was constructed of acacia wood and measured two and a half cubits in length.[21] Its width and height were one and a half cubits each. It was fully overlaid with pure gold inside and out (Exod. 25:10–16). The ark contained the two tablets of stone written by the finger of God containing the Ten Commandments (Exod. 25:16, 21). Moses was instructed to make a cover for it, of the same length and width as the ark itself. Over the cover he made two winged cherubim facing each other with their wings touching each other. The space over the cover and under the wings of the cherubim was called "the mercy seat" or "the covering," and it was where the LORD appeared and spoke to Moses (Exod. 25:17–22; Lev. 16:2). Anyone who dared to look upon the mercy seat without being authorized by God faced certain death. Even the high priest himself could not look upon the mercy seat; he had to burn incense before it on the Day of Atonement to cover himself from God's presence so that he

---

[21] A *cubit* is the standard unit of measure for length in the Old Testament. It is the length of an average forearm of an adult male. It measures from approximately seventeen to twenty inches, or forty-four to fifty-two centimeters.

would not die. The instructions given to Moses in this regard are vivid, reflecting the gravity of the risk: "And [Aaron] shall take a censer full of coals of fire from the altar before the LORD, and two handfuls of sweet incense beaten small, and he shall bring it inside the veil and put the incense on the fire before the LORD, *that the cloud of the incense may cover the mercy seat that is over the testimony, so that he does not die*" (Lev. 16:12–13). The ark was so holy that touching it brought instant death (see 2 Sam. 6:1–11). The Hebrew term used here to signify "covering" is *kapporet*. It literally means "cover." Because it was closely connected with the Day of Atonement as discussed in earlier chapters, the concepts of "atonement" and "covering" sins became associated with one another. In other words, *atonement* became synonymous for "covering" one's sins.

No one was permitted to enter this chamber at any time, not even Aaron or his sons. Aaron risked his own life if he were to enter this most holy chamber at any time. In this regard the LORD gave Moses this stern warning: "Tell your brother Aaron that he should not enter at any time into the sanctuary behind the curtain in front of the atonement cover that is on the ark, so that he might not die, because I appear in the cloud over the atonement cover" (Lev. 16:2, LEB). The high priest was allowed to enter this Holy of Holies every year on only *one* occasion—the Day of Atonement. Still, he could not appear before the LORD empty-handed but had to enter the presence of the LORD with the blood of sacrifices. On that day the high priest would enter this inner chamber twice—the first time to atone for his own sins with the blood of a bull as a sin offering (Lev. 16:11); the second time to atone for the sins of the people of Israel using the blood of a goat (Lev. 16:15–16). In both cases the high priest had to sprinkle the blood of the sacrifices on the cover (the mercy seat) and before the cover seven times. His entry on only one day every year symbolized how Jesus's sacrifice was offered only *once* for all (Heb. 7:27), meaning it is not a sacrifice that can, will, or should be repeated. Note that the number seven in the Bible signifies divine perfection. Thus, sprinkling the blood seven times before the presence of the LORD by the high priest signified the *perfection* of Jesus's sacrifice. Jesus is the high priest who offered perfect and complete atonement for the sins of his church in the presence of God the Father. That is, his sacrifice is sufficient to *fully* atone for *all* sins. Not only is Jesus's sacrifice not to be repeated but it is so perfectly sufficient.

Though initially nothing else was to be placed inside the Holy of Holies, an urn of manna was later placed before the ark to remind Israel of God's provision that he had supplied to them in the wilderness (Exod. 16:32–35). Based on Moses's instructions, Aaron took an omer of manna and placed it before the ark inside the Holy of Holies.[22] The rod of Aaron that budded was also placed in this most holy chamber, right in front of the ark, as a memorial against the Israelites for their rebellion. After Dathan, Abiram, and Korah rebelled against the LORD for choosing Moses and Aaron for his service, the LORD instructed Moses to bring a rod from each of the twelve tribes of Israel to the tabernacle with their names written on them. By the following morning the LORD had miraculously caused the rod that had Aaron's name on it to bud as a testimony that the Lord had chosen him for his ministry. The LORD then instructed Moses to bring Aaron's rod back and place it before the ark to become a sign against the rebels among Israel (Num. 17:1–11). This is what is meant by the author's reference to the urn of manna and the rod of Aaron that budded (Heb. 9:4).

This leads us to the first interpretive difficulty in this chapter (there are two of them). The Old Testament clearly states that only the tablets of the covenant were to be placed

---

[22] An *omer* is an ancient unit for measuring dry substances. It is equal to about two liters.

A diagram showing the tabernacle's chambers and furniture layout

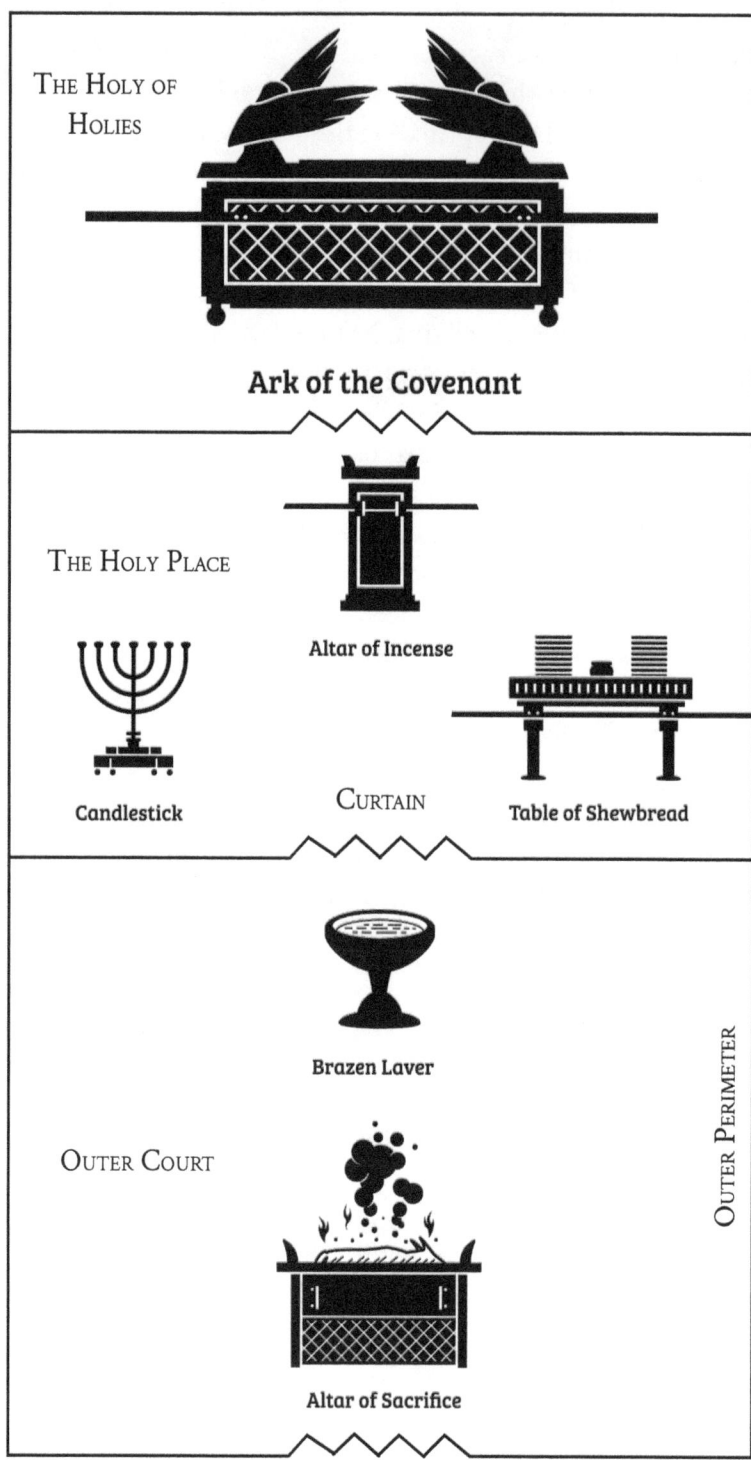

inside the ark, while our author states that it also contained the urn of manna and Aaron's rod.

It is hard to imagine that our author, so well-versed in the Scriptures as we have witnessed thus far, would commit such an obvious "mistake." So were the urn and the rod placed in front of the ark or inside it?

We know for certain that in the days of Moses they were placed in front of the ark. It is quite likely, however, that they were subsequently placed inside the ark as Israel journeyed through the wilderness for safekeeping, for the Levites removed and re-erected the tabernacle at every destination throughout the forty years of sojourning (Num. 4).

At the time of Solomon the ark was moved from the tabernacle, which David had built for it at the City of David (Zion), to the newly built temple (see 1 Chr. 15:1; 16:1; 2 Chr. 5:7). In that account we find this editorial note: "There was nothing in the ark except the two tables which Moses put there at Horeb, where the LORD made a covenant with the people of Israel, when they came out of Egypt" (2 Chr. 5:10, RSV). While this note may seem to contradict what the writer of Hebrews is stating, it is in fact an indication that there had been other items inside the ark, such as the rod and the urn, which were subsequently removed or lost. The way this editorial note reads shows that other items would have been expected to be found inside the ark but were not.

The Holy Place

The Holy Place contained three items related to the worship of the LORD. The first was the table of the showbread to the north (Exod. 40:22). To the west was the altar of incense in front of the curtain (or veil) that separated the Holy Place from the Holy of Holies (Exod. 40:26). Last, the lampstand stood toward the south (Exod. 40:24).

The table of the showbread (or "the bread of presence") was made of acacia wood and overlaid with gold, just as with the ark of the covenant. It was two cubits in length, one cubit in width, and one and a half cubits in height. On this table the Levites would place twelve loaves of bread (in two stacks of six each), representing the twelve tribes of Israel before the LORD—hence the term "the bread of presence," signifying Israel's continual presence before their God (Exod. 25:23–30). The Levites would eat the twelve loaves of bread and then replace them with freshly baked bread every Sabbath (Lev. 24:5–9).

Likewise, the altar of incense was made of acacia wood, overlaid with pure gold. It was placed directly before the veil that divided the Holy Place from the Holy of Holies. Aaron burned incense on it every morning as he tended the oil lamps of the candlestick. No sacrifice of any kind was offered on this altar; nothing was poured on it. It was used solely for the purpose of burning incense continually before the LORD. Only once a year, on the Day of Atonement, Aaron made "atonement for it" with the blood of the sin offering sacrificed on that day (Exod. 30:1–10). This brings up the second interpretive issue in this chapter.

The Old Testament is clear that the altar of incense was placed in the Holy Place, not in the Holy of Holies. Nevertheless, the author of Hebrews states that it was placed *behind* the veil within the Holy of Holies. Here is what he says: "Behind the second veil there was a tabernacle which is called the Holy of Holies, *having* a golden altar of incense and the ark of the covenant covered on all sides with gold, in which was a golden jar holding the manna, and Aaron's rod which budded, and the tables of the covenant" (Heb. 9:3–4, NASB). The keyword here is *having*. Though most English translations render it as if the Holy of Holies "had" or "contained" the altar of incense, the original Greek word (*echousa*) does not necessarily mandate that rendering. One of its common meanings is "adjoining," "neighboring," or "next to" a place or an object. It also signifies the notion of "being associated with" or "connected with" an idea or a concept. The writer of Hebrews uses a cognate of this exact word (*echomena*) elsewhere in the epistle to refer to matters that "belong to" or "accompany" our salvation (Heb. 6:9). Because of the close association between the Holy of Holies and burning the incense taken from off the altar of incense on the Day of Atonement, our author writes as though the Holy of Holies "had" (*echo*) the altar of incense within it, meaning that the two were closely associated one with another.

This association is not unique to Hebrews, nonetheless. As far back as the book of Exodus itself (the first mention of the altar of incense and the Holy of Holies), we find clear use of such an association. When all the furniture of the tabernacle, all its utensils, and all its coverings were made, the LORD gave this directive to Moses: "And you shall put the golden altar for incense *before* the ark of the testimony, and set up the screen for the door of the tabernacle" (Exod. 40:5, RSV). Though they were separated by a curtain, the altar of incense and the ark of the covenant were closely associated with each other. Thus, the author of Hebrews was not mistaken when he associated the two.

The lampstand (or "the candlestick"), on the other hand, was made of pure gold. It had three branches on one side and three on the other side, with one branch in the middle for a total of seven branches (Exod. 25:31–40). It was continually lit before the LORD, using seven lamps of pure olive oil. The lampstand was never to go out, and Aaron and his sons were instructed to tend it through the night, from evening to morning (Exod. 27:20–21).

A Word of Edification

Before we conclude our discussion concerning the earthly versus the heavenly tabernacle, I feel compelled once again to make a couple of side but crucial remarks.

It is significant and noteworthy that nowhere in the New Testament do we ever find any description of a physical design or layout of a tabernacle, a temple, or a church. Nor do we learn of any portrayal of altars, vessels, or utensils. Any mention of furniture items to be placed in the LORD's house is conspicuously absent from the New Testament writings. In our discussion of the patterns given to Moses and to David, we see the level of detail outlined in the plans that the LORD revealed to both men to construct his tabernacle and temple (see chapter 8). This speaks of how vital it is to God that his earthly habitation among his people be built according to a specific design, representative of his majesty and glory. The absence of any such design in all New Testament writings indicates that it is the LORD's intention to supplant his earthly, man-made dwelling and, as part of his new covenant, replace it with its permanent, heavenly counterpart.

The silence of the New Testament concerning the design of a church building under the new covenant compels the so-called "traditional churches" to construct their buildings according to plans or symbolic patterns primarily adopted from the Old Testament.[23] They also make vessels and utensils of carved work according to patterns similar to those mentioned in the Old Testament. Likewise, they fashion veils, coverings,

---

[23] Let me be clear concerning my reference to the "traditional churches" in this context. I am not referring to the Catholic Church *only*. My reference to "the traditional churches" includes all churches that claim themselves to be founded upon the Bible and the teachings of the early church fathers. In addition to the Catholic Church, this includes the entire Orthodox camp, such as the Greek and Russian Orthodox churches, the Assyrian Orthodox Church, and the Coptic Orthodox Church (my church from birth to the age of forty-four).

and cloths that resemble what we read about in the tabernacle and later in the temple (or introduce their own designs and fashions). They even ordain priests and anoint their altar utensils using "holy oils" formulated in the same manner that was given to Moses in the wilderness to use for anointing Aaron, his sons, and the furniture and the utensils of the tabernacle (see Exod. 30:22–38). Whereas no biological descent is required, these traditional churches are steeped in their belief and tradition of priesthood through "succession." This means that every new priest must be ordained by a predecessor priest traced back—as they believe—to the days of the twelve disciples of Jesus. These churches err in doing so—as the epistle to the Hebrews clearly shows—for they adopt patterns, designs, and practices that have been made obsolete, since they were all but a shadow and a copy of what was to come under the new covenant, which Jesus inaugurated with his blood!

Of equal import, I must point out that the Greek word for tabernacle in Hebrews, including in this chapter, is *skene*, which signifies *dwelling* or *presence*. This is the same word used by John when speaking of the Word of God—the second person of the Trinity (not the *written* word of God in the Bible!)—taking flesh and *dwelling* among us: "And the Word became flesh and *dwelt* among us, full of grace and truth" (John 1:14a, RSV). John is essentially saying that the person of Jesus of Nazareth has become the *new* tabernacle! Then immediately afterward, in the same verse, John goes on to say, "We have beheld his glory, glory as of the only Son from the Father" (John 1:14b, RSV). This is an unmistakable reference to the *shekinah*—the visible glory of God that appeared in the tabernacle and in the temple. It is hard to imagine stronger evidence to support the claims of the author of Hebrews that the incarnation of the Son of God, Jesus of Nazareth, has permanently replaced all previous forms of physical dwellings of God on earth. *God has sent his Son to dwell among mankind so that his Holy Spirit can dwell within them! As Jesus is our forerunner in many other aspects, by becoming the* new *tabernacle of God on earth, he has made us—all who believe in him—God's* new *dwelling place on earth.* All physical dwellings of God on earth have been thus abolished, and so have their design plans, patterns, and utensils.

Ministry within the Tabernacle

The writer of Hebrews reminds his original readers that the priests in the Old Testament performed their duties within the Holy Place without entering the Holy of Holies except, as explained above, on the Day of Atonement. The veil that separated the Holy of Holies from the Holy Place also separated the priests—as representatives of the people—from the presence of the LORD. The author points out that this signified the separation between God and his people. It is evident that this separation was the direct result of man's sin and disobedience.

Since God is infinitely holy, he cannot behold sin: "Your eyes are too pure to behold evil, and you cannot look on wrongdoing" (Hab. 1:13, NRSV). Nor can he dwell among sinners: "For you are not a God who delights in wickedness; evil may not dwell with you. The boastful shall not stand before your eyes; you hate all evildoers" (Ps. 5:4–5). This is why death was the immediate consequence for anyone who dared to enter God's presence without having his sins atoned for. The sinner had to die if he entered God's presence, since God and sin cannot co-exist in the same place. For this reason, in order for the Holy Spirit to dwell within New Testament believers, their old, sinful nature must die, and they must be given a renewed and sanctified nature to enable that dwelling. Paul explains this in Romans, saying, "How can we who died to sin still live in it? Do you not know that all of us who have been baptized into Christ Jesus were baptized into his death? We were buried therefore with him by baptism into death, so that as Christ was raised from the dead by the glory of the Father, we too might walk in newness of life" (Rom. 6:2-4, RSV).

The blood of animal sacrifices—foreshadowing the blood of Jesus, which atones for sins—represented acknowledgment of one's sins and his or her need for atonement. Therefore, the only occasion on which the high priest—representing the congregation—could enter the Holy of Holies was on the Day of Atonement when his and their sins were symbolically atoned for. Of course, the blood of animals never atoned for anyone's sins. This was nothing more than a symbolic act pointing to the true sacrifice of Jesus that forgives and atones for the sins of his congregation—those who believe in him—as the ultimate high priest. This is what Paul means in Galatians when he asserts that "the scripture *consigned all things to sin*, that what was promised to faith in Jesus Christ might be given to those who believe" (Gal. 3:22, RSV). Under the law, everyone was bound under sin but was promised forgiveness of sin and righteousness—a promise that awaited fulfillment in Christ.

In verse 8 the author of Hebrews, in his own style, illuminates how the rituals practiced in the Old Testament signified God's separation from the sinfulness of his people, emphasizing that this was not ordained by the hand of man but was revealed to us in the Scriptures by the Holy Spirit.[24] The phrase "the present age" in verse 9 points to the time when the tabernacle was "still standing," as stated at the end of the previous verse. As long as that priestly system was in place and the tabernacle was still standing, the presence of God was inaccessible to us, veiled behind the curtain. This is the same curtain that was torn from top to bottom in the same hour Jesus gave

---

[24] Though this is not a major emphasis of the author of Hebrews, it is a testimony that the Old Testament scriptures were written by the Holy Spirit. See also 10:15, in which the author conveys the same meaning concerning a passage from Jeremiah.

up his spirit on the cross—a detail captured by all the synoptic gospels (Matthew, Mark, and Luke): "And Jesus cried again with a loud voice and yielded up his spirit. And behold, the curtain of the temple was torn in two, from top to bottom; and the earth shook, and the rocks were split" (Matt. 27:50–51, RSV). Although there was no ark inside the Holy of Holies in the temple at the time of Jesus, this event symbolized that, from this point onward, the privilege of having direct access to and fellowship with the Father was granted. This was solely the result of his Son's death on the cross. In the same way that the veil of old symbolized the full blockage of our access to God, the torn veil signified our ability to have unimpeded access to him. (Recall our discussion in the previous chapter, as this was one feature of the "new covenant"—unmediated and direct access to God.)

The writer then reminds us that both the priests and the congregation participated in various kinds of rituals, including purifications and sacrifices, rightly referred to earlier, and in numerous places throughout the New Testament, as "the works of the law." Still, none of these could truly "perfect the conscience of the worshiper" (Heb. 9:9). This is a clear reference to the failure of these practices and animal sacrifices either to atone for the sins of those who offered them or to effect true transformation in their hearts or minds to overcome sin. These works of the law failed to justify the worshipers in the eyes of the LORD. Paul insists that "if a law had been given which could make alive, then righteousness would indeed be by the law" (Gal. 3:21, RSV). However, no one is justified by the works of the law (Rom. 3:20; Gal. 2:16).

Having outlined for his readers the practices of worship under the old covenant and continuing with his favorite theme of comparison to illustrate Christ's superiority, our writer rapidly moves to highlight how Jesus's ministry, as the high priest under the new covenant, is far greater than what he has just described.

Christ as the Mediator of the New Covenant (9:11–28)

If there is one passage in Hebrews that captures the mind of its author and the essence of his argument, Hebrews 9:11–28 is it! Over the next several verses, the author summarizes what he believes is the core of the gospel and the redeeming work of Christ in one neat sequence. At the end of the previous section our writer speaks of "the time of reformation" (Heb. 9:10). In this section he describes what that means.

Notice the preposition *but* (the Greek *de*) at the beginning of verse 11. This marker of contrast is the author's way of distinguishing the period that precedes the time of reformation from the period that follows it.

Here the author performs a three-tier comparison quite seamlessly. First he begins by comparing—in his unique style—the earthly tabernacle, which he just finished discussing, to the heavenly tabernacle in which Jesus ministers. The former was made by hand but—though intricate in design—was destined to vanish away. The latter is not made by hand, meaning it is not a creation of the present age. It is heavenly, nonmaterial, and thus cannot be seen or touched by hand. This, of course, is a reference to the heavenly presence of God the Father, where Jesus is now seated. Note here that Jesus entered the heavenly tabernacle *once.* This is a clear indication that he offered himself to the Father *only once* on behalf of all mankind to provide atonement for their sins and to impart his righteousness unto them. The heavenly tabernacle has once for all replaced its earthly counterpart, where the LORD dwelled among his people for generations.

The second layer of this comparison is the blood that Jesus took with him to enter the heavenly Holy of Holies. Whereas Aaron and his successors entered the innermost chamber once a year with the blood of animal sacrifice, Jesus appeared before the Father through the shedding of his *own* blood. Whereas the blood of goats and bulls could never atone for sins, Jesus's blood can and does—as the sinless Son of God and Son of Man. As the author puts it, Jesus's blood "[secured] eternal redemption" (Heb. 9:12, RSV).

The third and last layer of this comparison is the outcome of "sprinkling" Jesus's blood on his congregation. Here, the author briefly alludes to two Old Testament statutes in which the blood—and in one case, the ashes—of animals provided ritual purity, enabling the Israelites to dwell near the habitation where the LORD himself resided.

The author's reference to the blood of bulls and goats is a reference to the rituals of the Day of Atonement, when a bull was offered as a sin offering to atone for the sins of the high priest. To offer atonement for their sins, the people of Israel would bring two male goats. The high priest would then bring them both to the door of the tabernacle and cast a lot to determine which goat would be offered as a sin offering for the sins of Israel and which would carry the sins of Israel and be sent alive into the wilderness. After offering one of the goats as a sin offering, the high priest would then place both his hands on the head of the live goat "and confess over him all the iniquities of the people of Israel, and all their transgressions, all their sins" (Lev. 16:21, RSV). By the sacrifice of one of the two goats, the sins of Israel are "transferred" to the other one, which then carries them out of the camp and away from God's people. This ceremony symbolizes the *total* removal of sin from among the people of God.[25] The Psalter praises the

---

[25] While it is not within the scope of our discussion to interpret the text of Leviticus, it may be edifying to briefly comment on the meaning of *azazel* in the context of Leviticus 16. Many commentators have labored over what this unusual Hebrew word means, going as far as understanding it to signify one of the proper names of the devil. The Arabic word *'azl* (عَزْل) shares the same root with the Hebrew *azazel* (עֲזָאזֵל). Both terms signify "removal" or "separation" in their simple form. In Arabic the repetition of one letter in the middle of a word is a form of exaggeration (or intensity). For example, *kasara* (كَسَر) in Arabic is the past tense, singular masculine form of *break* (as in *shatter* or *split*). The form *kas-sara* (كَسَّر, with the repetition of the *s* sound) means to break something completely (*utterly*

LORD for this grace, saying, "As far as the east is from the west, so far does he remove our transgressions from us" (Ps. 103:12, RSV). Despite their solemn nature and precise symbolism, these ceremonies served only to foreshadow the true work of forgiveness and salvation that would be accomplished by Christ.

The author of Hebrews illustrates this, using the phrase "sanctify them for the ritual purity *of the flesh*" (Heb. 9:13, LEB), which underscores how these sacrifices were unable to "perfect the conscience of the worshiper" as discussed above (see verse 9). The best these rituals could do was to purify the flesh only so that the Israelites could stay in the camp and participate in worship in the tabernacle or in the temple.

It should be noted that the sprinkling in this verse directly refers to the ashes of the heifer, for the blood of bulls and goats was not sprinkled on the worshiper in the Old Testament for purification purposes. To understand the significance of the author's reference to the heifer, we must return to the book of Numbers.

To provide ongoing purification from coming in contact with a corpse, Eleazar the priest, the son of Aaron, was instructed to take a red heifer without blemish and slaughter her outside the camp. After sprinkling her blood seven times before the tent of meeting, her entire body was burned with fire outside the camp. Then her ashes were gathered and kept in a clean, known location outside the camp. Since anyone who touched a dead body—whether of man or beast—would become ritually unclean, to be cleansed, the defiled person had to be sprinkled with a mix of water and some of the ashes of this red heifer. Likewise, when someone died among the Israelites, everyone and everything in that household became ritually

demolish or *annihilate*). Thus, it becomes evident that *azazel* (with the repetition of the Hebrew equivalent of the *z* sound) is simply a form of exaggeration denoting complete removal or total separation between Israel and their sins.

unclean. That entire household, including the house itself and all the vessels in it, became unclean as well. Likewise, anyone who entered that house would become unclean. To restore ritual cleanness, they too had to be sprinkled with water mixed with the ashes of the red heifer.

Violating this statute was an extremely serious offense against the LORD; the text twice states that anyone who is not cleansed as prescribed "defiles the tabernacle of the LORD; and that person shall be cut off from Israel" (Num. 19:13, 20, NASB).

Compared to the effects of animal blood and ashes that could provide only ritual cleansing, Jesus's blood truly purifies not the flesh but our consciences from the blemishes of sin. Observe the mastery by which our author crafts his nuanced, underlying comparison. He intertwines his reference to purifying the flesh in verse 13 with the phrase "purify your conscience" in verse 14 to remind the reader of what he has just stated in verse 9: the sacrifices of the Old Testament could not "perfect the conscience of the worshiper." Not only did the rituals of the Old Testament fail to provide purification of the conscience (verse 9) but they scarcely offered outward cleansing (verse 13). In contrast, the blood of Jesus purifies our very consciences (verse 14).

The phrase "who through the eternal Spirit offered himself without blemish to God" may be puzzling at first, for how did Jesus offer himself up to the Father through the Spirit? Which "spirit" is that? To answer these questions, we must observe that the qualifying adjective "eternal" shows that the author is referring to the Holy Spirit, the Spirit of God. Other New Testament scriptures expound on how Jesus offered himself to the Father through the Holy Spirit.

First, Jesus was raised from the dead by the work of the Holy Spirit. Speaking of Jesus's suffering on our behalf, Peter writes, "For Christ also suffered once for sins, the righteous for the unrighteous, to bring you to God. He was put to death in the body but made alive in the Spirit" (1 Peter 3:18, NIV). Likewise, Paul in his introduction to Romans asserts that Jesus was "designated Son of God in power according to the Spirit of holiness by his resurrection from the dead" (Rom. 1:4, RSV). He also writes this short song to his disciple Timothy, confessing the mystery of our faith: "Great is the mystery of godliness: God was manifest in the flesh, justified in the Spirit, seen of angels, preached unto the Gentiles, believed on in the world, received up into glory" (1 Tim. 3:16, KJV). Hence, the New Testament scriptures show that the work of redemption offered by Jesus was completed by the work of the Holy Spirit in raising Jesus's dead body from the grave.

To fully understand this notion, it must be noted that the redemptive work of Christ was *not* completed through his crucifixion; it was *begun* by his crucifixion but *completed* in his *resurrection*! Paul definitively affirms this in his first letter to the Corinthians: "If Christ has not been raised, your faith is futile and you are still in your sins" (1 Cor. 15:17, RSV; see also 1 Cor. 15:14). Though Jesus offered himself up on the cross, his resurrection constituted the Father's acceptance of his sacrifice. Similar to the fire that came down from heaven, consuming the sacrifices of the Old Testament, the Father declared Jesus's sacrifice acceptable by raising him from the dead by the Holy Spirit. Thus, it is remarkable for the author of Hebrews to state that Jesus *offered* himself through the Spirit, who brought his salvific work to its fullness.

Second, another meaning of this phrase may be discerned by setting it as the antithesis of the author's previous reference to "the blood of goats and bulls" and the ashes of a heifer. While goats, bulls, and heifers perished by death and would never return to life again, Jesus came back to life through his bodily resurrection and now lives forever (hence the term "eternal"). As Peter reminds his audience in his first public address after Pentecost, death could not take hold of Jesus forever: "God raised him up, having loosed the pangs of death, because it was not possible for him to be held by it" (Acts 2:24, RSV). Thus, the phrase "eternal Spirit" refers not only to Christ's resurrection from the dead but also to his living forever, as he will not see death again. This is precisely what Jesus says to John in the opening chapter of Revelation: "Fear not, I am the first and the last, and the living one; I died, and *behold I am alive for evermore*, and I have the keys of Death and Hades" (Rev. 1:18, RSV).

We discussed the phrase "dead works" in chapter 6, explaining that it referred not to sins but to the dead "works of the law." Here, however, it signifies sin. The context associates it with the purification of one's conscience. Whereas reliance on the dead works of the law does not defile one's conscience, the works of sin do. This is also supported by the author's reference to the failure of animal sacrifices to cleanse the worshiper from his or her sins and provide atonement. Therefore, our author does not seem to use that phrase with the same meaning in both cases. The author then introduces a parallel from the civil law of his time (and ours) to argue his next point.

It is a widely accepted notion that when a person writes a will, it does not go into effect until his or her death. As long as that person lives, whatever inheritance pledged in his or her will does not get passed on to the heirs. It is noteworthy that a testator's will serves as a *covenant* between him and his heirs, effective only upon his death. In fact, the word *testament* comes from the Latin word *testamentum*, which literally means "covenant"—and not just any covenant but one between God and mankind![26] The first known use of the word *testament* in English (in the fourteenth century) signified that meaning. This is where the modern-day phrase "final will and testament" comes from. What is promised in the will of Jesus is

---

[26] Encyclopaedia Britannica, *Testament* Definition & Meaning, Merriam-Webster Dictionary, accessed April 18, 2024, https://www.merriam-webster.com/dictionary/testament.

eternal life to his heirs (brethren!)—those who believe in him as the Son of God. As the author of that will, he had to die so that his heirs could receive that inheritance. The writer then returns to the covenant ratification ceremony in Exodus to provide evidence for his argument from Scripture.

Since the particulars of that ceremony have already been covered in the previous chapter, it is sufficient to point out that, similar to Jesus's shedding his own blood, the old covenant was ratified through the shedding of blood, albeit the blood of animals. Building on this similarity of bloodshedding, the writer then draws a contrast.

Though shedding blood is a common element between the ratification of both the old and the new covenant, the blood of Jesus was shed only once, whereas the blood of animals was shed repeatedly. The author then nuances this argument by underscoring that the high priest under the old covenant did not shed his own blood, while Jesus did. The intended meaning here is that though there are similarities between the two, Jesus did not appear in the presence of the Father in an *identical* manner as the high priest in the tabernacle. The high priest did not offer his own blood but that of animals; thus, he had to offer his sacrifices repeatedly. Jesus, on the other hand, offered *himself*; therefore, it was sufficient to present his sacrifice only once. Had it not been so, the author affirms, Jesus—not the high priest—"would have had to suffer repeatedly since the foundation of the world" (Heb. 9:26a, RSV). This interjectory statement confirms that in the author's mind it is impossible for Jesus to have suffered multiple times. This squarely contradicts what most "traditional churches" practice today of offering the Eucharist or Communion every day on their altars—what they assert to be the true and literal body and blood of Jesus! They maintain that they offer that *same* "sacrifice" to the Father, to receive atonement and forgiveness of their sins. *According to Hebrews, Jesus suffered once—and only once*! The author makes this unambiguously clear in the second half of verse 26, using the same proposition *but* as in verse 11 (the Greek *de*) to show contrast between the animal sacrifices of the old covenant and Jesus's sacrifice under the new.

To emphasize the one-time nature of Jesus's sacrifice, the author writes, "*But* now he has appeared [before the Father] *once* at the end of the ages for the removal of sin by the sacrifice of himself" (Heb. 9:26b, LEB).

The writer then professes that "it is appointed for men to die *once*, and after that comes judgment" (Heb. 9:27, RSV). All claims of "reincarnation," as held by many Eastern religions, are dashed on the rock of this biblical truth, as declared by the Holy Spirit through our author. This is a clear doctrinal statement as to what we as Bible-believing Christians must believe concerning life after death. There is no ambiguity or occasion for debate that after our departure from this world, *judgment* is what comes next. In other words, after our bodily death, it is not "another chance of repentance" that follows but judgment. This brings to naught all claims that the dead may have a chance of repentance after death. Not only that, but it is asserted here with certainty that the judge is none other than Jesus Christ of Nazareth—*the same person who suffered to bear our sins*! Nor is there any doubt in the author's mind that upon his second return, Christ will bring deliverance to those who believe in him. Christ will return *not* to minister, evangelize, or call to repentance those who rejected him at first, giving them one last chance of repentance; he will return to bring eternal salvation to those who accepted him as the Son of God and *judgment* to those who did not. Paul affirms this, leaving no occasion for doubt: "For we must all appear before the judgment seat of Christ, so that each one may receive good or evil, according to what he has done in the body" (2 Cor. 5:10, RSV). This Christian doctrine is established beyond any skepticism or uncertainty.

Another note that I must insert in this regard is whether a Christian believer will be judged according to his faith or according to his deeds.

Though the Bible, the inerrant word of God, asserts time and again that every man will be judged according to his *deeds* (not the least of which is this last verse), entirely different theology is regularly taught from the pulpits of our modern-day churches. Those who adhere to what I called earlier "cultural Christianity" somehow find it defensible to uphold the belief that some believers will still enter the kingdom of God even though they have adopted for themselves a sinful lifestyle that contradicts God's commandments as set forth in Scripture. Many believe that anyone who has prayed the "sinner's prayer" and has confessed his or her faith in Christ has been eternally saved from the fires of hell, no matter how he or she continues living the rest of his or her life. Nothing could be farther from biblical truth!

Some even argue that while revilers and homosexuals will not "inherit" the kingdom of God according to 1 Corinthians 6:9–10, they will still "enter" the kingdom of God! I must say that this is the theology of someone who is playing with his or her eternal life as one plays with fire, for the Holy Spirit says through Paul that those who have died to sin through baptism can no longer continue living in it (Rom. 6:1–4). I must affirm that according to the Bible, every man will be judged according to his *deeds*, not his faith—for the Bible clearly teaches that faith that does not produce works worthy of the children of God and honoring to his name is a dead and worthless faith that should not be called such (see James 2:26). Do not rest assured in your salvation simply because you have made a verbal confession of faith if you continue living in sin—any sin—whether it is a same-sex relationship, revilement, use of profanity, drunkenness, fornication, or the like. John's words in the Scripture are clear:

> No one who abides in [God] keeps on sinning; no one who keeps on sinning has either seen him or known him. Little children, *let no one deceive you.* Whoever practices righteousness is righteous, as he is righteous. Whoever makes a practice of sinning is of the devil, for the devil has been sinning from the beginning. The reason the Son of God appeared was to destroy the works of the devil. No one born of God makes a practice of sinning, for God's seed abides in him; and he cannot keep on sinning, because he has been born of God. *By this it is evident who are the children of God, and who are the children of the devil*: whoever does not practice righteousness is not of God, nor is the one who does not love his brother. (1 John 3:6-10)

The Bible defines a believer as one who obeys the commandments of our Lord and keeps them—not merely as one who has confessed faith in Christ. If you have embraced a lifestyle or conduct that contradicts what the Bible describes as a holy and sanctified life in Christ, and you refuse to repent, no prayer or confession of faith will save you!

Returning to conclude our discussion on this ninth chapter of Hebrews, the author of Hebrews will pick up the topic of Jesus's ministry and sacrifice with even greater focus in the next chapter. This is because the doctrine of Christ as the ultimate high priest, who once for all sacrificed himself for our sins and entered the presence of his Father with his own blood to secure eternal salvation for us, is the author's most central theological theme. Though he has already dedicated much of this epistle to powerfully establishing it in the minds of his readers, he returns to it in the next chapter as he sees it as central to their faith and ultimately to their salvation.

Questions on This Chapter

1. Having read what this chapter of Hebrews teaches about life after death, what are your personal views on this topic? Do they align with the biblical truth as set forth in the word of God? Can you support your views—whatever they may be—from God's word?

2. In this chapter we discussed the idea of "covering" and its relationship to the notion of atonement. As a believer in the blood of Jesus, the next time you enter God's presence in prayer, envision that you are entering the heavenly Holy of Holies—the very presence of God the Father. He would normally look at you and see a fallen nature, covered in sin and iniquity, in which case the only outcome would be your death. Nonetheless, because you take refuge in the blood of Jesus, all the Father can see, as it were, is a curtain, a blanket of the blood of his Son, Jesus, covering you. Thus, he no longer sees your sins, but he sees you covered by the blood. This is the only reason you can enter his presence and not die. Meditate on this vision and make it a source of praise and worship, but, above all, a cause for appreciation of what Jesus has done for you.

CHAPTER TEN

Hebrews 10:1–39

"Therefore, brethren, since we have confidence to enter the sanctuary by the blood of Jesus, by the new and living way which he opened for us through the curtain, that is, through his flesh, and since we have a great priest over the house of God, let us draw near with a true heart in full assurance of faith, with our hearts sprinkled clean from an evil conscience and our bodies washed with pure water."

—Hebrews 10:19–22, RSV

The First Abolished, the Second Established

We arrive at this chapter having covered most of the content of the epistle in terms of its written text (that is, the proportion of text covered thus far compared to what remains). Nonetheless, in the author's mind this tenth chapter falls right at the center of his theological argument. In other words, the first few chapters of the letter (specifically chapters 1–7) were meant to lay the foundation for the author's climactic theme that unfolds starting in chapter 8 and onward. Thus, in chapter 10 he continues to convincingly argue for the supremacy of the sacrifice of Christ, using the Old Testament to support his views, as it was the authoritative Scripture of his original audience.

In this chapter we also encounter for the first time what may be considered a summarized thesis statement in the author's own words, starting in verse 19 and following. The way these verses read gives the reader the impression that the author desired to spell out his main points for his readers, as he felt very strongly about them. The themes outlined in this chapter constitute beliefs that are central to the salvation of the author's original recipients. Therefore, he did not wish to let his readers draw their own conclusions and risk his audience missing his core message; thus, he spelled out the heart of his argument.

The Single Sacrifice That God Desired (10:1–18)

The doctrines presented in this section of the epistle, chapter 10:1–18, have been introduced previously elsewhere. However, the author approaches them from a slightly different angle in this passage, putting it all together and then moving to exhortation in the second half of this chapter.

The first new notion introduced in this passage is the argument that if the animal sacrifices of the Old Testament had been effective in forgiving sins and in "perfecting the conscience of the worshiper," they would not have been offered repeatedly—meaning that they were offered repeatedly for this reason: they were never perfect! A work that is repeated can never be considered perfect. This is another argument against the traditional churches that *repeatedly* offer the sacrifice of Christ multiple times a week! A work that is perfect does not need to be repeated; if it is truly perfect, there should not be a need to add anything else to supplement it or complete it. In the author's mind—and rightly so—the very fact that the sacrifices of the Old Testament were repeated year after year proves that they were never perfect or complete.

Remember: his original recipients were in danger of abandoning the sacrifice of Christ and reverting to the Old Testament sacrifices—the exact sacrifices under discussion here. For this reason he categorically and unequivocally declares to them that it is *impossible* for those sacrifices to atone for sins. Notice that he does not say "it was impossible" for those sacrifices to take away sins; rather, he says "it *is* impossible" for them to do so. The present tense used here aims to tell his readers that these sacrifices are incapable of doing so *now* just as much as they were in the past. In other words, by the advent of Jesus, these animal sacrifices did not gain any efficacy or acquire any new value that they did not have before. They continue to be equally ineffective.

The following couple of verses are a direct quotation from Psalm 40. As has been his approach, our author employs Old Testament scriptures to argue and support his points, knowing that it is the body of text that his readers held and accepted as the authoritative word of God. This quotation, nonetheless, produces some interpretive challenges of its own. First the author quotes that psalm as if it is spoken by Jesus. Second, the text, as he quotes it, differs from what we see in our Bibles today.

Though the first difficulty has been fiercely debated among scholars, it is quite evident that the Psalter is replete with examples where what was uttered by the psalmist could not have applied to him directly or exclusively. One prime example of this is Psalm 22, in which the psalmist states that his enemies have pierced his hands and feet (Ps. 22:16). He cries out to God, for they have divided his garments and have cast lots for his raiment (Ps. 22:18). (Remember that the title of this psalm undeniably attributes it to King David.) We find no mention or even a suggestion that such atrocities were committed against King David. While it may be interpreted as a general outcry of the persecution David endured at the hands of Saul, as it stands, this text cannot be applied to David's life—even metaphorically. It is beyond debate that these words were written not to be applied to David's life but to Jesus's suffering and crucifixion.

Psalm 16 is yet another example of a similar typological application of an Old Testament text to the life of Christ. In

Acts, Peter uses this psalm to demonstrate precisely that point. After he quotes Psalm 16:8–11, Peter says—

> Brethren, I may say to you confidently of the patriarch David that he both died and was buried, and his tomb is with us to this day. Being therefore a prophet, and knowing that God had sworn with an oath to him that he would set one of his descendants upon his throne, he foresaw and spoke of the resurrection of the Christ, that he was not abandoned to Hades, nor did his flesh see corruption. (Acts 2:29–31, RSV)

Clearly this shows that in writing this psalm, David was not speaking of himself; rather, he knew he was speaking of the one who would descend from his seed and whom the LORD would set upon his throne forever—the Christ whose flesh would see no corruption.

It must be also noted that the verses quoted here from Psalm 40 could not have been strictly intended for King David even in their original Old Testament context when they were first composed. Nowhere in the Old Testament scriptures do we find it prophesied of David that he had come to do God's will (Ps. 40:7–8). Having been written during his own lifetime, such prophecy would have needed to be written of David before his time if this verse were to apply to him—something we do not find in the Old Testament books that predate him. It is thus evident that when writing these words, David knew that he was speaking of someone else. Therefore, it is not an issue to be reckoned with that the author of Hebrews takes Psalm 40 and directly applies it to Christ as if it had been spoken by him.

The second interpretive difficulty we must contend with is the text of the quotation itself. The author of Hebrews frequently relies on the Septuagint translation of the Bible rather than the Masoretic Text. It is important to understand the

The First Abolished, the Second Established

differences between the two texts since the Septuagint is quoted elsewhere in the epistle and in other parts of the New Testament apart from Hebrews.

The Septuagint is the Greek translation of the Old Testament text. It is commonly denoted by the abbreviation LXX—Latin numerals for the number seventy. It was completed during the reign of Ptolemy Philadelphus (285–247 BC[27]) in Alexandria, Egypt. About seventy scholars were assembled to translate the Old Testament from its original Hebrew to Greek—the *lingua franca*, or the common language of the time. This was the first time any part of the Bible had ever been translated. Attributed to these seventy scholars, the translation received its LXX designation. As Greek became more widespread in the Mediterranean basin, the Septuagint became the commonly used translation of the Old Testament outside Israel. By the time the New Testament was written (in the second half of the first century AD[28]), it became the default source of Old Testament quotations for the New Testament writers, especially in material written to predominantly Gentile Christians, such as Paul's letters and Hebrews. Recall that the New Testament itself was written exclusively in Koine Greek, which made frequent quotations from the LXX all the more natural.[29]

The Masoretic Text, on the other hand, is the Hebrew Old Testament. To this day it is the standard text used in the land of Israel and recited by Jewish children and adults alike. It was the text read in the temple in the Old Testament period and in the synagogues during the New Testament period. This text is generally considered superior to all others, including the LXX.

---

[27] BC stands for "before Christ."

[28] AD stands for the Latin *Anno Domini*, signifying "in the year of our Lord," that is, after the birth of our Lord Jesus.

[29] Koine Greek was the common language around the time the New Testament books were composed. It is a descendant of classical Greek, which was used at the time of Alexander the Great but with some Hebrew and Aramaic infused.

All extant translations of the Bible (in all languages) use this text as the basis for their translations. The Septuagint is referenced and compared only for accuracy in passages where the Masoretic Text is unclear.

On the following page, you will see a comparison table showing Psalm 40:6–8 in the Masoretic Text and in the Septuagint. The comparison also shows how our author quotes this passage in Hebrews 10. Note that in the Septuagint the numbering sequence in Psalms differs slightly from that of the Masoretic Text and from our modern Bibles. Thus, the chapters and verses shown have been adjusted as necessary. I used highlights and underlining to connect the related verses to each other across the three texts. You will notice that the author of Hebrews omitted the last part of what is known to us today as verse 8 of Psalm 40. (Remember that the Bible did not have chapter or verse numbers at the time Hebrews was composed and for centuries thereafter.) He also reversed the order of certain words in the last verse he quoted. The New Testament writers exercised liberty when quoting the Old Testament scriptures, sometimes using the LXX translation or their own translation to emphasize facets of meaning relevant to their arguments, but always remaining faithful to the text and never manipulating its intended meaning.

Notice a small but significant difference between the Masoretic and the LXX renderings. The Masoretic Text has the phrase "you have given me an open ear" in verse 6; the LXX has "but a body hast thou prepared me." This seemingly insignificant difference in translation is, in fact, central to the author's argument. In many instances in Hebrews the author intentionally quotes from the LXX, not only because it was readily available to his Greek-speaking audience but also because its rendering is central to his argument. On occasion the very foundation of his argument depends upon specific terms and phrases found only in the Septuagint. This is one such example.

The Masoretic Text (Ps. 40:6–8)	The Septuagint (Ps. 39:6–8)	The Epistle to the Hebrews (10:5–7)
V. 6: In sacrifice and offering you have not delighted, but you have given me an open ear. Burnt offering and sin offering you have not required.	**V. 6**: Sacrifice and offering thou wouldest not; but a body hast thou prepared me: whole burnt offering and sacrifice for sin thou didst not require.	**V. 5**: Sacrifices and offerings you have not desired, but a body have you prepared for me; **V. 6**: in burnt offerings and sin offerings you have taken no pleasure.
V. 7: Then I said, "Behold, I have come; in the scroll of the book it is written of me: **V. 8a**: I delight to do your will, O my God;	**V. 7**: Then I said, Behold, I come: in the volume of the book it is written concerning me, **V. 8a**: I desired to do thy will, O my God,	**V. 7**: Then I said, "Behold, I have come to do your will, O God, as it is written of me in the scroll of the book."
V. 8b: your law is within my heart."	**V. 8b**: and thy law in the midst of mine heart.	[omitted]

It is quite plain from the meaning of these verses that God never desired animal sacrifices in the first place—and that is precisely why our writer quotes them. Sacrifices were never God's delight. Using the Old Testament scriptures to demonstrate that to his readers, the author of Hebrews proves beyond a doubt that God's plan has always been to abolish animal sacrifices offered under the old covenant and to establish a new one. To put it differently, the coming of Christ and his sacrifice were never against the law but rather were the *ultimate fulfillment* of the law.

This is indeed what the writer underlines for his audience when he gives his own exposition of these verses from Psalm 40. The sacrifices and the burnt offerings were presented according to the law of the old covenant; but when it says, "I have come to do thy will," it shows that these sacrifices were not his will. The author then shows that the will of God has always been that we be sanctified. This was accomplished *only* through the offering of Jesus's sacrifice.

Notice how skillful this author is! I pointed out earlier the difference in rendering between the Masoretic Text and the LXX ("ear" versus "body"). The author uses the Septuagint to underscore the term *body* to show that it was the sacrifice of the *body* of Christ that the LORD desired, not the burnt offerings. Building on that difference in translation, when speaking of Jesus's sacrifice in this context, the author does not use phrases such as "the sacrifice of Jesus" or "Christ's sacrifice" as he does elsewhere in the letter; instead, he purposefully uses the phrase "the offering of the *body* of Jesus" (verse 10). He does this to firmly establish that the fulfillment of that prophecy from Psalm 40 *was none other than the Son of God*!

We are then given an explanation of the significance of Jesus's being seated at the right hand of his Father compared to the priests and ministers of the Old Testament, who could never serve inside the tabernacle or the temple sitting down. We have already covered this in chapter 1. As a reminder, the act of sitting down signifies that one's work has been completed. Since the work (the forgiveness of sins) was never accomplished in the Old Testament by the blood of bulls and goats (see verse 4), the priests under the old covenant were never able to sit down because they needed to continue offering sacrifices one after another (see verses 1–2). Nonetheless, Jesus's work was fulfilled, and thus he sat down at the right hand of his Father since his sacrifice is able to forgive and atone for the sins of all people at all times. The emphasis here is on the singleness of the sacrifice that Jesus offered (verses 12, 14).

The image portrayed here by our author is that of Jesus sitting on the right hand of his Father, "waiting" until his enemies are made his footstool (see our earlier discussion in chapter 2). This waiting involves death being defeated not only by Jesus himself—for that has already been accomplished—but also by his followers, which will be realized when those who have slept in the LORD are raised from death to inherit eternal life in non-corruption. Paul spells this out in his first letter to the Thessalonians: "For since we believe that Jesus died and rose again, even so, through Jesus, *God will bring with him those who have fallen asleep*" (1 Thess. 4:14, RSV). Paul then affirms that when our Lord Jesus returns with the sound of the trumpet, those who died in Christ (that is, believers in his name) will rise from the dead, and the believers who will be alive then will be caught up in the air with him (1 Thess. 4:16–17). Only then will *all* the enemies of Christ be defeated and made his footstool, for death is the last enemy to be overcome (1 Cor. 15:26).

Returning once again to the promise of the new covenant in Jeremiah, the author quotes a much more succinct version than that in chapter 8. He asserts that the Holy Spirit hereby testifies that it is through Jesus's sacrifice that the new covenant is ushered in and ratified. This is because total forgiveness of sins is an integral part of this promise; in fact, it *is* its ultimate outcome. Thus, whatever means provide such forgiveness are the same through which the promise is fulfilled—namely, the blood of Jesus!

The writer then uses the last verse of this section (verse 18) to definitively bring his argument to closure in preparation for his upcoming exhortation in the next section. Lest his readers remain attached to the rituals of their Jewish heritage, he categorically rules out the possibility that there may be any further need for sacrifices like those of the old covenant, now that the sacrifice of Christ has secured total forgiveness of sins. Notice how he positions the forgiveness of sins and animal sacrifices as mutually exclusives realities; that is, they cannot exist together at the same time and in the same realm. When these sacrifices prevailed, there was *no* forgiveness; where there *is* forgiveness, these sacrifices are abolished.

Exhortation to Persevere (10:19–39)

The last exhortation we encountered before this section was in chapter 6 (verses 11–12). Although we will come across more passages of exhortation in the remainder of the letter, here in 10:19–39 our writer offers his readers his most extensive exhortation in the entire epistle. If we connect this section with the previous chapters of Hebrews, it seems as though our author has been offering one argument after another in what appears to be a marathon of ideas, only to arrive at this section, where he finally reveals the reason for presenting those arguments in such speed and urgency. (This can be discerned only if Hebrews is read in one session—something I strongly encouraged you to do in the introductory chapters of this book.)

The first few verses of this section are among the most heartfelt encouragements found in the New Testament and perhaps the entire Bible. The writer is clearly concerned for the spiritual well-being of his audience. He also has many causes for the hope and confidence he offers them. Note that as a good teacher and preacher, he supplies his readers with practical applications to help them overcome the faith challenges they were facing at the time they received his letter. Although we are generations removed from our author, his words of encouragement still apply to many of us today, nearly two thousand years after he originally penned them.

The first consideration we see in this section is that entering the sanctuary—the heavenly equivalent of the earthly Holy of Holies—is made possible by nothing other than the blood of Jesus (Heb. 10:19). No good works, no membership in a certain church tradition, nor any earthly or ministerial status matters in this context. The only means to enter that heavenly sanctuary is the blood of the Son of God. Notice the author's insistence that through the blood of Jesus we not only enter the sanctuary of God the Father but also enter therein *with confidence*! Only those who put their faith in this sacrifice are found worthy to receive that privilege.

A close reading of this section raises a couple of questions. First, what does the author have in view when he says, "We draw near" (Heb. 10:22)? Second, in the same verse, where do the terms *sprinkled* and *washed with pure water* come from, and what do they signify to the author and to his original audience? And why does he use these terms specifically? Though he does not offer direct quotations here, this is where our author, through a seamless yet refined allusion, takes us back to the Old Testament scriptures once more.

One of the direct references we find in the Old Testament that speaks of being cleansed through the sprinkling of pure water is in the prophecy of Ezekiel. Speaking of his restoration of his people Israel, the LORD says, "I will *sprinkle clean water upon you, and you shall be clean from all your uncleannesses, and from all your idols I will cleanse you*" (Ezek. 36:25, RSV). The very words that our skillful author uses evoke this and similar Old Testament promises made by the LORD to his Israel. Note that the writer of Hebrews—with his subtle literary finesse and scriptural knowledge—uses the words of Ezekiel nearly verbatim! He relies on his audience's own knowledge of Scripture and on their understanding that these are, at their very core, *spiritual* promises distinct from God's promises of possessing land or establishing an earthly kingdom. Immediately after this promise, the LORD promises that he will give them a new, clean heart instead of their stony hearts: "A new heart I will give you, and a new spirit I will put within you; and I will take out of your flesh the heart of stone and give you a heart of flesh" (Ezek. 36:26, RSV). This promise can be fulfilled only *after* the LORD has restored Israel to their homeland, for he says earlier in the same chapter and as part of the same promise, "For I will take you from the nations, and gather you from all the countries, and bring you into your own land" (Ezek. 36:24, RSV).

Thus, the fulfillment of this promise could not have been completed before Israel returned from exile because the promise plainly ensures restoration; nor could it have been fulfilled between the time of their return and the birth of Christ, for the promise undoubtedly includes the spiritual restoration of Israel as well: "And I will put *my spirit* within you, and cause you to walk in my statutes and be careful to observe my ordinances" (Ezek. 36:27, RSV). During the 450 years from the time Israel returned from Babylon to the birth of Jesus, Israel was spiritually dead and could not have been said to have the Spirit of the LORD within them. Rebuking his people Israel for their unfaithfulness during the time of Malachi, the LORD sums up Israel's spiritual state at the time, saying, "I have no pleasure in you, says the LORD of hosts, and I will not accept an offering from your hand" (Mal. 1:10, RSV). Hence, there is no time in Israel's entire Old Testament history when Ezekiel's prophecy could have been said to have been fulfilled. Therefore, the writer of Hebrews is drawing the attention of his readers to the fact that these magnificent promises of God to his people Israel can be fulfilled only through his Son, Jesus.

The sprinkling of blood on people first appears in Scripture in the covenant ratification ceremony in the desert of Sinai. (For a fuller discussion of this, see chapter 8.) In this context, sprinkling the blood of bulls on the congregation of Israel symbolized their being consecrated and set apart from all other peoples as God's own people who are under his covenant (Exod. 24:3–8). There are two other references in the Old Testament scriptures to being cleansed by "sprinkling" and "washed with pure water."

The first one is during the annual ceremony of the Day of Atonement. Discussed on a few occasions elsewhere throughout this book, there is still more that should be said about that ceremony and what it reveals about the character of God and the infinite nature of his holiness.

As noted earlier, before giving the instructions for the Day of Atonement, the book of Leviticus reminds its readers that two of Aaron's sons, Nadab and Abihu, died because "they *drew near* before the LORD" and offered strange incense (Lev. 16:1). The LORD begins his direct instructions in the next verse, saying, "Tell Aaron your brother *not to come* at any time into the Holy Place inside the veil, before the mercy seat that is on the ark, so that he may not die" (Lev. 16:2). The phrase "not to come at any time into the Holy Place" uses nearly identical language to that used to describe Nadab and Abihu "drawing near." In both phrases the idea of approaching the presence of the LORD is in view. Doing so in the Old Testament was punishable by death in most cases. The LORD—in his fearsome holiness and righteousness—was unapproachable by sinful man. In contrast, the author of Hebrews emphasizes that we are *now* able to "draw near" and enter the LORD's presence with no risk of death. Through the blood of Jesus, any and all believers are not only authorized but in fact *invited* and encouraged to approach the holy presence of God. The writer of Hebrews uses these terms—packed with theological significance—to illuminate the transformation that has taken place in our relationship with the Father as a result of the sacrifice of his Son, Jesus.

To demonstrate this transformation in the Old Testament, the Day of Atonement became symbolic of Christ's sacrificial work. For one, it was the *only* day in the year when any of the Israelites—including the priests—could enter God's presence. Second, to enter therein, the shedding of blood was required. After atoning for his own sins so he could continue his ministry on that day on behalf of the congregation of Israel without risking his own life, the high priest would atone for the sins of the people in this manner. Thus it is written in the book of Leviticus,

> Then he shall kill the goat of the sin offering which is for the people, and bring its blood within the veil, and do with its blood as he did with the blood of the bull, sprinkling it upon the mercy seat and before the mercy seat; thus he shall make atonement for the holy place, because of the uncleannesses of the people of Israel, and because of their transgressions, all their sins; and so he shall do for the tent of meeting, which abides with them in the midst of their uncleannesses. There shall be no man in the tent of meeting when he enters to make atonement in the holy place until he comes out and has made atonement for himself and for his house and for all the assembly of Israel. Then he shall go out to the altar which is before the LORD and make atonement for it, and shall take some of the blood of the bull and of the blood of the goat, and put it on the horns of the altar round about. And he shall sprinkle some of the blood upon it with his finger seven times, and cleanse it and hallow it from the uncleannesses of the people of Israel. (Lev. 16:15–19, RSV)

Not only did atonement have to be made for the sins of the people but even the very objects (the furniture pieces of the tabernacle) that were used to offer sin sacrifices had to be cleansed from being defiled by the sins of the people. The sins of Israel did not defile them alone but also defiled the tabernacle of God and everything in it, all of which had to be cleansed on the Day of Atonement.

We find this principle in effect as early as the time of Adam. The LORD cursed the ground for Adam's sin (Gen.

3:17). Likewise, God warned his people Israel not to defile the land that he was about to give them, lest it "vomits" them, as it had vomited its previous inhabitants for their sins (Lev. 18:24–25). It is astonishing that in this passage the LORD declares that he had to punish the *land* for *its* sins: "Even the land was defiled; *so I punished it for its sin*, and the land vomited out its inhabitants" (Lev. 18:25, NIV). When the inhabitants of the land transgress against the LORD, in his eyes it is as if *the land itself* has sinned against him, thus meriting punishment. Because the sanctuary of God among his people was defiled by their sins, the high priest had to cleanse it by the blood of the sacrifices on the Day of Atonement.

The sprinkling of blood also had the effect of hallowing and consecrating people. Moses was instructed to sprinkle blood mixed with oil on Aaron, his sons, and their garments: "Then Moses took some of the anointing oil and of the blood that was on the altar and sprinkled it on Aaron and his garments, and also on his sons and his sons' garments. So he consecrated Aaron and his garments, and his sons and his sons' garments with him" (Lev. 8:30). Hence, being sprinkled with blood was known in the Old Testament for consecrating and setting apart people and objects as God's own and cleansing them from sin. This is precisely what the author of Hebrews has in view in his reference when he writes about "our hearts sprinkled clean from an evil conscience" (10:22, RSV). When our hearts are sprinkled by the blood of Jesus through our faith in him, they become cleansed from sin and set apart to love the LORD our God with all our heart and with all our soul and with all our might (Deut. 6:5).

The second reference related to being cleansed is found in Exodus, and it has to do with washing in pure water. One of the key furniture items Moses was instructed to make for the tabernacle is the bronze basin used by Aaron and his sons to wash themselves before they begin their ministerial duties before the LORD so that they do not die. Using the water contained in the basin, "they shall wash their hands and their feet, so that they may not die: it shall be a perpetual ordinance for them, for him and for his descendants throughout their generations" (Exod. 30:21, NRSV). In the immediate context, with their hands the priests handled God's holy vessels; with their feet they walked in his presence. Symbolically, hands signify one's deeds, whereas feet signify journeys and purposes. Taken in its entirety, the reference to hands and feet represents one's entire body. For this reason our author uses the phrase "our *bodies* washed with pure water" (10:22, RSV). The phrase "pure water" indicates that the water he has in view is not physical but spiritual. (The Bible typically uses another phrase to denote literal water that can be used for cleansing, and that is "running water.")

In New Testament theology, this pure water signifies the work of the Holy Spirit in the hearts and minds of the believers. In speaking of the whole church of Christ, set apart and consecrated to her Lord as were the Israelites in the Old Testament, Paul exclaims, "That he might sanctify her, having cleansed her by the washing of water with the word" (Eph. 5:26). Like the author of Hebrews, Peter writes to the believers who were in the dispersion, explaining the effect of this spiritual water in cleansing their consciences before God. Speaking of how God saved Noah and his family through the waters of the flood, he states, "Baptism, which corresponds to this, now saves you, not as a removal of dirt from the body but as an appeal to God for a *clear conscience*, through the resurrection of Jesus Christ" (1 Peter 3:21, RSV). Thus, the writer of Hebrews, in his reference to blood and water, is using Old Testament themes—well understood by his audience to signify cleansing and purification—to denote the spiritual work effected in them by the blood of Jesus and by the pure water of his Holy Spirit. He is bringing what was once practiced under the old covenant and giving it its true meaning and full significance under the new.

His next exhortation echoes his previous one in chapter 4: "Since then we have a great high priest who has passed through the heavens, Jesus, the Son of God, let us hold fast our confession" (Heb. 4:14, RSV). Notice that in both cases the author not only asks his audience to hold fast to their confession of faith or hope, but he also provides a basis for urging them to do so. In chapter 4 he finds Jesus's priesthood to be that foundation. In this chapter he reminds his readers that their hope of salvation is rooted in God's faithfulness. Thus, both their hope and their faith are founded upon a solid foundation. Note also that the "good works" he refers to here are the antithesis of "dead works" mentioned previously in 9:14. If the blood of bulls and goats could not purify the conscience of the worshiper, the blood of Jesus can, and as such, its cleansing work must therefore produce fruit worthy of repentance and inner transformation of heart.

To the author the gathering of believers to worship and fellowship with one another is paramount. It is well recognized and attested to in the New Testament that one of the roles of the church—as the community of believers—is to encourage and uplift one another. As members of the same body, it is part of God's design that believers are not isolated or alienated from one another but rather unified and strengthened by each other. Long before Hebrews was written, we are told in Acts that the believers "devoted themselves to the apostles' teaching and the fellowship, to the breaking of bread and the prayers" (Acts 2:42).

To understand the author's warning in the next section, I ought to say that in the Old Testament, among all the various sacrifices commanded to Moses, there was *no* sacrifice available to atone for *deliberate* sins. Sin and trespass offerings were available *only* to atone for unintentional sins. This is clearly outlined in the following passage from the book of Numbers:

If one person sins unintentionally, he shall offer a female goat a year old for a sin offering. And the priest shall make atonement before the LORD for the person who makes a mistake, when he sins unintentionally, to make atonement for him, and he shall be forgiven. You shall have one law for him who does anything unintentionally, for him who is native among the people of Israel and for the stranger who sojourns among them. But the person who does anything with a high hand, whether he is native or a sojourner, reviles the LORD, and that person shall be cut off from among his people. Because he has despised the word of the LORD and has broken his commandment, that person shall be utterly cut off; his iniquity shall be on him. (Num. 15:27–31)

The phrase "high hand" is an ancient Near East expression that denotes defiance or deliberateness. In this passage it is clearly the antithesis of "unintentionally." In Leviticus we also find that all sin and trespass offerings were commanded to those who committed *unintentional* sins, whether the anointed priest, the whole congregation, one of the rulers, or one of the Israelites (see Lev. 4:2, 13, 22, 27; 5:15). There is no law for intentional sins, for they were punishable only by death or by being "cut off" from the people. *If intentional sins were thus rewarded under the old covenant, which was ratified and ushered in by the blood of bulls and goats, how much greater would the punishment be for those who despise Jesus, the Son of God, who is far superior to the angels of heaven, to Moses, and to Aaron, and who is the author of the new covenant and the one who inaugurated it by his own blood, especially* after *they have come to the knowledge of the truth*! The author's answer is quite simple and has been articulated, though in passing, in chapter 6 (verses 4–6). Here, he elaborates it a bit more: there is no sacrifice that can be offered

The First Abolished, the Second Established

for apostasy. Because there is no higher sacrifice than that of the Son of God, there can never be atonement for those who reject it. This is the writer's stern warning to his original readers (and to us) mixed with his latest exhortation: those who reject the Son of God have made themselves subject to God's judgment and wrath.

The expression "outraged the Spirit of grace" in verse 29 finds parallels in both the Old and the New Testaments. In Isaiah, the LORD rebukes his people Israel, saying, "Yet they rebelled and grieved his Holy Spirit. So he turned and became their enemy and he himself fought against them" (Isa. 63:10, NIV). Paul also warns the Ephesians not to "grieve the Holy Spirit of God, with whom you were sealed for the day of redemption" (Eph. 4:30, NIV). Nonetheless, the Holy Spirit does not only become grieved; he also becomes outraged, which in some cases may result in death. We must bear in mind that these are warnings applicable *not* only to those who lived under the old covenant but also to those who live under the new.

Ananias sold his land, decided to keep part of the proceeds for himself, and gave the remainder to Peter, claiming that it was the full price. Peter rebuked him, saying, "Why has Satan filled your heart to lie to the Holy Spirit and to keep back part of the proceeds of the land?" (Acts 5:3, NRSV). Hearing these words, Ananias fell dead immediately. A few hours later, Peter did not hesitate to speak the same judgment on Sapphira, Ananias's wife. Before those who buried her husband had left the scene, they buried her too. Our Lord himself forthrightly warned us not to blaspheme against the Holy Spirit (that is, not to resist his work in us), calling it the only unforgivable sin: "Therefore I tell you, every sin and blasphemy will be forgiven men, but the blasphemy against the Spirit will not be forgiven" (Matt. 12:31, RSV).

Lest his readers believe he is being exaggeratory, our writer doubles down on this notion by citing the Old Testament scripture to show that vengeance belongs to the LORD and that he *will* judge *his* people. He quotes two consecutive verses from Deuteronomy using the Septuagint translation. The first verse comes from Deuteronomy 32:35, and it matches the Masoretic Text. The second one comes from Deuteronomy 32:36, and it does not match that text. It reads, "For the LORD will vindicate his people and have compassion on his servants" (Deut. 32:36). But in the LXX it is rendered, "For the LORD will *judge* his people, and he will relent on his slaves" (Deut. 32:36, LXX). This is another instance in which the author uses the Septuagint rendering because it contains terminology that bolsters his argument. The author aims to emphasize the notion that the LORD *will* judge everyone, even his own people who have gone astray and abandoned their faith.

Aligned with this notion, the author then delivers one of the most fearsome—and most avoided—verses of Scripture in the New Testament: "It is a fearful thing to fall into the hands of the living God" (Heb. 10:31). In a time when congregations want to hear only about the love of God, it is rare to find a preacher in church today preaching or teaching on the horrors of God's judgment and its dreadfulness. Most congregants know that "God is love," but they tend to forget that God is also a "consuming fire" (Heb. 12:29). Sadly, many preachers have led modern-day Christians to believe that they worship a different God than the "God of the Old Testament," who sent fire and brimstone on Sodom and Gomorrah and consumed Aaron's sons Nadab and Abihu because they dared to appear before his presence and offer strange incense, which he had not commanded (see Gen. 19:24–25; Lev. 10:1–3). I understand that this may not be easy to receive in a Christian culture in which most teachers and preachers assert that a believer "cannot lose his salvation" and is "once saved, always saved," as if these were indisputable biblical doctrines. Nonetheless, these doctrines have little basis in Scripture! The author's next section puts this beyond dispute.[30]

He reminds his original recipients of how they once endured suffering and hardships for their faith. To encourage them to stay the course and to keep walking the walk of faith, he brings to their remembrance how they served prisoners and joyfully accepted being dispossessed of their properties. For a time this was a widespread practice in the Roman Empire, for the government to seize the property—whether land or homes—of those who adhered to views, whether political or religious, perceived by Rome as oppositional to its ideologies. Christians were in that group for the first four centuries of Christian history and until the reign of Constantine.

By reminding them of the temporal nature of their presence on earth, he not only encourages and commends them for what they once did but also eloquently lays the foundation for his argument in the next chapter: that their fathers—Abraham, Isaac, and Jacob—were sojourners in this world, even though they had received the promise of a land inheritance (see Heb. 11:13–16). Believing that they have another, better possession—the kingdom of God, which they are about to inherit—they held loosely to what they owned in this present world. Likewise, the writer encourages his readers not to forego that heavenly inheritance. He then offers a word of encouragement—once again mixed with warning. He urges

---

[30] Recently, I heard a Bible teacher (more specifically, John McArthur) assert that a believer cannot lose (or "un-earn") his or her salvation because he or she did nothing to earn it in the first place. Such an assertion depends on how one defines "believer." Is a believer someone who has confessed faith in Jesus Christ and his redemptive work, or someone who has done so and also *lives* a life worthy of such a confession? Additionally, in both spiritual and earthly matters, every gift ever given or received, by definition, cannot be earned—otherwise, it would not be a gift. However, it is an undeniable truth that any gift might be misused, destroyed, or even lost due to negligence or other reasons. The manner in which one receives a gift does not guarantee one's ability to keep or preserve it.

them to persevere during the times of trials that they were experiencing; he also warns them that those who "shrink back" are destroyed (as in the RSV).

The author's exhortation in this section shows that his original readers were true believers who had experienced the joys and trials of genuine faith. It also shows that it was possible for these same believers to fall back, abandon their faith, and ultimately perish. This sequence of exhortation followed by a warning should make it plain that the risk of losing one's salvation is not only for weak or "fake" believers but also for the strong and real. After all, these believers were so genuine in their faith that, at some point, they accepted various persecutions joyfully.

Note that his encouragement comes in the context of God's faithfulness to his promises that he will not tarry. The promise quoted here comes from the Septuagint version of Habakkuk. In the table below, I have placed the Masoretic (Hebrew) Text and the Septuagint side by side for comparison. The bolded text indicates the difference between the two renderings.

Masoretic Text	Septuagint
For the vision is yet for the appointed time; it hastens toward the goal and it will not fail. Though it tarries, wait for it; for it will certainly come, it will not delay. **Behold, as for the proud one, his soul is not right within him**; but the righteous will live by his faith (Hab. 2:3–4, NASB).	Because there is still a vision for the time, and **he** will appear at an end, and not in vain; if **he** is late, wait for **him**, because one coming will be present, and **he** will not tarry. **If he draws back, my life does not find pleasure in it**, but the righteous one will live by my faith (Hab. 2:3–4, LXX).

In the first verse the LXX substitutes the third-person masculine pronouns *he* and *him* for the non-personal pronoun *it*. The Masoretic Text refers to the vision-promise given by the LORD; the LXX text refers to the LORD himself. As the author and the fulfiller of the promise, in the Septuagint the LORD and his promise are equated and referred to using the same terms for the purpose of promise fulfillment.

Though the fulfillment of the LORD's promise may tarry for a time, those who are waiting for it must not waver or allow their faith to wither away. Peter explains to readers in his second epistle that what may be viewed as "delay" is in fact the forbearance of the LORD in bringing judgment upon the world. Hence, it should not be viewed as lateness but as a chance of repentance to those who have not repented: "The Lord is not slow in keeping his promise, as some understand slowness. Instead he is patient with you, not wanting anyone to perish, but everyone to come to repentance" (2 Peter 3:9, NIV). What the LORD intends to be a chance for repentance to those who have not repented should never be a cause for apostasy for those who have.

The author closes this part of his argument by asserting his certainty that his audience is not among those who would relinquish their faith and perish. Notice that he includes himself among his audience by using the first-person plural pronoun *we*. This is an inclusion of solidarity. At times Paul used a similar technique to encourage his readers. Speaking of the hope of redemption we are waiting for at the second coming of Christ, Paul tells his readers in Rome that since "we hope for what we do not see, we wait for it with patience" (Rom. 8:25, NRSV). This is his way of encouraging his readers by including himself among those who are suffering and enduring present tribulations. The writer of Hebrews employs the same approach to reassure his readers. As they are encouraged to hold steadfastly to their faith and not waver, he indirectly reminds them that he is resolutely undergoing the same hardships. In that, he hopes, they should find comfort and encouragement to follow his example. His final reminder to them in this chapter is that only through endurance are the rewards and promises of God received.

Having exhorted his readers to hold steadfastly to their faith, the writer moves on to explain what faith is, using manifold examples of Old Testament characters—the ancestry of his original audience—to illustrate how they too contended for their faith and did not falter in the face of trials and hardships. Thus, in the next chapter we find a catalog of biblical characters and a listing of numerous tribulations endured.

Questions on This Chapter

1. As we approach the concluding chapters of Hebrews, what are the top key takeaways the Holy Spirit has spoken to you? Write them down in your journal for later reference.

2. You can clearly see how the author of Hebrews—and the rest of the New Testament writers—are so well versed in the Old Testament scriptures. Which part of the Old Testament have you not read yet? If none, which part would you say you should study more deeply? Write down your answers, as we will revisit this topic later, at the end of the book.

CHAPTER ELEVEN

Hebrews 11:1–40

"But now they desire a better country, that is, an heavenly: wherefore God is not ashamed to be called their God: for he hath prepared for them a city."

—Hebrews 11:16, KJV

The Miracles and Tribulations of Faith

Commonly known as the "faith chapter," the eleventh chapter of Hebrews comes as this letter is nearing its conclusion and can be viewed as its capstone chapter. Here the author provides a running list of nearly all who can be called "people or heroes of faith" in the Old Testament scriptures.

Except for a few principal characters (the likes of Abraham and Moses), the writer does not seem to be concerned with providing much commentary on the rest of the characters that he names. In the latter half of the chapter he offers a litany of trials and tribulations experienced by some Old Testament faith heroes without naming them. One reason for that may be that his original readers would have been intimately familiar with the biblical and extrabiblical narratives behind each character. Thus, the details he omits here would have been quite obvious to the letter's original recipients. Another possible reason is that the names attached to each act of faith are irrelevant to the author's argument. His emphasis is on the power of faith and what it can effect in one's life. It is the work of faith that he is focused on, not the heroes themselves.

Much has been speculated as to what these specific details refer to in the Old Testament history. Some extrabiblical sources have been consulted to aid with filling the gaps that our author leaves for us as we read this text more than twenty centuries after its original composition. Nevertheless, some of these attempts remain purely speculative and, in many cases, unsuccessful. For our purposes here, we will emphasize the characters who are known to us and on whom our writer seems to focus. As we attempt to fill the gaps in our current knowledge regarding the other details he offers, we will maintain focus on the central message that the author is trying to relay to us instead of getting absorbed in investigating specific historical references. As a result, this chapter will deviate from the familiar flow of discussion to which I have adhered thus far, as did some of the preceding chapters.

I should also add that there has been a great deal of debate as to why the writer of Hebrews mentions certain Old Testament characters by name while omitting others. For instance, he names Barak, Samson, and Samuel while omitting Othniel, Ehud, and Deborah. It must be noted that the author of Hebrews never intended his list to be all-inclusive. It is obvious from its literary elements that his listing was intended to be demonstrative, not exhaustive. Therefore, laboring over why the author chooses to name some while omitting the rest of the Old Testament heroes is a futile endeavor.

Faith Defined (11:1–3)

On the topic of faith, the first verse of this chapter is one of the most frequently quoted verses in the entire Bible, and rightfully so. It is the only verse in the Bible where we find a clear definition of faith spelled out rather than inferred. It is also one of the verses in the Bible whose essence most modern English translations do not capture. Perhaps the best (and simplest) rendering available is that of Young's Literal Translation: "And faith is of things hoped for a confidence, of matters not seen a conviction" (Heb. 11:1, YLT). Simply stated, to the author of Hebrews, faith means being confident that we will receive what we hope for, and being convinced—beyond any doubt—that the things we cannot see exist or will come into existence.

The author uses a relatively rare Greek word in the first half of the verse to relay this meaning: *hypostasis*. It appears only five times in the New Testament. The author of Hebrews uses it one other time in Hebrews to articulate that Jesus is the very essence or imprint of God (see Heb. 1:3 and the discussion in chapter 1). One of its common meanings is "substance" or "deed" (title of property). It is the same word used to refer to the legal instrument that proves land ownership. This is significant to understand, to fully comprehend the intended meaning of the author.

Faith, according to Hebrews, is *not* an unfounded *feeling* or perception of confidence based on one's emotional state or desire to "feel" confident. It is the certainty of ownership based on the legal instrument the LORD has provided—his word. In other words, it is the confidence founded upon and rooted in what God has "legally" provided, as a landowner is confident in his ownership based on the legal instrument (deed) that is in his possession—that is, God's promises as set forth in his word, backed by his character and faithfulness in bringing to pass all his past and future promises. As a result of what the LORD has assured, believers can be confident of receiving what they hope for.

The writer defines faith also as being convinced of things unseen. It must be noted that this conviction rests upon the "deed" provided in the first half of the verse. Since God has provided proof that we will receive what we hope for, it follows that we can be certain of the existence of what we cannot see, both present and future. For this reason, the author immediately proceeds to evidence his argument by asserting that the LORD—at the beginning of creation—spoke into existence the things that are now visible from that which did not exist. The underlying significance here is that since the LORD has done this once already to create the present world, he is able to do it again to create the world to come. In the author's view, the very world we now see should serve as the foundation of our faith in what is to come. He who believes the first verse in the Bible will have sufficient faith to believe the rest of it!

This is precisely what the author means in verse 3 when he asserts that by faith we know that the things that are now seen were *not* created from other things that were visible. When creating the world, God did *not* transform one material into another. Instead, he caused to exist things that were not previously. Through this biblical truth, all claims of the eternality of matter are proven false. The writer's declaration also disproves any worldview that asserts the preexistence of the physical world and that God used preexisting material to create what we see around us today. It is here affirmed that the world—and everything in it—was created *by the word of God*! By his word, it was created from *nothingness*. This too is significant as it contradicts ancient myths, some of which claim that the world was created through a series of struggles and wars among "the gods," causing the material world to come into existence. Evolution is another theory that is dashed to pieces on the rock of this solid biblical truth! The LORD spoke the world into existence *by his word* and *not* by a series of evolutionary happenings that eventually produced the world as we know it today. How do we know these truths to be true? The author's assertion is unequivocal: *only by faith can we know these realities to be true!* Apart from faith, not only can we not please God (v. 6) but we cannot even believe his word!

Abel, Enoch, and Noah (11:4–7)

The writer's choice of the biblical characters he highlights is neither random nor without literary strategy. First, those whom the author mentions in detail receive a homily-like commentary. This is consistent with the overall nature of the epistle. Second, his list is—for the most part—chronological based on the Old Testament scriptures. Third, since it is a listing of those whose faith serves as an example to model, it omits those who have disobeyed the LORD even if they were key figures not only in biblical history but also in human history at large. Adam is a notable example of that. Fourth, those who receive detailed commentary are those who demonstrated their strong faith by mighty acts of obedience.

Beginning with Abel, whom his brother Cain slew, the author attests that by faith he offered his acceptable sacrifice before the LORD. Recall that in the time of Abel, none of the Mosaic law had been written, nor had the ordinances of sacrifices been given. Therefore, Abel's sacrifice was solely based on his faith that if he were to present the best of what he had to the LORD, it would be looked upon with acceptance.

We see this notion articulated by the LORD not to Abel but to Cain, whose sacrifice was not regarded by God. The LORD indicated to Cain what he needed to have done so that his offering would be accepted: "Then the LORD said to Cain, 'Why are you angry? And why has your countenance fallen? *If you do well*, will not your countenance be lifted up? And if you do not do well, sin is crouching at the door; and its desire is for you, but you must master it'" (Gen. 4:6–7, NASB). In faith, Abel offered the "fat portions" of his animals—the best he had, out of his love for his God. Cain is said to have "brought an offering" of the fruit of the ground to fulfill a duty. Despite being warned by God, Cain succumbed to his envy against his brother and killed him. Hence, the author exclaims that Abel "still speaks" (Heb. 11:4, NASB). It is plain that the author does not intend to say that Abel *himself* still speaks as if he were still alive, rather, that his *blood* still cries out of the ground, demanding justice to be exacted against him who shed it! (See the next chapter for further discussion on Abel's blood.)

Generations after Abel's death, Enoch was another faith hero in the Genesis narrative about whom the Bible does not say much. Besides the genealogies of 1 Chronicles, Enoch is mentioned in the Bible in only three other books: Genesis, Hebrews, and Jude (who supplies us with a bit more detail about Enoch that would otherwise be unknown). Likely relying on extrabiblical sources, Jude tells us that Enoch preached the LORD's judgment to the sinners of his generation—something the Genesis narrative does not disclose. He writes, "Enoch, the seventh from Adam, prophesied about them: 'See, the Lord is coming with thousands upon thousands of his holy ones to judge everyone, and to convict all of them of all the ungodly acts they have committed in their ungodliness, and of all the defiant words ungodly sinners have spoken against him'" (Jude 14–15, NIV). As a testimony to his righteousness, God translated Enoch to heaven alive after he had lived on the earth for 365 years (Gen. 5:21–24). That Enoch is the youngest in the genealogy of Genesis 5 suggests that there may have been a pressing reason for which God took him—possibly some form of persecution he was experiencing in his generation because of his faith, and because he preached judgment to them.

Third, we come to Noah, who was doubtless the epitome of faith among his generation, for he believed God above all. At a time when wickedness had become widespread, Noah believed the LORD and chose to obey him by building the ark while enduring the ridicule that must have ensued from those who refused to believe that total destruction was imminent

(Gen. 6:13–7:24). Noah's faith was so great that in the midst of the wickedness of his generation, Scripture bears him witness that he did all that the LORD had commanded (Gen. 6:22; 7:5).

"Cain said to his brother Abel, 'Let us go out to the field.' And when they were in the field, Cain rose up against his brother Abel, and killed him" (Gen. 4:8, NRSV).

In this depiction, Cain is portrayed as fleeing from the presence of the LORD, while the body of his brother Abel lies on the ground—the earth having metaphorically "opened its mouth" to receive his blood, as described in Genesis 4:11.

Photo Credit: Morphart Creation/Shutterstock.com

We must remember that building the ark was an undertaking that lasted for a number of years. We can only conjecture about the contempt Noah must have endured from his wicked generation when they saw him expending the effort required and the years needed to build the ark. Yet at the only time in human history when the wickedness of mankind warranted total annihilation, Noah believed in the LORD and obeyed him. At no other time in the Bible do we find that the evil of man caused God to bring total judgment on every living soul. Even at the time of the overthrow of Sodom and Gomorrah, God's judgment and the ensuing destruction were limited to a specific region and to a few cities. In Noah's time, the destruction was total and the death was all-encompassing (Gen. 7:21–23).

Abraham (11:8–22)

As the father of all believers, Abraham receives a longer and more detailed mention than any other faith hero in this chapter. The author focuses mainly on two major events in Abraham's life that show his faith and commitment to God beyond any other character in the Bible: his departure from his homeland and his obedience in sacrificing his only son, Isaac.

When considered, Abraham's faith was nearly immeasurable. He left his father's tribe and his homeland to move to a land that was both far removed and unknown to him at the time. Though it is omitted in the biblical narrative, one can only imagine the criticism—and perhaps even the ridicule—that Abraham must have received from his household for leaving behind everything he knew to go to a foreign land, following a commandment from God, who had not yet promised him the inheritance of the land at that time. In this respect Abraham was probably similar to the other faith heroes mentioned above in being unique among their generation, thus inviting mockery and scorn. One can also envision such mockery and ridicule continuing much later in their lives and even after their deaths. Recall that Abraham, Isaac, and Jacob all received the same promise of the land from God but never inherited it in their lifetimes. Their only assurance was God's promise. The author of Hebrews recognizes this fact and un-

The Miracles and Tribulations of Faith

Abraham's hand was stayed from sacrificing his son, Isaac, as he received the oath-promise from the LORD that he would become the father of many (Gen. 22:1–19).

Photo Credit: Morphart Creation/Shutterstock.com

derscores it by stating, "These all [Abraham, Isaac, and Jacob] died in faith, not having received the things promised, but having seen them and greeted them from afar, and having acknowledged that they were strangers and exiles on the earth" (Heb. 11:13).

Placed under Abraham's faith is that of his wife, Sarah. Though Abraham received the promise of the land but did not inherit it in his lifetime, not all of God's promises to him followed the same pattern. God promised him a son, and that promise came to pass one year after God had "cut" a covenant with him through circumcision in the flesh (compare Gen. 17:1, 17, 21; 21:5). Within that year, Abraham received the three visitors by the oaks of Mamre (Gen. 18:1–15). Though Abraham had repeatedly received the promise of a son from God, it was essential that Sarah receive the same promise herself directly from the LORD. In verse 12 the writer of Hebrews points to the Genesis narrative where we are told that "Sarah laughed to herself, saying, 'After I am worn out, and my lord is old, shall I have pleasure?'" (Gen. 18:12). Considering the deadness of her womb—for "it had ceased to be with Sarah after the manner of women"—and the advanced age of her husband, Abraham, Sarah could not believe the LORD's promise at first. For this reason she laughed when she heard the LORD give his promise to her and to Abraham (Gen. 18:9–15). Despite the laughter and her attempt to hide it from the LORD, in her heart she believed that the one who promised was able to bring it to pass (Heb. 11:12). By faith, out of the dead womb of her who was ninety-nine years old, nations of innumerable descendants came forth!

In this somewhat detailed passage about Abraham and his faith, our writer adds a parenthetical note. He writes that although Abraham, Isaac, and Jacob all received the promise of the land and the numerous offspring directly from the mouth of the LORD, none of them lived to see it come to fruition.

The Scripture tells us that the LORD promised the land of Canaan to Abraham five times. The first occurred at the oak of Moreh shortly after he had entered Canaan (Gen. 12:7). After Lot strove with Abraham and separated from him, the LORD renewed his promise to Abraham (Gen. 13:14–17). The promise was subsequently reiterated to Abraham at the "covenant cutting ceremony," when the LORD made a formal covenant with him (Gen. 15:1–20). After the birth of Ishmael from Hagar, Sarah's maidservant, the LORD appeared to him yet again, promising him another son—from Sarah this time—and renewed his promise of the land of Canaan (Gen. 17:1–22).[31] The final promise came after Abraham obeyed the voice of the LORD and was about to sacrifice his son, Isaac (Gen. 22:16–18).

Unlike Abraham, Isaac received the promise of the land from the LORD only once. At the time of the famine in the land, God promised Isaac the land of Canaan as well as many descendants (Gen. 26:1–5). Similar to Abraham's strife with Lot, the LORD renewed his promise of numerous descendants to Isaac after his conflict with the herdsmen of Gerar. This promise, however, did not include any mention of land inheritance.

Jacob first encountered the LORD while he was on his way to Haran, fleeing probable death by the hand of his brother, Esau. The LORD appeared to him in a dream in which Jacob saw a ladder connecting heaven and earth, with angels ascending and descending on it (Gen. 28:10–15). To encourage Jacob after his contentious departure from the city of Shechem, God renewed his promise to him of the land a sec-

---

[31] At his initial calling the LORD instructed Abram to leave his kindred and go to the land that God would show him (Gen. 12:1–3). In this narrative there is no promise of *inheriting* the land. Similarly, though the LORD appears to Abraham in Genesis 18 and promises both him and his wife a son, no promise of the land is given there either.

ond time at Bethel after his daughter Dinah had been defiled by Shechem (Gen. 35:9–12).

It should be noted that in all these experiences of the patriarchs, the common element was the trials and hardships they endured. Despite the fact that the LORD had promised them the land on which they lived, they sojourned through it from one place to another like strangers rather than owners or heirs. This is what the author of Hebrews has in view when he remarks that they all lived and died without receiving the promises of God.

The writer of Hebrews is not the only biblical author who notes this fact about Israel's forefathers. They themselves acknowledged it in their lifetimes. After the death of his wife, Sarah, and in his search for a burial place for her in Hebron, Abraham tells the Hittites—the then-owners of the land—"I am a sojourner and foreigner among you; give me property among you for a burying place, that I may bury my dead out of my sight" (Gen. 23:4). Appearing before Pharaoh of Egypt for the first time, Jacob comments, "The days of the years of my pilgrimage are an hundred and thirty years: few and evil have the days of the years of my life been, and have not attained unto the days of the years of the life of my fathers in the days of their pilgrimage" (Gen. 47:9, KJV). Centuries later, King David himself recognizes this truth in his prayer when he writes, "For we are strangers before you and sojourners, as all our fathers were. Our days on the earth are like a shadow, and there is no abiding" (1 Chr. 29:15; see also Ps. 39:12). Those who have fixed their eyes on their heavenly inheritance always hold loosely to their earthly one—for the things that are seen are temporal, but the things that are not seen are eternal (2 Cor. 4:18).

Because they sought the LORD and the heavenly abode that he had promised them and knew that they belonged to him, God takes pleasure in calling himself their God—the God of Abraham, Isaac, and Jacob. In fact, God first introduced himself to Moses at the burning bush, saying, "I am the God of your father, the God of Abraham, the God of Isaac, and the God of Jacob" (Exod. 3:6, RSV). God used this formula two more times in the burning bush encounter alone (Exod. 3:15; 4:5). Our Lord Jesus himself reinforced this same formula—which is used to identify the LORD from among all other "gods"—in his encounter with the Sadducees, who believed that there was no resurrection of the dead, calling the LORD the God of the living and not of the dead (Luke 20:27–40).

Admittedly, it is hard to speak of the life of Abraham and not mention the most pivotal point of his life: when his faith was tested by the command to sacrifice his son, Isaac. What the author of Hebrews discloses to his readers here is among the most revelatory passages in the Bible concerning this episode of Abraham's life. Though the Genesis narrative does not *explicitly* state that Abraham knew that God would raise his son Isaac from the dead, the writer of Hebrews openly declares this to us (Heb. 11:19). He declares it in such a manner and without explanation, as if his original audience already knew it and thus did not need further evidence. Still, we do find a hint of this detail in the Genesis account.

After receiving the command from the LORD to sacrifice his only son, Isaac, Abraham sets out on a three-day journey to the mount that God had shown him (known today as Mount Moriah or the Temple Mount in Jerusalem, where both Solomon's Temple and the Second Temple stood). On the third day, seeing the mount from afar off, Abraham says this to the two young men who had accompanied him and Isaac on their journey: "Stay here with the donkey; I and the boy will go over there and worship and *come again to you*" (Gen. 22:5). The last part of this statement is particularly noteworthy. It shows that Abraham knew that, even though he was going to sacrifice his son, Isaac, somehow he was going to return to his servants with Isaac alive! Like the writer of Hebrews, this is what Paul alludes to in Romans when he speaks of the immense faith that Abraham had in the promises of God, stating, "No unbelief made him waver concerning the promise of God, but he grew strong in his faith as he gave glory to God, fully convinced that God was able to do what he had promised" (Rom. 4:20–21). Abraham had such a strong faith in God and in his word that he was persuaded that, even if Isaac were dead, the LORD would still raise him from the dead so that the promise of an offspring through Isaac would be fulfilled.

Speaking of Isaac, Jacob, and Joseph, our author remarks on how they, by faith, blessed their children and prophesied of things to come. Isaac blessed Jacob—who later became Israel—saying that he would receive the dew of heaven, eat from the fatness of the earth, and drink his wine from the wine of the land. As part of his blessing, Jacob's brothers (that is, Esau and his offspring) would serve him and bow to him. All of these blessings came to pass for Jacob's descendants, the people of Israel. Generations after Jacob, Moses relayed how Isaac's prophecy of increase would be fulfilled for the children of Jacob—the Israelites: "He will love you, bless you, and multiply you. He will also bless the fruit of your womb and the fruit of your ground, your grain and your wine and your oil, the increase of your herds and the young of your flock, in the land that he swore to your fathers to give you" (Deut. 7:13). The second half of the prophecy came to pass when the Edomites, the descendants of Esau, were subdued by David, the king of Israel, who put garrisons in Edom and made the Edomites his servants (2 Sam. 8:13–14). In turn, Jacob himself blessed his children, the heads of the tribes of Israel, before his death in Egypt.

Perhaps the most powerful prophecy that Jacob uttered during his patriarchal blessing was that of Judah, for he says of him, "The scepter shall not depart from Judah, nor the ruler's staff between his feet, until Shiloh comes. And to him shall be the obedience of nations" (Gen. 49:10, LEB). Shiloh (rendered in other translations as "to whom it belongs") is a clear reference to Christ. Notice here that the writer of Hebrews mentions Jacob's leaning on his staff before his death (Gen. 47:31). While the Masoretic (Hebrew) Text says that Jacob leaned upon the head of his bed, the writer of Hebrews uses the Septuagint rendering, that he leaned on his staff. Both renderings signify the same meaning, and that is, one's readiness to die as he acknowledges that his hour has come. In the ancient Near East culture, this act signifies one's announcement that he has completed all that he had set out to accomplish during his lifetime and is thus content to be succeeded by his descendants. King David bowed himself upon his bed at the end of his life after inaugurating Solomon, his son, as his successor (1 Kings 1:47).

Joseph, certain that the children of Israel would leave Egypt, requested that his bones be taken with them, out of the land of Egypt and back to his homeland (Gen. 50:24–25). About four hundred years later, when the Israelites came out of Egypt, they took Joseph's bones with them as they journeyed through the wilderness for forty years (Exod. 13:19). After they came to the promised land, Joshua buried Joseph's bones in Shechem, the modern-day city of Nablus (see Joshua 24:32). All three men spoke in faith and prophesied by faith of what was to come; because of their faith, all that which they had spoken came to pass.

Moses (11:23–28)

Proceeding to the next prominent faith hero of the Old Testament, the author of Hebrews highlights the life of Moses and the major milestones in his journey. The first major event in Moses's life was related not to his own faith but to that of his parents. After the death of Joseph and the coming of a new king to the throne of Egypt, an edict was issued to the two midwives, who helped deliver the Hebrew babies, that when they serve "as midwife to the Hebrew women and see them on

"Then Pharaoh's daughter went down to the Nile to bathe, and her attendants were walking along the riverbank. She saw the basket among the reeds and sent her female slave to get it. She opened it and saw the baby. He was crying, and she felt sorry for him. 'This is one of the Hebrew babies,' she said" (Exod. 2:5–6, NIV).

Photo Credit: ruskpp/Shutterstock.com

the birthstool, if it is a son, [they] shall kill him, but if it is a daughter, she shall live" (Exod. 1:16). Later Pharaoh issued the same order to all his people, saying, "Every son that is born to the Hebrews you shall cast into the Nile, but you shall let every daughter live" (Exod. 1:22). Thus, when Moses was born, death would have been his sure fate had it not been for the faith of his parents.

As Moses was born at such a time, his parents—in faith—refused to kill their own child or surrender him to be killed by the Egyptians. Instead, they hid him in their house for the first three months of his life. After making a basket of bulrushes and daubing it with pitch, they placed it in the Nile, committing their child to the care of God. Miriam, the older sister of the newborn baby, stood afar off to see what would become of the child. A short while later the basket was picked up by Pharaoh's daughter, who adopted the child Moses as her own son and hired his mother as a caregiver to nurse and care for him. While Moses's parents did not know what was to become of him, they placed their trust in God, believing that he would protect the child Moses—the very essence of faith. Because the LORD is the God who never fails those who trust in him, their child became the instrument that God later used to deliver his people Israel out of the land of Egypt and one of the most influential figures in both Jewish and human history at large.

As Moses grew into adulthood, he began to recognize his Hebrew roots. In defending his brethren, Moses killed an Egyptian who was beating a fellow Hebrew and secretly buried his body (Exod. 2:11–12). Moses believed that his people would understand that Gad had called him to deliver them.[32] In his address before being stoned to death, Stephen remarked on how the Israelites failed to see the significance of

---

[32] This suggests that Moses's encounter with God at the burning bush may not have been his initial calling to deliver Israel from bondage.

this event (Acts 7:25). Instead, one of them threatened to expose what Moses had done, forcing him to flee Egypt and escape to the land of Midian (Exod. 2:14–15).

In the mind of the writer of Hebrews, this was a deliberate choice made by Moses. As Stephen noted, by killing the Egyptian, Moses chose to share in the suffering of his people instead of enjoying the riches in Pharaoh's house. Due to the hardness of their hearts and refusal to recognize God's intervention, Moses had to flee to Midian, delaying God's deliverance by forty years.[33]

The mention of "the reproach of Christ" in verse 26 is significant and may have different meanings. It may signify a reproach *similar* to that of Christ's: Moses was rejected by his own people, Israel, in the same way Jesus was. They murmured and complained against him on numerous occasions; in one instance they were about to stone him (Exod. 17:4). Alternately, this phrase may denote the reproach Moses suffered by the hands of the Egyptian *along* with Israel, who are God's people and therefore Christ's. The latter view is more likely, as Moses would have known of the suffering that awaited him at the hands of the Egyptians, but could not have anticipated the grumbling of the children of Israel later in the wilderness. Under this view, this reference to Christ is weighty evidence for the deity of Jesus and his equality to God, insofar as the author of Hebrews is concerned.

As the author closes this passage on Moses, he cites two other key events in his life. Those who killed the Passover lamb—so that they could mark the lintels and the doorposts of their houses with its blood—did so in faith, for they had to believe the imminence and gravity of God's judgment. They also had to believe in the efficacy of the blood of the lamb and in God's promise of deliverance from certain death. Also, as

---

[33] It is noteworthy that the Israelites' arrival to the promised land would be delayed by yet another forty years due to their lack of faith (see Numbers 13 and 14; see also the discussion in chapter 3).

terrifying as it was, they had to take God at his word and believe that it was safe to cross the Red Sea with a wall of water on either side of them. This same water killed the Egyptians, who did not know the LORD and refused to recognize his sovereignty. Note that in this section—as in all the other sections in this chapter and in accordance with his definition of faith in verse 1—the writer portrays faith as the simple act of believing what God says. Faith is believing this basic fact: what the LORD says, the LORD does.

Other Heroes (11:30–32)

The acts of faith listed in this final passage of the chapter all exhibit deeds that normally would never lead to the desired outcome. Yet because of the power of the faith of those heroes, their actions were rewarded by God. In short, these acts of faith would have been mere foolishness in the eyes of a fleshly man, but in the eyes of a spiritual man, they are rooted in the wisdom of God.

As the writer provides a listing of the remaining faith heroes of the Old Testament, rapidly moving through its history, he highlights how their acts exemplify his definition of faith stated earlier in the chapter: being certain of the things hoped for and being confident of receiving the not-yet-seen rewards.

Marching around a well-fortified city such as Jericho while blowing trumpets for seven consecutive days—in the natural realm—would never lead to the collapse of its walls. Mere human logic would have informed Rahab that the Israelites would not be able to breach Jericho's walls. Hence, her covenant with the enemies of her people would have seemed like a foolish act of uncalculated risk. Nonetheless, by the power of faith, the walls of Jericho fell, and Rahab and her family were the only people in the city who escaped death.

Gideon was one of the judges of Israel who succeeded Joshua. It is remarkable that the writer of Hebrews mentions him by name, given that in his lack of faith he asked for not one but two signs from the LORD. Despite being personally called by the LORD to deliver Israel from the oppression of the Midianites, Gideon asked God that his fleece be full of dew while the ground around it remained completely dry. After receiving this sign, Gideon made a second request to God: to make the fleece dry and the ground around it full of dew. In his patience the LORD granted him that sign too (Judges 6:36–40). As the men went out to battle against the Midianites, the LORD reduced Gideon's army from 32,000 to just 300 men (Judges 7:2–8). This was the number of men that God used to defeat an army of 135,000 of Israel's enemies by the hand of Gideon. Despite his initial lack of faith, Gideon displayed strong faith in trusting in the LORD's victory against an army that was 450 times the size of his own. It required a great deal of faith to take this level of risk in battle.

The mention of Barak comes in reverse chronological order since he precedes Gideon in the book of Judges. Barak, who was not named a judge himself, fought alongside Deborah, the prophetess and judge of Israel, against Jabin, king of Hazor, and Sisera, the commander of his army (Judges 4:4–7). With 10,000 men from the tribes of Naphtali and Zebulun, the LORD caused the army of Sisera to flee before Israel. Seeking refuge in the tent of Heber the Kenite, Sisera was killed shortly thereafter by Heber's wife, Jael. Through the faith and obedience of Deborah and Barak, God brought total victory to Israel over their enemy.

The story of Samson and Delilah has been the object of mainstream pop culture for decades. From a biblical standpoint, however, Samson stands as an example of repentance and return to God despite one's flaws, shortcomings, and erroneous decisions. Doubtless, Samson attached himself to foreign women against the commandment and the will of God. He trusted the daughters of the enemies of Israel; for that, he paid a hefty price of servitude to the Philistines, which included his eyes and eventually his life. In a final act of faith, nonetheless, Samson placed his trust in God to avenge him of those who had conspired against him. As the Philistines celebrated their victory over Samson and over Israel, he placed his hands on the pillars that supported the house where they were and cried out to his God one last time. At his death, Samson

Samson and Delilah, Cornelis Massijs, 1549. Samson is sleeping with his head on Delilah's lap while she cuts his hair. Three Philistines are ready to capture Samson.

Photo Credit: Morphart/Shutterstock.com

killed more of Israel's enemies than he had during his lifetime (Judges 16:30).

Jephthah is listed here after Samson, though in the narrative of Judges he appears before Samson. This aligns with the writer's lax adherence to the chronological order of the Old Testament. As an illegitimate son, Jephthah was ridiculed and rejected by his half-brothers but chosen and called by God (Judges 11:1–3). To help Israel defeat the Ammonites, he became a judge over Israel.

Jephthah's inclusion among the heroes of faith is particularly striking: as the son of a prostitute, he was not supposed to be admitted into the assembly of Israel up to the tenth generation—let alone be named among the faithful in the New Testament (see Deut. 23:2).[34] This meant that he could not be circumcised, partake of the Passover, offer sacrifices, or even marry an Israelite woman. His inclusion in this "cloud of witnesses" is due to nothing other than the gracious faithfulness of God. Jephthah's faith was honored and recognized by God, though he was not part of the congregation of God. The LORD has no respect of persons; he honors those who believe in him, even if they were the descendants of sin.

Armed with his faith in the God of Israel, Jephthah crossed over the Jordan and fought against the Ammonites, and the LORD delivered them into his hands (Judges 11:32). His vow to the LORD was that whatever came out of his

---

[34] In this context it is noteworthy to point out that the genealogy of King David at the conclusion of the book of Ruth plays an important role in legitimizing David's—and Jesus's!—right to the throne of Israel (see Ruth 4:18–22). In fact, it is often argued that legitimizing David's claim to the throne is the sole reason the book of Ruth was written and included in the Old Testament canon (see Ruth 4:17). As the illegitimate son of Judah, Perez and his descendants could not be admitted into the congregation of Israel for ten generations (see Gen. 38:29). David is the tenth from Perez, and thus his claim to the throne becomes legitimate. Theologically this plays an important role in our Lord Jesus's reigning forever on the throne of his father David. If David's claim to the throne were nullified, so would Jesus's.

house first to meet him upon his return would be sacrificed to the LORD as a burnt offering. It was his own daughter who came out first to greet him as he returned home. Thus, she was dedicated to God as an unmarried virgin for life (Judges 11:37).[35]

No list of faith heroes would be complete without mentioning David. Perhaps the most faith-filled moment in his life is his defeat of Goliath—a well-known story that warrants but a brief mention of its main highlights. No one from the army of Israel dared fight Goliath, nine feet tall, who spent forty days taunting the Israelites (1 Sam. 17:16). David, however, trusted in God, who had delivered him from the mouths of a lion and a bear (1 Sam. 17:34–36). He took five smooth stones and slung one of them, hitting Goliath in the forehead. David then grabbed Goliath's own sword and separated his head from his body (1 Sam. 17:40–51). In a spectacular display of faith, David was the instrument whom God used to deliver Israel from certain defeat before their archenemy.

Samuel is listed here after David since the latter was a much more prominent figure in Israel's history during that period. Samuel was the last judge of Israel. He was the son of Hannah, who had been barren prior to his birth. She had vowed to the LORD that if she were to bear a child, she would

---

[35] While some interpreters have chosen to adopt the view that Jephthah actually killed and sacrificed his daughter to the LORD, there is nothing in the biblical text that suggests this. In fact, the daughter's request to her father to allow her two months to mourn her virginity strongly suggests her knowledge of the manner in which she would be "offered" to the LORD (Judges 11:37); that is, she would not be able to get married. This is unambiguously clear from what the Bible states a couple of verses later: "At the end of two months she returned to her father, who did to her according to the vow which he had made; *and she had no relations with a man.* Thus it became a custom in Israel" (Judges 11:39, NASB). On several occasions the God of the Bible strictly prohibits child and human sacrifice, calling it a sacrifice he "never had in mind" (see Lev. 18:21; 20:1–5; Deut. 12:31; 18:10; Jer. 7:31; 19:4–5; 32:35). Thus, sacrificing Jephthah's daughter would never have been a sacrifice that the LORD would accept from Jephthah.

dedicate him to the service of God. As the child grew up in and around the house of the LORD, he learned to hear the voice of God by faith (1 Sam. 3:1–14). For his mother's and his own faith, God sent Samuel to anoint Saul, Israel's first king, and David, Israel's greatest king (see 1 Sam. 10:1; 16:13).

The Miracles of Faith (11:33–35)

Through faith the heroes who remain in this chapter—though unnamed—performed miracles, defeated death, and finished the work that God had sent them to accomplish. The author of Hebrews moves rapidly through this list in no particular chronological order and without providing much detail as to who in the Old Testament performed each act of faith. For one, he relies on his readers' knowledge of Scripture and extrabiblical Jewish sources. Secondly, he intends his list to be an illustrative set of powerful acts achieved by faith and through the work of the Holy Spirit.[36] Thus, the sequence and the individuals who performed each specific act are irrelevant. In fact, not naming his faith heroes from this point forward supports the writer's argument that it was the power of faith that performed all these acts rather than the qualities of each individual. In short, true faith works with no respect of persons.

Another observation that should be noted regarding this rapid inventory of faith acts is that, in the first half, the author recounts the miracles performed by the power of faith and the rewards received by those faith heroes; in the second half, he enumerates the trials and hardships others suffered for their faith. This is an important consideration for our modern-day believers. Faith is not only about performing miracles, casting out demons, raising the dead, or walking on water. The other

---

[36] Though the work of the Holy Spirit and the form in which he abided in the saints of the Old Testament remain a topic of debate, it is evident that these faith heroes were filled with his presence, as without the Holy Spirit there can be no faith.

side of faith *necessarily* involves enduring persecution, patiently and faithfully waiting on the LORD, and holding steadfastly to God's promises amid difficult times when everyone around us may see our faith as the epitome of foolishness. Those who are not willing to resolutely endure the trials of faith will never reap the joy of its rewards and miracles.

The author of Hebrews employs this literary device to bolster his argument. As he hastily moves through his list, the underlying message is clear: just as these past heroes of faith endured great tribulations and were ultimately rewarded, so too should his original readers accept their own trials—not only with patience and fortitude, but also with joy and thanksgiving. James puts it this way: "Count it all joy, my brothers, when you meet trials of various kinds, for you know that the testing of your faith produces steadfastness" (James 1:2). By implication, this miracle-tribulation paradigm includes us too. This is what the author means by his closing statement: "God had provided something better for us, so that apart from us they would not be made perfect" (Heb. 11:40, NASB).

Conquering Kingdoms

Most of the references that the writer points out in this passage are found in Scripture. Others refer to the intertestamental (deuterocanonical) documents—otherwise known as the Apocrypha in some church traditions.[37] Two references (addressed below) are based on Jewish tradition. Some of the author's brief references may refer back to the deeds of some faith heroes already mentioned by name earlier.

For example, the author's reference to "conquered kingdoms" may refer to the Israelites' exodus out of Egypt with the strong arm of the LORD against the powerful war machine of Pharaoh and his army. It may also refer to Gideon, who defeated an army of 135,000 with a small band of 300. The more

---

[37] See the introduction for my views on these writings.

likely reference, nevertheless, would be to Moses's defeat of Sihon, king of the Amorites, and Og, king of Bashan. In addition to being Israel's first grand triumph against existing kingdoms after their exodus out of Egypt, these two victories were the first to enable Israel to conquer foreign land possessed by other peoples. After defeating the Amorites, the Scriptures tell us, "Israel took all these cities, and Israel settled in all the cities of the Amorites, in Heshbon, and in all its villages" (Num. 21:25). After coming out against Israel with all his might, Og was humbled by the Israelites as "they defeated him and his sons and all his people, until he had no survivor left. And they possessed his land" (Num. 21:35).

While not mentioned by name here, the phrase "administered justice" (so rendered in most translations) may be a reference to the just rule of David, but more likely to Solomon's wisdom and discernment in judgment. Psalm 72 (by Solomon) reflects his earnest desire to exercise justice and righteousness in judging the poor and needy. When presented with what would otherwise be a moral dilemma, Solomon applied the divine wisdom that the LORD had conferred upon him to discern proper judgment and sound counsel. Two women with an infant child came to him, each claiming the child as hers. After hearing their claims, Solomon called one of his guards and commanded him to kill the child, divide him in two, and give each woman a half. When one of the women accepted that judgment while the other refused to see the child killed, Solomon immediately discerned that the woman who had agreed could not have been the child's real mother and ordered that the child be given to the other. After this incident, we are told, "When all Israel heard of the judgment which the king had handed down, they feared the king, for they saw that the wisdom of God was in him to administer justice" (1 Kings 3:28, NASB).

Though Abraham received Isaac through the promise of God, it is likely that the author intends to refer to the general notion that, through faith, the promises of God were attained. There are numerous examples of this throughout the Bible, perhaps the most prominent of which is that of David, to whom the LORD promised a Son to reign forever upon his throne (2 Sam. 7:4–17). This promise, received by David in faith, came to pass through the kingship of Jesus the Messiah.

Quenching Fires

Next, the writer of Hebrews appeals to two miraculous acts of God from the book of Daniel. The only instance in the Bible where the mouths of lions were shut by the power of faith is when Daniel was cast into the lions' den as a result of his faithfulness to God. Through the envy of his enemies, Daniel was cast into the lions' den by order of Darius the Mede, who ruled over Chaldea after the Persian conquest of Babylon. The king had decreed that anyone found making a petition to any god or man other than him would be cast into the lions' den (Dan. 6:7). Daniel was then seen through the windows of his upper room on his knees, praying to his God three times a day as he faced Jerusalem.[38] After spending the night in the den, Daniel walked out unharmed because the LORD God had "sent his angel and shut the lions' mouths so that they would not hurt [him]" (Dan. 6:22, NRSV). It was the power of Daniel's faith and faithfulness to the LORD that delivered him from the

---

[38] I find the mention of this detail in the book of Daniel fascinating. During the dedication of the temple in Jerusalem, Solomon prayed one of the most beautiful prayers in the Bible. In it he asks the LORD that if the Israelites were exiled for their sins, but then "repent with all their heart and with all their soul in the land of their captivity to which they were carried captive, *and pray toward their land,* which you gave to their fathers, the city that you have chosen and the house that I have built for your name, then hear from heaven your dwelling place their prayer and their pleas, and maintain their cause and forgive your people who have sinned against you" (2 Chr. 6:38–39). Praying with his face toward Jerusalem, Daniel was doing exactly that.

mouths of the lions, for he "was found innocent" in God's sight.

The second miracle that the author of Hebrews refers to from the book of Daniel is that of three young men, Hananiah, Mishael, and Azariah, who were thrown into the fiery furnace by Nebuchadnezzar, king of Babylon. Having defiantly refused to worship the image the king had created, these three were thrown into the blazing furnace. When asked by the king why they had refused to bow before the image he had created, their answer was a remarkable example of faith:

> O Nebuchadnezzar, we have no need to present a defense to you in this matter. If our God whom we serve is able to deliver us from the furnace of blazing fire and out of your hand, O king, let him deliver us. But if not, be it known to you, O king, that we will not serve your gods and we will not worship the golden statue that you have set up. (Dan. 3:16–18, NRSV)

Outraged at their defiance and trust in their God, the king commanded that the furnace be heated up seven times more than its usual intensity. Because of the intense heat, the guards who threw the three young men into the furnace were themselves consumed by its fire. Yet the three young men were seen by the king and his companions walking unharmed and unbound in the midst of the fiery furnace—and with a fourth person who appeared to the king as "a son of the gods" (a bodily manifestation of what the king understood to be divine). As the three young men held steadfastly to their faith in God, he delivered them.

The Edge of the Sword

We find a direct reference in the life of Moses to his escaping the edge of the sword. His second son, Eliezer—signifying "my God is a help"—was named as such, for Moses said, "The God of my father was my help, and delivered me from the sword of Pharaoh" (Exod. 18:4, NRSV). In faith, Moses spoke this. Not only did the LORD deliver him from the sword of Pharaoh by protecting him as he escaped to the land of Midian, but he also protected him yet again during the exodus from Egypt.

Another example of God's delivering his people from the edge of the sword is that of Elijah's escape from Jezebel. Elijah had challenged the prophets of Baal to have him send down fire from heaven to consume their offering. Despite their cries to Baal for hours, no fire came. When he in turn offered his sacrifice to the LORD, God sent down fire from heaven that consumed not only the burnt offering but also the altar stones, the wood, and even the water in the trenches around it (see 1 Kings 18:38). Seeing this, Elijah commanded the people of Israel to seize the prophets of Baal and slay them. When Jezebel, the wife of Ahab, king of Israel, heard the news of what Elijah had done to the prophets of her god Baal, she sent messengers to him, saying, "So may the gods do to me and more also, if I do not make your life as the life of one of them by this time tomorrow" (1 Kings 19:2). As he sought refuge for himself from the face of Jezebel, the angel of the LORD appeared to Elijah and gave him bread to eat and water to drink that sustained him for the next forty days as he made his way as far as Mount Horeb (1 Kings 19:4–8). The LORD rewarded Elijah's steadfast faith in the face of persecution by protecting him and keeping him alive to prophesy the death of Jezebel, who had schemed to take his life (1 Kings 21:23).

The Weak Made Strong

The author then follows with a reference to the weak made strong. This can be a repeated reference to Samson, David, Solomon, or a new reference to Jeremiah. Samson lost the source of his strength when his hair was cut, breaking his Nazirite vow to God—a vow symbolized by the locks of his uncut hair. While he was in captivity, his hair grew longer, and he regained enough strength to destroy the house in which 3,000 Philistines were celebrating their god Dagon, who they thought had given them victory over Israel (Judges 16:21–30). David was the youngest and thus physically the weakest among his brothers. In fact, he was the forgotten son in his father's house, so when Samuel entered the house of Jesse asking to see all his sons, Jesse passed his seven older sons first, overlooking the fact that his youngest son, David, was in the field tending his sheep. It was not until Samuel asked if these were all of Jesse's sons that he found out that there was one missing (see 1 Sam. 16:6–13). Nonetheless, the LORD chose David to become the mightiest and the greatest ruler of Israel. To this day he continues to be the sole military leader in recorded human history who did not experience even a single defeat in battle!

In turn, when God appeared to Solomon at the beginning of his reign, Solomon wisely did not ask for riches, power, or longevity. Instead, he asked for wisdom, for he said that he was "but a little child," who did not know how to go out or come in (1 Kings 3:7). The LORD also made him one of the greatest kings in Israel, expanding the borders of his kingdom even beyond what his father, David, had done. Likewise, Jeremiah was weak in his own eyes, so when the LORD called him to be his mouthpiece to Judah, he said, "Ah, LORD God! Behold, I do not know how to speak, for I am only a youth" (Jer. 1:6). He too became one of Israel's greatest prophets. All four men, as well as others, through the power of faith and obedience, were instrumentally useful to serve greater causes than they could have ever dreamed or imagined.

Next comes the writer's reference to being "mighty in war" (Heb. 11:34). There are manifold instances of this in the Old Testament. One notable example is when the Israelites fought against the Amalekites at Rephidim shortly after their departure from Egypt. This was an unprovoked attack by the

Amalekites against the people of God. Moses stationed himself at the top of a hill with his hands lifted up to heaven and with "the staff of God in [his] hand," as the Israelites defended themselves against their archenemy of the time, under Joshua's leadership (Exod. 17:8–16). When Moses let his hand down, the Amalekites prevailed; when he held his hand up, Israel prevailed. Aaron and Hur supported Moses's hands until sunset so that Israel might defeat their enemy. This back-and-forth in battle shows that it was not the strength of the Israelites that awarded them victory but rather the might of their God through faith and obedience. Lifting up Moses's hands—in natural terms—never would have caused Israel to overcome the Amalekites. This act of faith and obedience activated the power of God to their advantage, thus yielding supernatural results.

One of the most compelling passages in the Bible concerning the power of faith in the face of foreign enemies is the story of Hezekiah, king of Judah, as he faced the mighty army of Sennacherib, king of Assyria (2 Kings 18:13–19:37). Rabshakeh was among the three emissaries whom Sennacherib had sent with a large army to besiege Jerusalem and to speak to Hezekiah, asking him to surrender without a fight. After Rabshakeh's extended speech of disparagement, Hezekiah went into the house of the LORD, covered himself with sackcloth (a sign of mourning and humbling oneself before the LORD), spread the letters of threat he had received from the Assyrians before the LORD in his temple, and prayed. After sending a message of encouragement through Isaiah, the son of Amoz, the prophet in Judah at the time, the LORD sent his angel, who struck down 185,000 men in the Assyrian camp in a single night—forcing the enemy to retreat to their land in defeat and humiliation. Following this defeat, Sennacherib was later killed by two of his sons as he prayed in the temple of his god Nisroch.

The Dead Received Alive

The last of the miracles of faith that we find in this section is women receiving back their dead sons. Elijah raised the son of the widow of Zarephath, and Elisha raised the son of the Shunammite woman.

During the drought that the LORD brought upon the land of Israel through the word of Elijah, there was neither flour nor oil to make bread (both are the produce of the land). At the command of the LORD, Elijah went and stayed with a widow in Zarephath who had only one son. She had but a little flour in a bowl and a small measure of oil left in a jar—scarcely enough to feed her and her son for one meal. Elijah promised her that if she were to make him bread *first*, the flour would not be exhausted, nor would the oil run out. In faith she took the man of God at his word. For many days afterward, neither the flour nor the oil ran out. But calamity struck a short time later: the widow's only son became sick and died shortly thereafter. Moved with compassion for the woman, Elijah took the dead body of the boy and went up to his chamber, laid him on his own bed, and prayed. Hearing Elijah's prayer and seeing the faithfulness of the widow, the LORD returned the boy's soul to his body and restored his breath in him. Then we read that "Elijah took the child, brought him down from the upper chamber into the house, and gave him to his mother; then Elijah said, 'See, your son is alive'" (1 Kings 17:23, NRSV).

In a similar setting, Elisha, Elijah's disciple and successor, raised the son of the Shunammite woman who hosted him in her house. As Elisha frequented her small town, she built him a small room in the upper chamber of her house so that he could turn in there whenever he passed by. With the woman's husband being old and having no children of her own, Elisha desired to reward her by promising her a son from the LORD. The following year she gave birth to a son, as Elisha had spoken. Then her son suddenly died. In a remarkable act of faith and while Elisha was not at her house, she carried the body of her dead son and placed him on Elisha's bed in the upper room where he stayed. Although she refused to tell Elisha what had become of the child, the LORD revealed to Elisha that her son had died. Elisha then went into his room and prayed for the child's life to return to him. The boy's flesh immediately "became warm," he sneezed seven times, and then he opened his eyes. Elisha called the woman up to his room and said to her, "Pick up your son" (2 Kings 4:36, LEB). Then "she came and fell at his feet and bowed down to the ground; then she picked up her son and went out" (2 Kings 4:37, LEB).

While the Scripture is silent concerning the faith of these two women before and after their encounters with Elijah and Elisha, the writer of Hebrews has spoken well when he said that through faith women received their dead alive once more. Their faith was indeed remarkable!

The Tribulations of Faith (11:35–40)

Having established the power of faith in effecting miracles, the author now moves to discuss the trials and tribulations experienced by the men of faith. In his mind it is equally critical that his audience see the alternate side of the faith experience. While faith can perform miracles beyond what can be comprehended in the natural realm, those who possess such a strong faith can be the object of trials and hardships that no human mind can conceive. Through faith they can withstand these trials with unimaginable resolve, unbelievable fortitude, and even with joy.

Accepting Torture

In verse 35 the author of Hebrews refers to women receiving their dead sons alive through faith. Intriguingly, in the same verse he also refers to a well-known, though sad, incident in the Jewish intertestamental history in which a mother witnessed all of her seven sons being tortured and violently murdered for their refusal to renounce their faith. None of them came back to life again.

In the second century B.C. Antiochus IV Epiphanes ruled over the Seleucid kingdom, which at the time encompassed the land of Israel. In his brutality against the Jews, he desecrated the temple by sacrificing swine on the LORD's altar and forced some of the Jews to eat of the sacrifices. In 2 Maccabees (among the deuterocanonical books) we read the story of a mother of seven sons who refused to eat of the swine sacrificed on the altar in Jerusalem (2 Macc. 7). In an extraordinary display of faith and courage, all of her seven sons refused to obey the king's command, enduring extreme forms of torture with steadfastness and bravery. When offered relief from the torture to which they were subjected, they all refused, citing their hope and conviction that the LORD would raise them again from the dead and grant them eternal life because they died holding fast to his laws and to the faith of their fathers. The most remarkable testimony comes from the second son, who testified against the king as he was gasping his last breath, saying, "You accursed wretch, you dismiss us from this present life, but the King of the universe will raise us up to an everlasting renewal of life, because we have died for his laws" (2 Macc. 7:9, RSV). After watching all of her seven sons die brutal deaths, the mother herself died, refusing to urge any of her children to renounce their faith to save their lives.

Chains and Imprisonment

Had the author of Hebrews been writing concerning New Testament history, the likely candidate for this reference would have been none other than the great apostle Paul, but this is unlikely. The most probable Old Testament event to which this refers is Jeremiah's imprisonment for refusing to be silenced concerning the future calamities surrounding the kingdom of Judah and its future exile.

When Pashhur, the chief officer in the house of the LORD at the time of Jeremiah, heard what Jeremiah had been prophesying against Jerusalem, he beat him, imprisoned him, and placed him in the stocks (Jer. 20:1–2). Still, when released the next morning from prison, Jeremiah remained faithful to his prophetic office and continued to prophesy against the city, foretelling its impending destruction by the hand of Nebuchadnezzar:

> And [the LORD] will give all Judah into the hand of the king of Babylon. He shall carry them captive to Babylon, and shall strike them down with the sword. Moreover, I will give all the wealth of the city, all its gains, all its prized belongings, and all the treasures of the kings of Judah into the hand of their enemies, who shall plunder them and seize them and carry them to Babylon. (Jer. 20:4–5)

In fact, in the boldness of his faith, Jeremiah prophesied against Pashhur himself and against his family, saying, "And you, Pashhur, and all who dwell in your house, shall go into captivity. To Babylon you shall go, and there you shall die, and there you shall be buried, you and all your friends, to whom you have prophesied falsely" (Jer. 20:6).

The writer's next reference to stoning almost certainly refers to Jeremiah. (This makes it likely that he had Jeremiah in view in the previous section.) According to Jewish tradition, Jeremiah died by stoning in Egypt. We know from the book of Jeremiah that he was taken down to Egypt against his will by the rebellious, unbelieving Jews of his time. Because they had refused to hearken to the voice of the LORD through Jeremiah and after most of the inhabitants of Judea were taken captive by Nebuchadnezzar, Johanan, the son of Kareah, and all the officers of Judah took all the remnant of Judah along with Jeremiah the prophet and Baruch, the son of Neriah, his scribe, and led them to the land of Egypt against the command of the LORD. Later Jewish sources tell us that Jeremiah was stoned to death and buried in Egypt.

According to other extrabiblical sources, Isaiah the prophet, the son of Amoz, was sawn in half by Manasseh, the evil king of Judah. While his father, Hezekiah, was a righteous king, Manasseh, his son, committed numerous abominations in the eyes of the LORD, from idolatry and witchcraft to passing his own son through fire as a form of sacrifice to his pagan gods (2 Kings 21:1–9). There was little evil that Manasseh did not commit before the LORD. Noncanonical Jewish sources from the early first century AD tell us that Isaiah refused to bless Manasseh—who began to reign at twelve years of age—predicting his sinful reign and abominable deeds. Manasseh ordered that Isaiah be sawn in half using a log.

Killed by the Edge of the Sword

Among the many prophets and faith heroes who were murdered for doing the work of the LORD, Uriah the prophet stands recognized as a clear example of a man of God who is explicitly said in the Scriptures to have been murdered by the edge of the sword. He was a contemporary of Jeremiah, prophesying a similar message of impending destruction against Jerusalem for its disobedience and apostasy. Because Jehoiakim, king of Judah, was angry with the message Uriah was preaching, he sought to kill him; so Uriah fled to Egypt. Still, the king sent men to Egypt to search him out and bring him back to Judah, where Jehoiakim "struck him down with the sword and dumped his dead body into the burial place of the common people" (Jer. 26:23).

The Miracles and Tribulations of Faith

According to Jewish tradition, the prophet Isaiah was murdered by being sawn asunder. He is depicted here looking up to heaven, holding a pen in one hand and a large saw in the other.

Photo Credit: Morphart Creation/Shutterstock.com

Epilogue

As the author closes this section of the epistle, he makes passing references to sheepskins and goatskins worn by men of faith. In the Old Testament we find that Elijah was known for wearing "a garment of hair, with a belt of leather about his waist" (2 Kings 1:8). Though not part of the Old Testament scriptures but still before Christ began his earthly ministry, John the Baptist—who would have been well known to the author and to his original readers—wore camel's hair and girded his waist with a leather girdle (Matt. 3:4).

Likewise, wandering in caves and deserts is a reference that well suits Elijah. When he fled from the face of Jezebel, he came down to Mount Horeb and stayed there in a cave for a time (1 Kings 19:8-9). A similar occurrence is found shortly before this event in 1 Kings. At that time Obadiah was over the household of Ahab, the evil king of the northern kingdom of Israel. But Obadiah feared the LORD. So when he heard that Jezebel was seeking all the prophets of God to destroy them, he took one hundred of them and hid them by fifties in caves and provided them with food and water (1 Kings 18:4).

The writer closes by remarking that all these men and women of faith had received the promises but did not see their fulfillment. While some promises did not come to pass in their lifetime (such as David and his descendant, the promised Messiah), some did (such as Isaac's birth). The main promise that the author has in view, however, is the promise of eternal rest, vindication, and everlasting joy. In other words, though they believed in God and in his eternal promises and suffered and died for that belief, none of them received the promises for which they died here on earth. They refused to forsake their God and their faith. Many of them paid for that choice through tribulations; some paid with their lives. Regardless of the immediate outcome, all of them gained approval and pleased God by their faith. Nonetheless, they were not "made perfect" before we—their successors in the faith walk—can join them, following in their footsteps and imitating their faith. This is the "higher purpose" that God had in mind when he let them pass from this transitory world without receiving the promises that he had given them. None of God's believers will witness the ultimate fulfillment of his promises until the number of God's children is completed, and until all the "other sheep" that belong to our Lord Jesus have been brought into his fold: "And I have other sheep that are not of this fold. I must bring them also, and they will listen to my voice. So there will be one flock, one shepherd" (John 10:16).

Questions on This Chapter

1. After reading this chapter and seeing the power of faith in the lives of these faith heroes, can you relate to any of their experiences? Have you ever experienced trials or tribulations because of your faith?

2. While different church traditions have different views on this issue, do you believe that faith still performs miracles? Why or why not? What do you think this chapter of Hebrews says about this controversial issue?

Chapter Twelve

Hebrews 12:1–29

"Fixing our eyes on Jesus, the originator and perfecter of faith, who for the joy that was set before him endured the cross, disregarding the shame, and has sat down at the right hand of the throne of God."

—Hebrews 12:2, LEB

A New and Precious Covenant

In this chapter the author brings to a close his argument outlined in the previous chapters. He knows that he is approaching the end of his letter; hence, he uses this last opportunity to underscore the conclusion of what he desires to articulate to his readers. He summarizes his main points, exhorting his readers not to forsake their faith in the face of the pressures and the persecutions they have been experiencing. Despite the warning and admonishing tone with which he writes this chapter, a careful reading readily reveals his true motivation behind writing in this manner.

Though his tone may seem harsh at first, there is an undertone of deep concern for the salvation and the eternal destiny of his recipients. It is evident that his personal relationship with his audience compels him to warn them against the pitfalls of renouncing their faith. He is not writing to them this beautifully crafted letter with all his eloquence and finesse because he wants to prove them wrong or because he desires to "win" an argument. He is more concerned for their salvation than he is with "being right." This clearly shows throughout this chapter.

God's Chastisement of His Children (12:1–13)

This chapter opens with what can be termed "a marker of strong inference": the Greek word *toigaroun*, typically rendered *therefore*. This marker denotes that what follows is firmly built on what preceded and is closely related to it.

In the writer's mind this "cloud of witnesses" that he detailed in the previous chapter is (or should be) a cause for encouragement to his readers. This cloud of witnesses—faith heroes—serves as motivation to cast aside every "weight" or sin encompassing them. The word he uses here for "weight" (or "encumbrance" in some translations) is particularly interesting. It signifies *hindrance* or *impediment*, but it may also mean *weight* or *mass*. The image he has in view here is that of a runner in a race who must cast down any weight and overcome all obstacles so that he can run and win the race! This is made even plainer in his use of the phrase "let us run with endurance the race that is set before us" (Heb. 12:1, NASB). In connection with sin surrounding us, notice the adverb he employs—*easily*. The writer recognizes that not every sin can be cast down, for some sins cannot be so easily shunned. Some sins require struggle—sometimes for years—to overcome! Nonetheless, we must rid ourselves immediately of those sins that do not cling to us as hard.

In this regard, Jesus is the example to follow. He fixed his eyes on what he considered to be his prize—our salvation. Here the writer of Hebrews uses the term *joy*. He immediately defines it as "enduring the cross." This "joy" is what enabled Jesus to run the race with endurance and patience, looking at the finish line—Golgotha! Nowhere else in the Scriptures do we find the term *joy* used to describe the redemptive work of Jesus on the cross. This "joy" that was set before Jesus—on which he fixed his gaze—is not only what caused him to leave his heavenly glory behind and take the form of a humble servant, but it is also what kept him walking from Galilee toward Jerusalem, and from Pilate's praetorium to the place called the Skull! Not only that, but that joy strengthened Jesus to *despise* the shame that comes with being hung on a cross.

For one, the law of Moses says that anyone who is hung on a "tree" is cursed by God (Deut. 21:23; Gal. 3:13).[39] Second, execution by crucifixion was the most humiliating form of death in the time of Jesus, under Roman rule. Yet not only did Jesus *endure* this pain and shame, but he also despised it as a thing not to be regarded altogether! Therefore, our author invites his original readers—and us—to fix our eyes on Jesus himself. Observe how the writer does not exhort his audience to fix their eyes on any other prize or reward. Instead, he considers Jesus himself to be the perfect reward and the ultimate prize!

The phrase used here of Jesus—"the author and perfecter of faith," or in other translations, "the founder and finisher of faith"—is used nowhere else in the Bible to describe our Lord Jesus, and is thus unique to Hebrews. The writer of Hebrews uses a similar expression when he refers to Jesus as "the author of [our] salvation" (Heb. 2:10). As the inaugurator of the new covenant ratified by his own blood, Christ is he who provides a new pathway to the Father and is the first to walk in that path, paving it with his blood. Jesus not only instructed us on how to live—enduring pain and tribulations with patience and resolve—but he also lived that way first, setting himself as

---

[39] For the English reader, the word "tree" in Deuteronomy may be problematic, especially when used to refer to the cross of Jesus in the New Testament. The Hebrew word *'eits* (עץ) literally means *tree*, but it also means *wood*. Hence, to the New Testament Jewish writers both concepts were used interchangeably. The word signifies any relatively large woody plant, or any large wooden object made from it that is vertically positioned (such as a cross or a pole). See Deut. 21:22–23 in the NIV).

a model to be followed. This is what the writer of Hebrews refers to elsewhere as Christ's being our "forerunner" (Heb. 6:20). With Christ as our forerunner, who suffered *first* on our behalf for sins he did not commit, God the Father rewarded and glorified him by seating him at the right hand of his throne.

Like the aforementioned heroes of faith, the author of Hebrews emphasizes that looking at Jesus—as the forerunner who ushered in the new covenant and sanctified our pathway to heaven by his blood—should be a cause for encouragement and a source of perseverance to the suffering audience. If the heroes of old are distant and removed from these persecuted first-century readers, Christ—contemporary to their own time—is the archetype of enduring suffering to achieve victory and glory. As the original recipients of Hebrews were unjustly persecuted for their faith, Jesus underwent similar trials as he sustained injustice by sinful Jews and Gentiles and betrayal by his own disciple. This persecution did not cost Jesus private property or possessions as it did the original readers (Heb. 10:32–34)—but rather his blood. This is significant to the author as he admonishes his readers to struggle against sin even to the point of shedding their own blood as Jesus shed his (Heb. 12:4).

Then the writer—for the first time—quotes from the book of Proverbs. This quotation from Proverbs 3:11–12, as in previous instances, more closely aligns with the Septuagint rendering than with the Masoretic Text. The main difference between the two renderings is in the second half of verse 12, though the overall meaning is similar. Here are the two texts side by side (the italicized text indicates the variations between the two translations):

The Masoretic Text	The Septuagint
My son, do not despise the LORD's discipline or be weary of his reproof, for the LORD reproves him whom he loves, *as a father the son in whom he delights* (Prov. 3:11-12, RSV).	My son, despise not the chastening of the LORD; nor faint when thou art rebuked of him: for whom the LORD loves, he rebukes, *and scourges every son whom he receives* (Prov. 3:11-12, LXX).

The point that the author intends to demonstrate to his readers with this quotation is that the discipline and the chastening of the LORD are not a sign of God's enmity toward them but rather are the hallmark of his fatherhood. To impress this point upon his audience further, the writer uses a relatable, real-life experience: that is, earthly fathers and how they discipline their children. Note that the underlying premise of this argument rests upon God's fatherhood to those who fear him—a premise that the author already established with this quotation from Proverbs. The psalmist echoes the same truth as he writes, "The LORD has chastened me severely, but he has not given me over to death" (Ps. 118:18, NIV). Though the LORD may discipline his children at times, in his fatherly love he will never deliver them to death.

Earthly fathers discipline their children out of love, not motivated by hostility or for the purpose of exacting punishment. In fact, the main motive for which fathers chastise their children is their love toward them and concern for their well-being. If a father did not correct his children's wrongful behavior, one would wonder if they were his own children or why he has no concern for their welfare. Thus, not only should correction be endured with patience but it should also be received with joy and thanksgiving, for it is a sure sign of one's sonship to God. The author suggests that the absence of the LORD's discipline should be a cause for concern. Those whom the LORD does not correct, he does not consider as his children but, as it were, illegitimate offspring. Doubtless this is a literary metaphor that ought not be taken literally or out of context, for the LORD does not have "illegitimate" children in the literal sense. The intended meaning here is that God's correction shows his love; the lack thereof indicates separation from him.

In his first Epistle to the Corinthians, Paul explains the saving nature of God's chastisement. As God chastises his children, he does so out of love, that they may not be condemned with the rest of the world. He writes, "But when we are judged by the Lord, we are chastened so that we may not be condemned along with the world" (1 Cor. 11:32, RSV).

The author concludes this passage of encouragement by exhorting his original recipients to strengthen each other so that he who is weak and is stumbling does not fall down completely and be destroyed. The role of the shepherd—our author in this case—is to encourage and strengthen the flock; the role of the flock is to strengthen and encourage each other.

Holiness (12:14–17)

By now we should be accustomed to the literary style of the writer of Hebrews. For him, theological exposition of biblical passages is usually followed by encouragement and exhortation; exhortation is then followed by warning and admonition. We have seen the exhortation in the previous section; in the next one we find his harshest warning yet.

Here I must note that as a shepherd of the flock, the author sees his role toward his flock not only to encourage and strengthen but also to warn and admonish when needed. This is a noticeable pattern in Hebrews, although it is evident elsewhere in the New Testament writings. When the sheep have become weak, they need strengthening; but when they have gone astray, they need warning and correction. Teachers and preachers who constantly preach on the love of God toward mankind, for "God is love" (1 John 4:8, 16), must also remember (and preach!) that indeed "our God is a consuming fire" (Heb. 12:29, RSV).

The author's assertion that without *holiness* no one will see the Lord militates against the false teaching that a "Christian believer" who lives a lifestyle of sin will not lose his or her salvation but will still inherit the kingdom of God! Seeing the Lord in this context is a clear metaphor for entering the kingdom of God. Notice that the author does not say "without *faith*" but "without *holiness.*" He has already stated in the previous chapter that without faith it is impossible to please God (Heb. 11:6). Hence, if faith is a prerequisite to pleasing God and holiness is required to see him, then *both* faith *and* holiness are necessary to have an everlasting fellowship with him. Separating the one from the other contradicts sound biblical teaching and proper theology.

Following his pattern of drawing on Old Testament anecdotes to deliver compelling theological views, the writer employs the example of Esau as someone who lived in lawlessness and defilement and yet desired and sought blessing. The author uses the example of Esau as the epitome of those who live unholy lives and yet expect blessings and salvation.

In biblical times the firstborn son usually became the head of his siblings. We read in Genesis that Esau was the firstborn of Isaac and thus was in line to receive the birthright and inherit the blessing of his father. While Jacob is described as "a peaceful man, living in tents," Esau is described as "a skillful hunter, a man of the field" (Gen. 25:27, NASB). One day as Esau was returning from the field, exhausted and hungry, he was greeted by his brother, Jacob, whom he asked for a bowl of red lentil stew and some bread. Unlike his brother, Jacob recognized the blessing of being the firstborn. Thus he asked his brother, Esau, to forfeit his birthright and sell it to him. Esau's response is appalling: "I am about to die; of what use is a birthright to me?" (Gen. 25:32). As the writer of Genesis himself writes, it is clear from this response that "Esau despised his birthright" (Gen. 25:34).

Later in the Genesis narrative, we see that Jacob, at the beseeching of his mother, deceived his father, Isaac, by impersonating Esau so he could steal the blessing of the firstborn. Not realizing that his blessing had been stolen by his brother, Esau came to his father asking to be blessed. Aghast at what had happened, Isaac told his son Esau that he had made his brother his master (Gen. 27:37). Realizing the enormity of his loss, Esau wept and sought with tears to be blessed by Isaac, who told him that the blessing had already gone out and been bestowed upon his brother, Jacob. Still, Esau received this "blessing," which made him inferior and a servant to his brother, as it was the only blessing Isaac had left for him:

> Behold, away from the fatness of the earth shall your dwelling be, and away from the dew of heaven on high. By your sword you shall live, and you shall serve your brother; but when you grow restless you shall break his yoke from your neck. (Gen. 27:39–40)

Esau's insistence that a blessing be bestowed upon him is what would later cause his descendants, the Edomites, to be subjected to the yoke of Jacob's offspring, Israel. Had these words not been prophesied by Isaac, they would not have come to pass on the Edomites. Generations later, David, king of Israel, subdued the Edomites, and they became his servants. We find this testimony during David's reign: "And David made a name for himself when he returned from striking down 18,000 Edomites in the Valley of Salt. Then he put garrisons in Edom; throughout all Edom he put garrisons, and all the Edomites became David's servants. And the LORD gave victory to David wherever he went" (2 Sam. 8:13–14). This was a direct fulfillment of Isaac's prophecy over his son Esau.

Edom remained under Israel's control until the reign of Joram (or Jehoram) during the divided monarchy of Israel and Judah (2 Kings 8:20-22). At that time, they rebelled against Israel, set up their own king, and regained independence, fulfilling the second half of Isaac's prophecy that Esau's descendants would eventually grow restless and rebel against Israel.

As Esau despised his birthright and sold it for a single meal, the author warns that so will be regarded those who apostatize from Christ, despising their heavenly inheritance. The neuter pronoun *it*, which the writer uses in verse 17, may refer to "repentance," meaning that Esau sought repentance with tears; or it may refer to "blessing," signifying that he sought after his father's blessing with tears. Nonetheless, from the narrative of Genesis it is clear that Esau never sought to repent. He was never remorseful for what he had done. When he wept with tears, he wept seeking to be blessed, not to be forgiven.

A Mountain Trembling (12:18-24)

The author now moves on to yet another anecdote from the Old Testament to further illuminate his argument to his readers—the LORD's encounter with the Israelites at Sinai.

In this section of the passage the author compares—one last time—the old covenant to the new. The old covenant was established at Mount Sinai when the people of Israel heard the voice of the LORD and witnessed fire and smoke. The new covenant, on the other hand, was ratified by the blood of Jesus, which was shed in Jerusalem (hence the reference in Heb. 12:24), and points to a new kingdom established at Mount Zion and a new assembly gathered in the new city—the heavenly Jerusalem that will be revealed from heaven.

When the Israelites first came out of Egypt, the LORD led them to Mount Sinai. To establish his covenant with them, the LORD appeared to them on the mountain where they heard the audible voice of God (Exod. 19:9; Deut. 4:12, 36). Immediate death was the punishment for any person or animal touching the mountain or coming near its borders. The mountain on which God descended to speak with his people was so holy that any person or animal touching it became holy as well. To kill them, they could not be touched, but rather had to be stoned or shot through with arrows from a distance (see Exod. 19:12–13). The presence of the LORD was so fearsome that the mountain trembled and burned with fire and smoke (Exod. 19:18). Seeing this scene, the Israelites were terrified and asked Moses to speak to them on the LORD's behalf because they were afraid to die as they heard the voice of God (Exod. 20:19).

Some skeptics may see a contradiction between what the author is asserting and what is reported in Exodus concerning Moses saying that he was afraid of the presence of God on Mount Sinai. In the Exodus narrative, we do not have a direct reference where Moses reportedly said that he was fearful and trembling. Nonetheless, we see a clear mention that "all the people in the camp trembled" (Exod. 19:16). The phrase "all the people in the camp" likely included Moses as well. We are also told that "when all the people saw the thunder and the flashes of lightning and the sound of the trumpet and the mountain smoking, the people were afraid and trembled, and they stood far off" (Exod. 20:18). Thus, the writer of Hebrews is attributing to Moses what Exodus collectively attributes to the assembly. In other words, he is explicitly including Moses with the assembly of Israel, whereas Exodus does so only implicitly.

Though Mount Sinai is a real, geographical location present to this day—likely in northwest modern-day Saudi Arabia—the author's reference to Mount Zion is of a different nature. In Jewish literature and tradition Mount Zion is what is known to us today as the Temple Mount (otherwise known as Mount Moriah where Abraham was instructed to sacrifice his son Isaac). As the most significant site in Jerusalem, the ex-

An 1890 depiction of the traditional Mount Sinai in the Sinai Peninsula, Egypt. Although Jabal el Lawz in northwest Saudi Arabia is more likely to be the true location of Mount Sinai, tradition dating back to the early fourth century AD identifies this mountain, in the Sinai Peninsula, as the site where the LORD met with Israel.

Photo Credit: Morphart Creation/Shutterstock.com

pression "Mount Zion" was later used to signify the whole city of Jerusalem. However, the author speaks not of a literal mountain but of a metaphorical one. This is evident by the use of the phrase "the heavenly Jerusalem" (Heb. 12:22), setting it apart from the earthly one. Since "the city of the living God" can be none other than Jerusalem, it follows that the phrase "Mount Zion" refers to the heavenly Jerusalem. This is aligned with the Jewish understanding and use of "Mount Zion" to denote the earthly Jerusalem. In short, the three phrases used here ("Mount Zion," "the city of the living God," and "the heavenly Jerusalem") all refer to the same concept—God's new heavenly city in the age to come.

Though the old covenant was established by a scene so magnificent and fearsome at Sinai, the new covenant looks forward to a new, not-yet-realized reality that will surpass its earthly predecessor. The writer reminds his audience that in the new Jerusalem they will witness the presence of the heavenly angels and the spirits of those who were "made perfect." The author uses this last phrase to refer to the faith heroes of old who received God's promises in faith and died not having seen them fulfilled (Heb. 11:39). This is the author's preferred expression to refer to those who died perfecting (completing) their earthly walk in faith. Since Christ is the firstfruits of God as the first to be resurrected from bodily death and to inherit his glorified body, his whole church—as his body—is rightfully called "firstfruits" (see 1 Cor. 15:20, 23; 2 Thess. 2:13; James 1:18; Rev. 14:4). As members of the resurrected body of Christ, the church herself will be resurrected from the dead in the last day. As the head of the church, Christ will infuse his life, which flows through his resurrected body, to the church, and thus she will be brought back to life herself. The scene that the writer has in view is the rejoicing heavenly Jerusalem—whose inhabitants are the resurrected saints who had slept in the LORD—with the angels surrounding the throne of God at the center of it all. This very scene is what John sees in Revelation:

> After this I looked, and behold, a great multitude that no one could number, from every nation, from all tribes and peoples and languages, standing before the throne and before the Lamb, clothed in white robes, with palm branches in their hands, and crying out with a loud voice, "Salvation belongs to our God who sits on the throne, and to the Lamb!" And all the angels were standing around the throne and around the elders and the four living creatures, and they fell on their faces before the throne and worshiped God, saying, "Amen! Blessing and glory and wisdom and thanksgiving and honor and power and might be to our God forever and ever! Amen." (Rev. 7:9-12)

Whereas Hebrews was likely written decades before Revelation, the similarities between what the two books describe (and *how* they describe it) are intriguing. It is significant that the author of Hebrews uses the term *enrolled* to refer to those who will be in heaven with the LORD. John in Revelation describes how no one will enter the heavenly Jerusalem except those whose names are written in the book of life of the Lamb of God (Rev. 21:27). The Greek word that is translated "enrolled" literally means *to be registered*, as in a governmental record or census.[40] The language used in Hebrews is also reminiscent of what Jesus told his disciples after they had rejoiced that the evil spirits obeyed them in his name: "Behold, I have given you authority to tread upon serpents and scorpions, and over all the power of the enemy; and nothing shall hurt you.

---

[40] James Swanson, *Dictionary of Biblical Languages with Semantic Domains: Greek (New Testament)* (Oak Harbor: Logos Research Systems, Inc., 1997), entry 616. Logos Software.

Nevertheless do not rejoice in this, that the spirits are subject to you; but rejoice that your names are *written* in heaven" (Luke 10:19–20, RSV). Those who will enter the kingdom of God will have their names written—as it were—in the official registry of heaven, just as the citizens of a country have their names registered in the government records.

Having made previous reference to Abel among the faith heroes, the writer of Hebrews reminds us once more that as the blood of Abel was crying for justice against Cain, who had unjustly shed it, the blood of Jesus still cries out, seeking not justice against those who shed it but rather forgiveness and justification for those who believe in its redemptive power. This caused the author to describe the blood of Jesus as a "better" blood than that of Abel. Recall that the overarching theme of Hebrews is the "betterness" of everything Jesus came to offer compared to what had been offered under the old covenant. Not only does Jesus offer better promises, better hope, better sacrifice, and better priesthood than those under the old covenant, but his blood is better than any man's blood —even that of the righteous Abel—for Jesus's blood offers forgiveness and mercy.

Final Admonition (12:25–29)

The author of Hebrews now arrives at his last opportunity to warn his original readers against apostatizing from their Christian faith. You may recall from our discussion on the occasion of writing Hebrews that this was his main concern and objective as he sat down to pen this deep and rich epistle (see the introductory chapter on the purpose of writing Hebrews). As such, the strong and direct warning language of this passage cannot be overlooked, nor its urgency.

The writer begins this section by exhorting his readers not to dismiss his admonition to them. Recognizing the urgency and the importance of what he is about to tell them, he makes a clear appeal to his audience to have an ear to hear and not to reject his warning, despite its repetitive nature. With his familiar literary style, he proceeds to build upon the illustration he just gave them from the Old Testament concerning the Israelites at Mount Sinai. When God spoke to the Israelites, he spoke to them through fire and smoke, to establish a covenant ratified by the blood of animals. The manifestation of the LORD's glory was seen there on an earthly mountain, which was shaken at God's presence. Yet the glory of God itself remained unseen. In comparison, the new covenant was inaugurated by the blood of Jesus, by which God calls his people not to an earthly mountain shaken and burning with fire but rather to a heavenly city surrounded by the visible glory of God in its fullness. If those who rejected the old covenant did not escape God's punishment, how much greater would the judgment then be on those who reject a covenant established by the blood of the Son of God!

To help answer this question, the author follows with a quotation from the book of Haggai. Haggai lived around the time of Zerubbabel and Joshua, the son of Jehozadak, both of whom were involved in the rebuilding of the temple after the return from the Babylonian exile. Seeing how modest the second temple was compared to the glory of Solomon's Temple, the Israelites had become discouraged. To encourage his people Israel to complete the rebuilding effort, the LORD sent his prophecy by the hand of Haggai, telling Israel what would eventually become of this second temple and how its latter glory would exceed that of the first temple, which had been destroyed at the hands of the Babylonians. In the book of Haggai the LORD promises that the heaven and the earth would be shaken "yet once more"—which our author exposits as "one last time" (Hag. 2:6)—meaning that this would be the last time they would be shaken. Since the existing earth is always subject to shaking via naturally occurring events such as earthquakes, volcanoes, and the like, it follows that the earth that would not be shaken would be a different earth and, by association, the heaven would also be a different heaven. This is how the writer of Hebrews expounds the significance of that verse (Heb. 12:26–27).

Nonetheless, this understanding is not unique to Hebrews or to Haggai for that matter. Centuries before the exile and before Haggai, Isaiah prophesied the same things. In the words of Isaiah, the LORD promises the creation of a new heaven and a new earth as part of his promise of restoration to his people: "For behold, I create new heavens and a new earth, and the former things shall not be remembered or come into mind" (Isa. 65:17). Earlier in Isaiah the LORD also promises the removal of the existing heaven: "All the host of heaven shall rot away, and the skies roll up like a scroll. All their host shall fall, as leaves fall from the vine, like leaves falling from the fig tree" (Isa. 34:4). Hence, the exposition that the author of Hebrews offers here would not have been foreign to the ears of his original recipients.

In the New Testament we also find similar prophecies. John the Seer saw a scroll sealed with seven seals, which no one in heaven or on earth was worthy of opening except the slain Lamb of God. After the plagues that followed the opening of the first five seals, the Lamb opened the sixth seal, at which point John testified that "the sky vanished like a scroll that is being rolled up, and every mountain and island was removed from its place" (Rev. 6:14. See also 2 Peter 3:11–13).

The author concludes this rather bleak imagery with another, which is full of hope and joy, as he reminds his audience that a kingdom awaits them that will never be shaken or destroyed. This same language is found in the book of Daniel, where Daniel interprets a dream seen by Nebuchadnezzar, king of Babylon. Daniel explains to Nebuchadnezzar that following the collapse of his kingdom, three more kingdoms would rise and fall (Medo-Persia, Greece, and Rome). After these four earthly kingdoms, Daniel writes, "In the days of those kings the God of heaven will set up a kingdom that *shall never be destroyed*, nor shall the kingdom be left to another people. It shall break in pieces all these kingdoms and bring them to an end, and it *shall stand forever*" (Dan. 2:44). This is an unmistakable reference to the kingdom of God, which would start during each of these kingdoms but would be fully established by the advent of Christ. Unlike the previous four earthly kingdoms, this kingdom will never be destroyed but will stand forever!

With this reminder the writer of Hebrews closes by exhorting his audience to remember that the end of all things is at hand. Hence, they must hold fast to the faith that they have received with fear, knowing that all evil will be condemned and that even the existing creation—having been corrupted by sin—will be burned with fire! God in his righteousness will not allow even the material creation to stand before his eyes forever, having been cursed due to man's sin. The LORD's righteousness is a consuming fire that burns sinful, unrepentant men and defiled creation alike.

Questions on This Chapter

1. When chastised by the LORD, complaining is usually our initial reaction. Our immediate desire, when experiencing pain, is for the pain to go away. Can you recall a time when you were chastised by the LORD? How did that make you feel?

2. Reflecting on this, jot down in your journal the blessings (and growth) you would have missed out on had the LORD done what you asked and caused the pain to immediately abate.

Chapter Thirteen

Hebrews 13:1–25

"Now may the God of peace who brought again from the dead our Lord Jesus, the great shepherd of the sheep, by the blood of the eternal covenant, equip you with everything good that you may do his will, working in us that which is pleasing in his sight, through Jesus Christ, to whom be glory forever and ever. Amen."

—Hebrews 13:20–21

The Final Benediction

As the writer of Hebrews concludes the epistle, he does not neglect to impart to his readers what constitutes acceptable worship before the LORD. This is especially important at this point in the letter, given that he has just warned them against rejecting the Christian faith and exhorted them to offer sacrifices acceptable to God in awe and reverence (Heb. 12:28).

His final benediction and greeting carry some resemblance to the Pauline style, found at the end of nearly every one of Paul's letters, but it lacks the somewhat detailed listing of names for which Paul is known.

Acceptable Sacrifices (13:1–6)

The last chapter of the letter ended with this exhortation: "Let us offer to God acceptable worship, with reverence and awe"

(Heb. 12:28). In this chapter the author gives a brief but rapid list of what that "acceptable worship" entails. Hospitality, visiting the imprisoned, remaining faithful in marriage, and avoiding greed are at the top of his list. Notice that this short list begins with two virtues that the author urges his audience to practice and concludes with two vices from which he admonishes them to refrain.

Written in a time when travel was mostly done on foot or on the backs of donkeys and mules, hosting strangers and travelers was an important practice that showed one's consideration and sacrificial love toward others. This practice was what earned Abraham the honor of hosting the LORD himself with his two angels at the oaks of Mamre.

Sitting at the door of his tent in the heat of the day, Abraham saw three strangers passing by from afar. He urged them to turn aside, rest, and be nourished by some bread and milk. As was the custom in the ancient Near East, guests must eat first before those in the household could do so.[41] Thus, Abraham stood under a tree as he watched his distinguished guests eat (Gen. 18:8). Unbeknownst to Abraham, the LORD was one of these three visitors in one of God's preincarnation Old Testament appearances. During this blessed visit, both Abraham and Sarah received directly from the LORD's mouth the promise of a son (Gen. 18:10–14).

Shortly after this passage we read that Lot—who then lived in Sodom and Gomorrah—hosted the two angels sent by God to save him and turn the cities into ashes. As he sat at the gate of Sodom, Lot impressed upon the two strangers to come into his house to stay for the night (Gen. 19:1–3). As the night wore on, the people of the city surrounded his house and demanded that the two guests be brought out so that they may

---

[41] In some regions in the Middle East, this custom is still in effect today. The point of this custom is to make sure that guests get the best of the food and drink offered before the host family begins to eat and drink. Members of the household then eat and drink what is left of the meal.

"know them" (a biblical euphemism for sexual relations. See also Gen. 4:1). The narrative eventually concludes with Lot and his two daughters being saved alive, while Lot's wife turned into a pillar of salt and the two cities (and the cities around them) burned with sulfur and fire (Gen. 19:23–26). Being hospitable toward strangers afforded one man a face-to-face interaction with the LORD, while earning the other deliverance from certain death!

The second form of an acceptable sacrifice the author names is that of remembering the imprisoned (in this context, serving or visiting them). In 10:34 as he reminds them of their faithfulness in the past, he commended them for having compassion on those in prison. Here he exhorts them to continue in that good deed. Though it is not certain that the writer of Hebrews had read what is written of Jesus in the synoptic gospels, the language employed here is quite reminiscent of what Jesus utters in the account of Matthew. When the Son of Man comes in his glory, he will judge all nations based on these six criteria: (1) feeding the hungry, (2) giving drink to the thirsty, (3) welcoming the stranger, (4) clothing the naked, (5) visiting the sick, and (6) visiting the imprisoned (Matt. 25:31–46). Those who will have done these things to "the least of these [his] brethren" will be welcomed into his kingdom. Those who will not have done so will be cursed into eternal damnation! (See Matt. 25:46.)[42] Hence, the author of Hebrews rightly urges his readers to heed his advice and continue presenting this acceptable sacrifice before the LORD. Having

---

[42] In light of these verses from Matthew, I must assert my belief that salvation comes by faith, not by works! (See Eph. 2:8.) Although our Lord will judge us based on our deeds, these deeds should be an outward sign of an inward transformation—they should be the *natural* outcome of the Holy Spirit's abiding within us by faith! By themselves, righteous works cannot save anyone. The deeds our Lord enumerates in this Matthew passage show one's love for his neighbor, which—second to loving the LORD with all one's heart, mind, and strength—constitutes the heart of the law of God (Matt. 22:37–40; Mark 12:29–31; Luke 10:25–28).

done so, he highlights that their main motive for such service should be that they are members of "the [same] body"; that is, the body of Christ. In turn, this echoes what Paul articulates in his letter to the Corinthians—concerning the unity of the church as the body of Christ—that "if one member suffers, all the members suffer with it; if one member is honored, all the members rejoice with it" (1 Cor. 12:26, NASB).

It is remarkable that the next item on the author's list is faithfulness and fidelity in marriage. As the marriage covenant between one man and one woman is an extension of Christ's covenant with his bride, the church, it is worthy of the marriage bed to be kept undefiled. Though marriage is the *only* context in which sexual relations are permissible from a biblical standpoint, the bed of a married couple may itself be defiled. The author offers two possibilities as to how this may happen—sexual immorality and adultery.

His admonition directly confronts "Christians" who subscribe to the notion that consuming pornographic material in the context of marriage is biblically permissible! The biblical truth exposited here opposes those who insist that, if consented to by both spouses, it is allowable to engage in sexual relations with a third person instead of, or in addition to one's own spouse! Take note of the pair of Greek words used here: *pornos* and *moichos* (typically translated "[sexually] immoral and adulterous" respectively, or similar in most translations). The first term is where the English word *porn* gets its origin. It encompasses all sexually immoral behaviors. More specifically, it signifies "a person who is known for their sexual profligacy"[43] (that is, licentiousness or extreme indulgence). The second word (*moichos*) is equally plain in meaning; it denotes a person who commits adultery or fornication. Doers of either of these deeds "God will judge" (Heb. 13:4).

The last vice that the author admonishes his readers to avoid is the love of money. Similar to other phrases, this too

---

[43] Bible Sense Lexicon. Logos Software.

resembles language used by both Jesus and Paul. The first is found in the gospel accounts where Jesus plainly says, "No servant can serve two masters, for either he will hate the one and love the other, or he will be devoted to the one and despise the other. You cannot serve God and money" (Luke 16:13). The second is where Paul uses the exact phrase used in Hebrews—"the love of money." In his first letter to his disciple Timothy, Paul writes, "For the love of money is the root of all evils" (1 Tim. 6:10).

The second half of this exhortation is likewise similar to Jesus's and Paul's.[44] In the Sermon on the Mount, Jesus commands his audience not to be anxious about what they would eat or what they would wear, stating, "For life is more than food, and the body more than clothing" (Luke 12:23, NRSV). Likewise, Paul reminds Timothy that we bring nothing into this world and cannot take anything out of it. Hence, "if we have food and clothing, we will be content with these" (1 Tim. 6:8, NRSV). These same concepts are echoed by the author of Hebrews, who quotes similar meanings from the Old Testament (see Deut. 31:6, 8; Joshua 1:5; Ps. 118:6).

Godly Leaders (13:7-9)

The author's concern for his audience is supplemented in 13:7-9 by exhortation to follow in the footsteps of their leaders (that is, those who have authority over them). Doubtless the writer does not have the authorities of the civil government in view, but rather those who have led his readers to Christ, for he says, "Who spoke the word of God to you" (Heb. 13:7, NASB). As in Paul's appeal elsewhere (1 Cor. 4:16; 11:1;

---

[44] These and other similarities between the diction and phraseology used in the gospels and in the general epistles directly contradict the skeptical claims that both bodies of writings are theologically and historically disconnected. It is plenty evident that the writers of the non-Pauline epistles were well familiar with both Paul's writings and the gospel accounts (for example, see 2 Peter 3:15–16).

Phil. 3:17), the writer of Hebrews encourages his original recipients to imitate the faith of those faithful and righteous leaders; that is, to have a faith similar to theirs (see the same theme in Heb. 6:12).

The unchanging nature of Christ guarantees that those who remain faithful in the present time and in the future will reap the same rewards as those who have come before them in times past. The Lord who has been faithful to those who have patiently endured tribulations and trials to the end of their time on earth will likewise reward those who hold fast to their faith with patience (Heb. 13:8).

Since the original recipients of Hebrews were Christians from Jewish origins, it is only appropriate that the writer of the epistle—who has just cautioned them against forsaking their Christian faith—advises them not to be entangled once again in the sacrificial ordinances of the Old Testament. Under the new covenant of Christ, the hearts and minds of believers are filled with grace and kept righteous not by eating or drinking but by growing in faith and in the knowledge of the Lord Jesus Christ. For this reason the author of Hebrews pleads with his readers not to follow strange teachings that prioritize tangible elements of worship at the expense of its spiritual reality. Peter asserts the same meaning—almost verbatim—in his second epistle, saying, "You therefore, beloved, since you are forewarned, beware that you are not carried away with the error of the lawless and lose your own stability. But grow in the grace and knowledge of our Lord and Savior Jesus Christ. To him be the glory both now and to the day of eternity. Amen" (2 Peter 3:17–18, NRSV). Paul too cautions the Colossians against being in bondage to these ordinances, saying, "Therefore do not let anyone judge you with reference to eating or drinking or participation in a feast or a new moon or a Sabbath" (Col. 2:16, LEB). Paul exhorts this to the Colossians for the same reason as the writer of Hebrews; that is, all these ordinances "are a shadow of what is to come, but the reality [or substance] is Christ" (Col. 2:17, LEB). None of these ordinances was able to sanctify or save those who adhered to them, for they were all mere shadows of what would become real in Christ.

A Different Altar (13:10-14)

The notion of an altar in 13:10-14 has been erroneously interpreted by most traditional churches to refer to *their* altar, on which they offer "the body and blood of Jesus" anew to God the Father—or so they believe! This is further complicated by the author's comment that "those who serve the tabernacle have no right to eat" from that altar (Heb. 13:10, NASB). Those traditional churches immediately understand this to be a reference to the Eucharist, which the Jews cannot receive. Nonetheless, the context of this verse clearly does not speak of literal eating or drinking.

The writer has just finished warning his audience against being in bondage to the things of old, which included eating and drinking, stating that it did not benefit those who followed them. Thus, he admonishes his readers to have their hearts strengthened by grace and not by different foods (Heb. 13:9). The foods he is referring to here are the animal sacrifices that are offered to the LORD according to the Old Testament laws (Heb. 13:11). The mention of strengthening the heart that he uses in verse 9 is unmistakably referring to literal—not spiritual—eating, for in the Old Testament food is said to strengthen one's heart (see Gen. 18:5; Judges 19:5; Ps. 104:15). Hence, it is this literal eating that the author is cautioning against. In this context it is unlikely—when he is speaking of an altar—that he has yet another altar in mind where literal eating and drinking take place! In fact, the very reason he mentions *this* other altar is to show contrast between the altar of old, where *literal* eating and drinking took place, and the New Testament altar, where eating and drinking happen spiritually rather than literally. Thus it is evident that what the author has in view is the sacrifice of Jesus, of which we eat and drink not literally as of the animal sacrifices of the Old Testament—which were a type and a foreshadowing—but spiritually. In the same sense Paul beseeches the Romans to "present [their] bodies a living sacrifice, holy, acceptable unto God, which is [their] reasonable service" (Rom. 12:1, KJV). The eating and drinking the author of Hebrews is referring to happens by praising God and communing with him—a notion the author presents in verse 15 (see the next section).

Those who serve the tabernacle of old—who still live under the old covenant—do not have the right to "eat" in this manner from Christ's sacrifice (that is, partaking of the privilege and grace imparted on those who are now under the new covenant). Animal sacrifices symbolized Christ; and literal eating foreshadowed spiritual nourishment. As Jesus's sacrifice was substituted for animal offerings, spiritual food replaced the physical. It is worth noting that in the Old Testament the sin offering was burned outside the camp (Exod. 29:14; Lev. 4:12, 21; 9:11; 16:27; Num. 19:3). In fact, sin offering was the *only* sacrifice that was to be burned outside the camp. Being removed from the camp signified the removal of sin from among the congregation.[45] Burning the sacrifice *wholly* symbolized the *total* abolishing of the consequence of sin that was borne by the sacrificed beast. When Paul referred to Christ, who did not know sin, as becoming sin for our sake,

---

[45] Strictly speaking, not every sin offering was burned outside the camp. In Leviticus 4:22-35 there are three kinds of sin offering that were to be burned on the altar of burnt offering (i.e., the brazen altar. See illustration in chapter 9). Though no clear instructions are given for the first of these three sacrifices (a male goat), there is no indication that it was burned outside the camp. As for the latter two sacrifices (a female goat and a female lamb, respectively), they are clearly said to be burned on the altar. As burning the sin offering symbolized the removal of sin, burning it on the altar is said to be a "sweet savor unto the LORD," signifying the acceptableness of Christ's sacrifice in the eyes of his Father (see Lev. 4:31).

he did *not* mean that Christ became a *sinner*; rather, Jesus became the sin *offering* on whom the Father transferred all the sins of those who would later believe in his death and resurrection. This transfer of sin is foreshadowed in the Old Testament by placing one's hands upon the head of the animal sacrifice before it was to be slaughtered and burned outside the camp (Lev. 4:4, 15). As the sin offering in the Old Testament was burned outside the camp bearing the sins of the congregation, so was Christ crucified outside the walls of Jerusalem bearing the sins of his people!

Those who are persecuted for the name of Christ—as the original recipients of Hebrews were—should therefore rejoice in bearing his reproach as he carried theirs. Jesus was made a byword of shame and ridicule before, during, and after his crucifixion. Believers who are called Christians should expect no less shame than that of their Lord and teacher, for Jesus has already forewarned us that "a servant is not greater than his master. If they persecuted me, they will persecute you also. If they obeyed my teaching, they will obey yours also" (John 15:20, NIV).

The Sacrifice of Praise (13:15–16)

In the Old Testament the people of God were instructed to worship him via various kinds of sacrifices and offerings, such as peace offerings, burnt offerings, meal and drink offerings, and freewill offerings. Under the new covenant we are to offer praise and thanksgiving through the fruit of our lips. Recall that in the Old Testament, singing to the LORD and praising his name were also forms of worship. Nevertheless, they were not sufficient. They had to be supplemented by the aforementioned offerings. In the New Testament, as the sacrifice of Jesus replaced the outgoing sacrificial system of the old covenant, praise became the means by which we can offer true worship to the Father through his Son. This is precisely what

Jesus alluded to in his conversation with the Samaritan woman, when he said:

> Woman, believe me, the hour is coming when *neither on this mountain nor in Jerusalem will you worship the Father.* You worship what you do not know; we worship what we know, for salvation is from the Jews. But the hour is coming, *and now is,* when the true worshipers will worship the Father in spirit and truth, for such the Father seeks to worship him. God is spirit, and those who worship him must worship in spirit and truth. (John 4:21–24, RSV)

In contrast to worshiping in Spirit and truth, the Holy Spirit spoke through Isaiah rebuking Israel, for "this people draw near with its mouth, and with its lips it honors me, and its heart is far from me, and their fear of me is a commandment of men that has been taught" (Isa. 29:13, LEB). For this reason the author of Hebrews warns that we should not neglect good works and "sharing" (a common New Testament term for financial contributions sent to those in need). This is reminiscent of a parallel reference in which Paul extends gratitude to the Philippians for having received what they had sent him by the hand of Epaphroditus, "a fragrant offering, an acceptable sacrifice, well-pleasing to God" (Phil. 4:18, LEB).

Presenting the sacrifice of praise is nothing new under the new covenant. David entreats the LORD, saying, "Let my prayer be counted as incense before thee, and the lifting up of my hands as an evening sacrifice" (Ps. 141:2, RSV). We thus discover that offering the fruit of our lips is one of many forms of acceptable worship under both the old and the new covenants, similar to fasting, giving, and the like.

The Last Prayer and Benediction (13:17–25)

The author reiterates his request that his original readers honor those who have authority over them (compare Heb. 13:7). Again, he has the spiritual leaders in mind, not those in government or civil duties. His greetings to "your leaders" in verse 24 suggest that he is referring to specific individuals who were shepherding the congregation of his original readers at that time.

It is imperative that I note that this is *not* an absolute commandment of obedience to those in spiritual authority over us; it is, however, a charge to obey those who "keep watch over [our] souls," and those who conduct themselves as ones who will give an account before the LORD for how they lead (or mislead) their congregations. In other words, spiritual leaders, guides, and counselors who lead us astray from the LORD, teach that which is contradictory to the word of God, or put their own interests first before their flock's are excluded from this directive!

In his literary finesse, the author contrasts this notion with how he views himself as a spiritual leader to his readers. With eloquence he poses himself as an example of those leaders whom the congregation should obey and for whom they should pray. He appeals to them to pray for him (among unnamed others), stating that they "have a good conscience, desiring to conduct [themselves] honorably in all things" (Heb. 13:18, NASB). He asks for their prayers that the LORD may grant him to continue doing so. It was already discussed in the introductory chapters that the author likely knew his audience, and being away from them, he was hoping that he would be reunited with them once more. This also shows that his audience was located in a specific city or a particular locale (see the introductory chapter on the audience of Hebrews).

The consistent appeals of the New Testament writers to their readers for prayer show how much they believed in the efficacy of prayer, especially by the congregation on behalf of their leaders. It is noteworthy that nearly all New Testament epistles close with a similar request. In one instance Paul pleads with his readers, saying, "Pray for us as well that God will open to us a door for the word, that we may declare the mystery of Christ, for which I am in prison" (Col. 4:3, NRSV). This intimates how the shepherds of the flock of Christ are in more need of prayers than—arguably—anyone else in the flock. The devil tends to target for destruction those of high spiritual stature or those in positions of authority or leadership. When a believer who is not in a leadership position falls, he is likely to fall alone. But when a shepherd of a flock falls, he is likely to bring down with him many sheep. Contemporary church history is sadly replete with examples of fallen church leaders who have become stumbling blocks to many! Our Lord Jesus put it this way on the night in which he was betrayed: "I will strike the shepherd, and the sheep of the flock will be scattered" (Matt. 26:31; quoted from Zech. 13:7).

The writer's reference to the God of peace unquestionably brings to remembrance Paul's usage of the same phrase in Romans (Rom. 15:33). In fact, the phrase "the God of peace" is exclusively Pauline (see our discussion on the authorship of Hebrews). Notice that describing Jesus—who is the only one to be resurrected and still lives—as the great shepherd is an unambiguous testimony of his deity. In the Old Testament, Isaiah refers to the LORD as the shepherd of Israel:

> Behold, the LORD GOD comes with might, and his arm rules for him; behold, his reward is with him, and his recompense before him. He will feed his flock like a shepherd, he will gather the lambs in his arms, he will carry them in his bosom, and gently lead those that are with young. (Isa. 40:10–11, RSV)

The Final Benediction

In Ezekiel we find this clear testimony spoken by God himself, stating that he is the shepherd who seeks and saves the lost sheep of his flock:

> For thus says the LORD God: Behold, I, I myself will search for my sheep, and will seek them out. As a shepherd seeks out his flock when some of his sheep have been scattered abroad, so will I seek out my sheep; and I will rescue them from all places where they have been scattered on a day of clouds and thick darkness. (Ezek. 34:11–12, RSV)

Thus, it is beyond debate that Jesus, who is here called "the great shepherd" and who has repeatedly called himself "the good shepherd," is equal to the God of Israel (see John 10:11, 14).

Last, the author refers to the entire epistle as a "word of exhortation" that he has briefly written (Heb. 13:22). This is telling, as it shows what has been on his mind all along as he sat down to write this epistle. He did not intend to write a theological treatise—though he has crafted one of the deepest and most eloquently written in the entire New Testament. He is *mainly* anxious for the salvation of his original readers and anyone who would come after them to feed off the richness and depth of this epistle.

His final comment about Timothy suggests that Timothy had likely been imprisoned and was awaiting release. This is a strong indication that whoever penned this letter was in the company of Timothy (and possibly Paul, though the epistle's diction and phraseology suggest that Paul was not its author). It is the intent of the author that Timothy would visit them soon (possibly to bring a financial offering back to the author and the other churches he served).

It is not clear if the phrase "those from Italy" means those who are *located* in Italy or those who *came* from Italy. This same phrase is used elsewhere in the New Testament to refer to those who came from Italy. In Acts we learn that Paul left Athens and came to Corinth, where he found Aquila, *a native of Pontus*, with his wife, Priscilla, both of whom had recently come *from* Italy to Corinth, "because Claudius had commanded all the Jews to leave Rome" (Acts 18:2, RSV). In this context, it is clear that Aquila had only recently arrived from Italy, but it was not his homeland.

In some ancient versions of the Bible, such as the KJV and some ancient non-English translations, there appears an editorial note to the effect that the epistle was written to the Hebrews by the hand of Timothy from Italy. This note is absent in nearly all modern English translations and cannot be verified by the historical or literary context of the letter.

Questions on This Chapter

1. Having learned from this chapter that praising God with our lips is a form of worship, do you find that most of your prayers are requests and petitions you ask the LORD for, or do you spend enough time worshiping him for who he is?

2. If we want to find a reason to complain and murmur, we will. Likewise, if we want to find a reason to thank the LORD, we will. It is all about the posture of our hearts. The next time you find yourself complaining, make it a point to look around you for something to glorify and thank the LORD for. You will find a few!

3. Do you pray for your leaders? Do you make mention in your prayer of the pastor of your local church, for example? I encourage you, the next time you go to church, approach your pastor and explain that you are praying for him. I assure you, it will be a great encouragement to him.

Conclusion

I stated at the beginning of our journey through Hebrews that my primary goal was for you to read this epistle with joy and understanding, and to appreciate its depth and richness. If you have made it this far on our journey, I certainly hope and pray that I have been successful in achieving that goal.

Hebrews stands as one of the richest and deepest bodies of writing in all the Bible. Its unique theological features set it apart from the rest of the New Testament—and also the Old Testament for that matter! For instance, nowhere else in the Bible do we find Jesus so overtly—and repeatedly—referred to as the high priest. The letter is not vague about what it sets forth. There is little space for ambiguity and even less room for interpretation regarding what the author intended to intimate to his readers at the time of composition.

Though it may be compared to Romans in its richness and depth, Hebrews is far more straightforward in its theology. Written with a sense of urgency and concern, the author spares no effort in arguing his main theological and doctrinal points.

In the introduction of this book I mentioned that Hebrews is deeply rooted in the Old Testament scriptures and that, to fully understand it, one must be familiar with the Old Testament writings. By now I hope you have observed how this remarkable author has used these writings to make the person of Jesus Christ the focal point of the epistle. Hebrews stands as a notable example of how vital it is for the modern-day Christian not only to read the Old Testament but also to live it and breathe it!

Recently while I was working on this book, my wife Michelle, who is a voracious Bible reader, asked me this question: "What am I supposed to take away from the Old Testament? There's so much context that I don't grasp as a Western Christian, making it difficult for me to apply it to my life right now." For context, at the time she asked me these questions, she had been reading the historical narratives of the Old Testament, following a daily Bible reading plan. She had been struck by the vivid and violent nature of some of the killings, beheadings, dismemberments, and the like found in the Old Testament accounts (for example, see Judges 19:29; 2 Sam. 4:7–8). Michelle genuinely wanted to understand why she—as a New Testament Christian living under the new covenant—still needs to read all this and how it may edify her walk with the LORD. Her inquiry was genuine. But how do Michelle's questions relate to our study of Hebrews? Read on!

After I had pondered Michelle's questions for a bit, I reflected on how the writer of Hebrews so frequently referred to and used themes and events found in the Old Testament to illuminate who Jesus is. Having been so deeply entrenched in my study of Hebrews, I began explaining how crucial the Old Testament is to one's understanding of God's plan of salvation for mankind! For one, the Old Testament is a description of the state of mankind *without* a savior. The violent and bloody nature of the Old Testament narratives is not coincidental; it is indeed intentional. It is intended to convey the depravity to which mankind had arrived in the absence of a savior who can renew and wash away sin and iniquity. The Holy Spirit, the ultimate author of Scripture, deliberately desired to underscore the endless downward spiral of moral corruption and spiritual decay in which man was entangled before the Savior arrived on the scene. Reading about the extreme degeneracy of the human race, the desperate need for a savior becomes ever so evident!

Many Bible skeptics (and even Christians) understand "the God of the Old Testament" as a violent, bloodthirsty God, whereas "the God of the New Testament" is seen as a merciful and gracious Lord. Both perspectives could not be farther from the truth. What these perspectives fail to recognize is that it is not *God* who is different in both Testaments—it is the *people*! Though they often describe God's character, these biblical narratives are not exclusively about who God is, but also about who man is. The development of the biblical narrative—emphasizing, at first, judgment as a result of sin and then highlighting grace as a result of Jesus's salvific work—is not an indication of *any* change in the character of God but rather of a transformation in the nature of man as a direct outcome of the redemption Jesus has provided on the cross and through his empty tomb!

Second, it must be noted that the Old Testament is mainly concerned with God's relationship with his people Israel. As such, some readers tend to accuse—and even judge—Israel as a nation that disobeyed God, broke his commandments, and violated their covenant with him. In our modern day, some church traditions (particularly in the East) have gone as far as claiming that the atrocities committed against the Jews over the centuries have been a just punishment against them for what they have done against God. It is true that the LORD often chastises his people through hardships and tribulations. It is equally true—as we saw in our discussion on chapter 12—that the LORD may choose to discipline his children—because they are his—more than the sinners and the wicked, who are not his. Nevertheless, one must remember that disobeying God is not unique to Israel. Every nation and people who have ever existed have broken God's commandments and have disobeyed him in the same manner, if not more! While the Old Testament primarily describes the history of the Jewish nation, Israel is only an example and an illustration of the violence and evil that were taking place in other nations back then, and to our present day. Extrabiblical history—contemporary to that of the Old Testament—shows how depraved other nations were in the ancient Near East and beyond. From witchcraft and idolatry to child sacrifice and bestiality, these nations did it all! In fact, these extreme forms of decadence are widely practiced in our (supposedly) civilized world today! So if we are to accuse and condemn Israel for being so ungodly and disobedient, a similar judgment must be equally applied to every nation that has ever existed since the advent of the human race. It was never a part of God's plan for mankind that they would reach so depraved a state. Those accounts are a reminder of what we can become—without a savior—under sin and disobedience. They exemplify our extreme need for a deliverer.

After I had answered Michelle's questions, I discovered that she had an even harder task for me. She asked, "Why does the Scripture refer to Israel's deliverance out of Egypt so frequently, and why is it such a pivotal event in the biblical narrative?" Almost anyone who reads either the Old Testament or the New would concur with her observation.

As seen throughout our study, the exodus constituted a covenant between the LORD and the children of Israel, like the covenant formed with Abraham when God instructed him to leave his land and go to Canaan. Every event that followed in the history of Israel was founded upon the LORD's covenant with Abraham and later with Israel. In fact, the reason the LORD gave Israel the law at Sinai is that he was establishing not only a nation but a people—his people. Therefore, breaking his covenant through disobedience resulted in one's "being cut off from his people" (see Gen. 17:14; Exod. 31:14;

Lev. 23:29, and so on). It is important to recognize that the law given at Sinai was never intended to be a list of commandments, prohibitions, and ordinances. A careful examination of the law shows that it reveals God's *own* character. By revealing his law to man, God desired that—through it—man would know who God is. Thus, the ultimate purpose of the law was *communion* with the LORD. But because mankind failed to keep God's law, Jesus came to fulfill it; that is, to keep it all and observe it all. To be righteous before the LORD, man had to keep his law unbroken—and that was an impossibility. For this reason Jesus, who was the only one able to keep God's law, came "so that in him we might become the righteousness of God" (2 Cor. 5:21).

The observations that Michelle made strike at the very core of Hebrews as an expository sermon on the Old Testament, intended to show who Jesus is! In fact, as a case study of the New Testament use of the Old Testament, Hebrews shows that no part of God's word can or should be set aside as invalid, inapplicable, or obsolete. It is one of the most eloquently crafted books of the Bible, especially in its ability to connect the Old Testament to the New, both literarily and theologically. As seen throughout this book, the author of Hebrews is masterful in using the Old Testament scriptures. He does this to show who Jesus is and to illuminate the significance of his sacrificial work. Jesus came to declare himself the Son of God by fulfilling the Scriptures. Had it not been for the Old Testament scriptures, it would not have been possible for us to know and believe that Jesus of Nazareth is the Messiah. Writing about the Old Testament scriptures—for at the time the New Testament had not yet been written—Paul spoke the truth when he exhorted his disciple Timothy, saying, "All Scripture is *breathed out by God* and profitable for teaching, for reproof, for correction, and for training in righteousness, that the man of God may be complete, equipped for every good work" (2 Tim. 3:16–17). All of Scripture was written for our teaching and edification (Rom. 15:4; 1 Cor. 10:6, 11).

As I write the last few words in this book, I must reiterate that this book was written with only one goal in mind: to encourage you to develop an intimate relationship with the word of God. As you read it, study it, and meditate on it. I pray that you become so saturated with God's word that it will be on your heart when you are awake and when you sleep! It is my hope that you establish a daily Bible-reading routine for yourself so that the Bible becomes an integral part of your everyday life. It is hard to imagine a true Christian who does not read his or her Bible daily. It is even harder to imagine a *growing* Christian who does not do that! The Bible is a balm to the broken soul and sustenance to the weak and hungry—and who among us is not? Listen to what the LORD declares regarding his word by the mouth of Isaiah: "The grass withereth, the flower fadeth: But the word of our God shall stand for ever" (Isa. 40:8, KJV). To God—and to him alone—be all glory forevermore. Amen!

Questions on the Conclusion

Now that we have come to the end of our journey, the following questions are meant to both challenge and enhance your Bible-reading experience. I hope and pray that this journey through Hebrews has been a blessing to your life!

1. When you read God's word, do you wonder why God inspired each author to write what he wrote specifically and nothing else?

2. Based on your answer to the previous question, do you discern the literary connection between one section of Scripture and the one that comes before and/or after it?

3. When reading your Bible, try to put yourself in the shoes of the original readers. Does that change the way you understand the text?

My Personal Journey with Hebrews

Our Lord Jesus said concerning the Holy Spirit, "He will teach you all things and bring to your remembrance all that I have said to you" (John 14:26). Writing this book is a living testimony of this! I speak the truth when I say that I have learned and continue to learn from my own writing. As I started writing this book it became evident that it was not I who was writing but the Spirit of my Father writing through me. When I repeatedly read the contents of this book during the review and editing process, I often wondered, "Who wrote this? Whose words are these?" I knew from the beginning that I was only an instrument, a vessel that our Lord would use to pour his words into, so that they reach those who are eager to soak it up and be enriched by it—that is, you!

Finally, as we come to the end of our journey through Hebrews, I have a personal testimony to share with you. I mentioned in the preface that the idea of writing this book began during my studies at Moody Theological Seminary. But there is a more personal side to this story. Most authors choose the topic they write on; in my case it is fair to say that I did not choose Hebrews—it chose me!

I grew up in a conservative Christian family in the trenches of the Coptic Orthodox Church—one of the oldest and most traditional churches in existence today. In this regard my journey is remarkably similar to that of Paul's! I was quite involved in my church: A Copt, the son of a Copt; well-versed in the history of my church; a teacher of Coptic hymns; and discipled at the hands of the best teachers of its rituals, symbolism, and dogma. I was truly "a Pharisee, the son of Pharisees" (Acts 23:6). Up until recently I believed—as I once stated—that "I am a Copt; I will live as a Copt; and I will die as a Copt!" God, however, had a different plan in mind.

The final thesis of my master's program was titled *The Priesthood of Christ in Hebrews*, a study of Hebrews 7. As I was working on this capstone project—through the leading of the Holy Spirit—I began reading the first few verses of chapter 8. Mind you, Hebrews 8 was not the chapter I was researching. That was when I came across this verse: "For every high priest is appointed to offer gifts and sacrifices; hence it is necessary for this priest also to have something to offer" (Heb. 8:3, RSV). As I read this verse over and over again, I realized that priesthood existed for the sole purpose of offering sacrifices and that every priest *must* have something to offer. I was then forced to ask myself the inevitable question: since every priest must have a sacrifice to offer, what kind of sacrifice do the priests of the Coptic Church offer? Their claim that they offer the body and blood of Jesus must be untrue, for that was offered once and *only* once (see Heb. 7:27; 9:12; but especially 10:10). But since they cannot be offering the body and blood of Jesus, and since priesthood exists only to offer sacrifices, and given that all other sacrifices were abolished, what need is there for priesthood under the new covenant? It quickly became evident that the form of priesthood that they represent has ceased to exist in the New Testament! If priesthood exists to offer sacrifices, when the need for sacrifices goes away, priesthood goes away with it. Put differently, if in the New Testament all sacrifices have been done away with, what need do we have for priesthood? That was the moment when my mind was illuminated to see that all forms of priesthood under the new covenant have been abolished (except that of Jesus of course).

All this happened—and God is my witness—in the few minutes it took me to finish typing the last page of my thesis, about 300 words double-spaced! This unfolded in the last class of my coursework, and in the very last assignment of that class. Was that a "coincidence" or was it something that the LORD all along had intended to open my eyes to see but was only waiting for the right moment? You be the judge. From my perspective I am indebted to the grace of God for opening my eyes to see the light of his word (Ps. 119:18, 105).

As I continued to "search the Scriptures" further, I continued coming face-to-face with other biblical truths that supported this conclusion. For instance, the silence of the New Testament writings about human priesthood, the physical design of a church, and the ordinances of offering sacrifices under the new covenant was deafening! As detailed as the Old Testament was on these topics, the New Testament is completely silent; we do not find even as little as a brief description of church construction. The LORD provided a thorough blueprint of the tabernacle to Moses, and later of the temple to both David and Solomon. He also gave a detailed description of the various kinds of sacrifices in the Old Testament, including the animals that must be sacrificed for every occasion, the means of sacrificing them, and precise instructions on how every sacrifice must be offered—all of which were a copy and a shadow. If the LORD provided such detailed instructions for the sacrificial system involving animal sacrifices, would not he have provided an even more comprehensive description of the worship and sacrificial ordinances related to the true body and blood of his Son if it had truly been his intention that such a system exist?

It was not long after I had started studying Hebrews and shortly after I had asserted my strong attachment to the Coptic

Church that the LORD revealed to me that I was to be a Copt no more! To say the least, the experience of studying Hebrews was transformative and life-changing. I must add that it was equally liberating. It was as if the LORD was setting me free from decades of bondage to "the tradition of men" (Mark 7:8). This catalyst is what compelled me to study Hebrews even more deeply and what set the writing of this book in motion.

This experience, though personal, may resonate with some of you. I share it here not to disparage any one church doctrine or another, but to simply bear witness to the transformative power of the word of God—if studied seriously—and by doing so, to encourage you to study it. Those who are genuine in their study of Scripture are bound to come face-to-face with revelations that they may find uncomfortable, but if submitted to, they will prove emancipating!

I can think of nothing more satisfying than eating the word of our God (Jer. 15:16; Ezek. 3:1–3; Rev. 10:9–10). From experience I can say that if you do not see yourself being transformed by the word of God, then you are simply not growing and maturing spiritually. If that is the case, I invite and encourage you to take your study of Scripture more seriously—because without it you will "have a name that you are alive, and you are dead" (Rev. 3:1, LEB).

To our Lord Jesus belongs all glory, honor, and praise. Amen!

About the Author

David Adeeb is a graduate of Moody Theological Seminary. He holds a master's degree in biblical studies with the highest honors, summa cum laude. Studious as he is, David has always had a hunger for knowledge, which is now being put to good use for the glory of God through diligent and careful study of God's word. It was not easy for David to grow up as a Christian in a predominantly Muslim country—Egypt—where he was born and raised. Growing up in that environment has given him a deeper appreciation of the Lord's work in his life. It has also enabled him to read the Bible through the eyes of ancient Near Eastern culture—a culture with which he is well acquainted. This enriches his reading experience of Scripture and adds elements of practical significance.

David was born and raised in the Coptic (Egyptian) Orthodox Church. As he studied God's word for himself, he realized that much of what the Coptic Church is founded upon doctrinally contradicts the word of God. Believing in the authority of the word of God above all, at the age of forty-four, he left the church he had grown up in and now does not adhere to any specific denomination. His work on Hebrews, presented in this book, was a turning point in his life in this regard.

David aspires to serve the Lord with all the gifts and talents that the Lord has given him by ministering to those who seek the Lord with all their hearts.

We encourage you to contact us, as we would like to hear from you. We are always encouraged when we hear the testimonies of others and how the Lord works and manifests himself in the lives of his children. May the peace of Christ abide in you.

The Significance of the Book Cover

As the slain Lamb of God, our Lord Jesus—the central figure in Hebrews—is shown on the altar that he chose for himself: the cross. On one side the ark of the covenant of God is shown, signifying God's covenant with his people Israel and with all who abide by the commandments contained therein. On the other side the candlestick points to the continual light of the presence of God. Both are central themes in the Old Testament and in the Epistle to the Hebrews.

To learn more about Adeeb Christian Publishing, read sample chapters, and stay up-to-date on our upcoming publications, visit our website. We also publish new blogs that explore insightful biblical topics to enrich your spiritual journey.

adeebchristianpublishing.com

Scripture Reference Index

For your convenience, the following is a comprehensive list of scriptural references cited in this book, intended to guide you to key biblical passages discussed throughout the text. Arranged by book, this index provides chapter and verse numbers, followed by the page number(s) where they appear, making it efficient to locate each passage.

Genesis
- 1:26, 29
- 1:28, 47
- 2:2, 80
- 2:15, 80
- 3:15, 80
- 3:17, 208
- 3:17–19, 80
- 4:1, 285
- 4:6–7, 225
- 4:8, 227
- 5:1, 29
- 5:3, 29
- 5:21–24, 226
- 6:13–7:24, 227
- 6:22, 62, 227
- 7:5, 63, 227
- 7:21–23, 228
- 12:7, 231
- 13:14–17, 231
- 14:18, 127, 138
- 15:1–20, 231

Genesis (*continued*)
- 15:7–21, 162
- 16:10, 43
- 17:1, 230
- 17:1–22, 231
- 17:14, 300
- 17:17, 230
- 17:21, 230
- 18:1–15, 230
- 18:5, 289
- 18:8, 284
- 18:9–15, 230
- 18:10–14, 284
- 18:12, 230
- 19:1–3, 284
- 19:23–26, 285
- 19:24–25, 214
- 21:5, 230
- 22:1–19, 116, 229
- 22:2, 116
- 22:5, 233
- 22:11–18, 43

Scripture Reference Index

Genesis (*continued*)
22:16–18, 117, 231
23:4, 232
25:27, 269
25:32, 270
25:34, 270
26:1–5, 231
26:35, 112
27:37, 270
27:39–40, 270
27:41, 112
28:10–15, 231
28:16, 130
28:22, 130
35:9–12, 232
47:9, 232
47:31, 235
49:10, 135, 234
50:24–25, 235

Exodus
1:16, 237
1:22, 237
2:5–6, 236
2:11–12, 237
2:14–15, 238
3:6, 233
3:13–15, 4
3:15, 233
4:5, 233
4:22–23, 133
13:19, 235
16:32–35, 171
17:4, 238
17:8–16, 251
18:4, 249
19:9, 272
19:12–13, 272
19:16, 272
19:18, 272
20:18, 272
20:19, 272
24:3–8, 206
24:8, 162
25:1–8, 152

Exodus (*continued*)
25:8, 168
25:9, 152
25:10–16, 169
25:16, 169
25:17–22, 169
25:21, 169
25:23–30, 174
25:31–40, 175
25:40, 152
26:30, 152
27:20–21, 175
28:1, 95
28:29–30, 150
29:14, 290
30:1–10, 174
30:21, 210
30:22–38, 177
31:14, 300
31:16, 82
31:16–17, 81
32:15–16, 160
33:20, 139
34:1, 160
34:6, 113
34:28, 160
34:33–35, 27
40:5, 175
40:16, 63
40:22, 173
40:24, 173
40:26, 173
40:34, 154

Leviticus
4:2, 212
4:3, 93
4:4, 291
4:12, 290
4:13, 212
4:15, 291
4:20, 150
4:21, 290
4:22, 212
4:27, 212

Leviticus *(continued)*
 5:15, 212
 8:30, 209
 9:7, 84
 9:11, 290
 10:1-2, 87
 10:1-3, 148, 214
 16:1, 207
 16:2, 87, 169-170, 207
 16:6, 85
 16:11, 170
 16:11-16, 85
 16:12, 121
 16:12-13, 170
 16:13, 86
 16:15, 121
 16:15-16, 170
 16:15-19, 208
 16:17, 85
 16:21, 182
 16:27, 290
 18:24-25, 209
 18:25, 209
 20:1-5, 118
 23:11, 53
 23:29, 301
 24:5-9, 174

Numbers
 8:4, 152
 12:6-8, 62
 12:7, 62
 13:4-15, 68
 13:20, 71, 77
 13:33, 68
 14:32-33, 69
 15:27-31, 212
 15:32-36, 44
 17:1-11, 171
 19:3, 290
 19:13, 184
 21:4-9, 79
 21:25, 246
 21:35, 246

Deuteronomy
 4:12, 272
 4:13, 160
 4:36, 272
 5:22, 160
 6:5, 209
 7:13, 234
 9:10, 160
 10:8, 135
 17:2-5, 44
 17:12, 44
 18:1-5, 135
 18:15, 64
 18:18, 61
 18:18-19, 64
 21:23, 265
 23:2, 242
 31:6, 287
 31:8, 287
 31:24-26, 160
 32:10, 111
 32:36, 214
 33:2, 44
 34:10-12, 61

Judges
 4:4-7, 240
 6:22, 43
 6:36-40, 240
 7:2-8, 240
 11:1-3, 242
 11:32, 242
 11:37, 243
 16:21-30, 250
 16:30, 242
 19:5, 289
 19:29, 298

First Samuel
 3:1-14, 244
 10:1, 244
 16:6-13, 250
 16:13, 244
 17:34-36, 243
 17:40-51, 243

Scripture Reference Index

Second Samuel
 4:7–8, 298
 6:1–11, 170
 7:4–17, 247
 7:12–16, 135
 8:13–14, 234, 270

First Kings
 1:47, 235
 3:7, 250
 3:28, 246
 8:10, 154
 17:23, 252
 18:4, 258
 18:38, 249
 19:2, 249
 19:4–8, 249
 19:8–9, 258
 21:23, 249

Second Kings
 1:8, 258
 4:36, 253
 4:37, 253
 8:20–22, 271
 18:13ff, 251
 21:1–9, 256

First Chronicles
 15:1, 173
 16:1, 173
 23:13, 95
 29:15, 232

Second Chronicles
 5:7, 173
 5:10, 173

Psalms
 2, 31, 95
 2:7, 32, 53
 2:7–8, 64
 2:12, 32
 5:4, 139
 5:4–5, 178
 8, 46–47
 8:4–8, 46
 8:6, 47

Psalms (continued)
 8:7–8, 47
 10, 3
 16:8–11, 198
 22, 197
 22:16, 197
 22:18, 197
 33:6–9, 30
 39:6–8 LXX, 201
 39:12, 232
 40, 197–198, 200–202
 40:6–8, 200–201
 40:7–8, 198
 44:1–3, 111
 45:6, 33–34
 45:7, 33
 68:17, 44
 72, 246
 95, 67, 82
 95:10, 67
 95:11, 82
 102, 33–34
 102:25–27, 33–34
 102:26–27, 34
 103:12, 183
 104, 32
 104:4, 32
 104:15, 289
 110, 15, 34, 49, 95, 125–
  127, 129, 131–132, 136–137, 154
 110:1, 35, 49, 126
 110:2, 131
 110:4, 126, 131, 138
 118:6, 287
 118:18, 267
 119:18, 307
 119:105, 307
 141:2, 292

Proverbs
 3:11–12, 266–267
 8:31, 81

Ecclesiastes
 7:8, 114

318

Scripture Reference Index

Isaiah
  2:2–4, 156
  5:1–7, 110
  5:7, 111
  6:4, 154
  6:5, 139
  7:14, 32
  9:6, 32
  25:8, 51
  29:13, 292
  34:4, 278
  40:8, 302
  40:10–11, 294
  42:8, 4
  53:3, 86
  53:9, 86
  63:10, 213
  65:17, 278

Jeremiah
  1:6, 250
  15:16, 308
  20:1–2, 255
  20:4–5, 255
  20:6, 255
  26:23, 256
  31:31–34, 156
  31:32, 159
  31:33, 160
  31:34, 160, 164
  39–41, 156
  52, 156

Ezekiel
  3:1–3, 308
  34:11–12, 295
  36:24, 206
  36:25, 205
  36:26, 205
  36:27, 206

Daniel
  2:44, 279
  3:16–18, 248
  6:7, 247
  6:22, 247
  7:10, 32

Hosea
  11:1, 133

Joel
  2:13, 113

Jonah
  4:2, 113

Habakkuk
  1:13, 178
  2:3–4, 216

Haggai
  2:6, 277

Zechariah
  13:7, 294

Malachi
  1:10, 206

Matthew
  1:1–16, 133
  2:15, 133
  3:4, 258
  3:9, 61
  3:16–17, 99
  4:1–11, 94
  5:17, 158
  5:21–22, 64
  5:33–37, 120
  7:13–14, 113
  8:4, 68
  12:31, 213
  13:20, 78
  13:21, 78, 114
  16:16, 64
  16:18, 64
  19:28, 112
  21:33–46, 111
  21:45–46, 111
  22:41–46, 35
  22:42, 131
  22:43–45, 131
  25:31–46, 285
  25:46, 285
  26:28, 161
  26:31, 294

Matthew (*continued*)
26:37, 98
26:39, 98
26:61, 150
27:42, 115
27:50–51, 180
27:51, 27

Mark
1:11, 99
1:44, 68
7:8, 308
11:28, 96
12:1–12, 66
12:6, 67
12:9, 66
15:29–30, 151

Luke
1:2, 45
1:32, 133
2:14, 82
2:40, 100
2:51–52, 100
3:8, 115
3:23, 134
3:23–38, 134
9:1–2, 112
9:5, 68
9:33, 100
9:35, 100
10:19–20, 276
10:26, 158
10:28, 158
12:23, 287
16:13, 287
20:27–40, 233
21:24, 163
22:14–23, 112
22:20, 161
22:43–44, 98
24:25, 101

John
1:1, 4, 34, 99
1:3, 34
1:14, 44, 177

John (*continued*)
2:21, 151
3:31, 151
4:21–24, 292
5:31–32, 96
5:45, 61
7:16, 96
8:23, 151
8:39, 61
10:11, 295
10:14, 295
10:16, 259
14:9, 27
14:26, 305
15:20, 291
17:4, 63
17:5, 4, 48, 99
17:24, 4, 99
18:12–24, 92
19:30, 31

Acts
2:24, 186
2:29–31, 198
2:42, 211
5:3, 213
7:25, 238
7:30, 42
7:35, 42
7:44, 153
7:53, 42
10:44–46, 78
13:33, 32
18:2, 296
18:24–26, 10
18:24–28, 10
18:28, 10
19:1–2, 10
21, 3
21:40, 3
22, 3
23:6, 306
28, 11

Scripture Reference Index

Romans
  1:3–4, 32
  1:4, 185
  3:20, 44, 180
  3:31, 158
  4:20–21, 234
  5:12–17, 49
  6:1–4, 189
  6:2–4, 179
  6:4, 52
  6:5, 48
  7:12, 157
  7:14, 158
  8:17, 52
  8:25, 217
  8:29, 29
  11:25, 164
  11:26, 163
  12:1, 290
  15:4, 302
  15:33, 294

First Corinthians, 50
  1:12, 10
  3:1–3, 102
  3:4, 10
  3:22, 10
  4:16, 287
  10:6, 302
  10:11, 70, 302
  11:1, 287
  11:23–26, 138
  11:25, 161
  11:32, 268
  12:26, 286
  15:14, 185
  15:17, 185
  15:20, 274
  15:23, 274
  15:26, 203
  15:28, 50

Second Corinthians
  3:13, 27
  3:13–14, 27
  4:13, 68

Second Corinthians (*continued*)
  4:18, 151, 232
  5:10, 188
  5:21, 301
  6:2, 113

Galatians
  2:16, 44, 158, 180
  2:20, 44
  3:2, 77
  3:5, 78
  3:10, 109
  3:11, 44
  3:12, 158
  3:13, 159, 265
  3:19, 42
  3:21, 180
  3:22, 179
  3:29, 120
  4:4, 47
  4:4–5, 159

Ephesians
  1:19–20, 30
  3:12, 86
  4:30, 213
  5:26, 210

Philippians
  2:7–8, 46, 97
  2:8, 101
  3:17, 288
  4:3, 9
  4:18, 292

Colossians
  1:15, 28, 52
  1:18, 53
  2:9, 27
  2:16, 288
  2:16–17, 152
  2:17, 140, 289
  3:1, 30
  4:3, 294

First Thessalonians
  4:14, 203
  4:16–17, 203

Scripture Reference Index

Second Thessalonians
2:13, 274

First Timothy
3:16, 185
6:8, 287
6:10, 287

Second Timothy
3:16, 2, 12
3:16–17, 302

Hebrews
1:2, 33
1:3, 27–28, 30, 223
1:5, 35
1:5–14, 60
1:8, 33–34
1:10–12, 34
1:13, 35
2:3, 10, 60, 66
2:8, 49
2:9, 52
2:10, 52, 265
2:15, 49
2:17–18, 92
2:18, 54
3:1, 66, 84
3:5–6, 65
3:7–8, 113
3:12–13, 69
4:1, 79
4:2, 76, 79
4:9, 83
4:11, 83
4:13, 83
4:14, 86, 211
4:15, 94, 97
5:1, 93, 140
5:2, 94
5:2–3, 93
5:5, 95
5:6, 99
5:7, 97
5:9, 99
5:12, 101
5:13, 109

Hebrews (*continued*)
5:14, 102, 109
6:1–3, 108
6:4, 110, 112
6:4–5, 110
6:6, 115
6:7, 110, 112
6:8, 112
6:9, 115, 175
6:9–10, 115
6:10, 15
6:11, 116
6:12, 288
6:13, 120
6:20, 266
7:2, 133
7:3, 128–129, 133–134, 137
7:5, 135
7:7, 135
7:10, 135
7:11, 140
7:11–14, 137
7:15–19, 138
7:18–19, 140
7:20–21, 138
7:20–22, 140
7:22, 137
7:23–24, 140
7:25, 139
7:27, 137, 170, 306
7:27–28, 17
8:1–2, 149
8:2–5, 163
8:3, 140, 306
8:3–5, 17
8:4, 150
8:5, 140, 153
8:6, 163
8:9, 159
8:12, 163
8:13, 163
9:3–4, 174
9:4, 171
9:7–8, 17
9:9, 180

Hebrews (continued)
9:10, 181
9:12, 139, 141, 182, 306
9:13, 183
9:25, 17
9:26, 187–188
9:27, 188
10:1, 140
10:1–3, 17
10:4, 141
10:10, 306
10:19, 204
10:19–22, 86, 139
10:22, 205
10:31, 214
10:32–34, 266
11:1, 121, 223
11:4, 226
11:6, 269
11:12, 230
11:13, 230
11:13–16, 215
11:19, 233
11:34, 250
11:39, 274
11:40, 245
12:1, 264
12:2, 84
12:4, 266
12:15, 76
12:17, 112
12:22, 274
12:24, 271
12:26–27, 278
12:28, 283–284
12:29, 214, 269
13:4, 286
13:7, 287, 293
13:8, 288
13:9, 289
13:10, 289
13:10–11, 17
13:11, 289
13:18, 293
13:19, 10–11, 15, 109

Hebrews (continued)
13:22, 26, 295
13:23, 10, 15, 109
13:24, 11, 14

James
1:2, 245
1:18, 274
2:26, 189
5:12, 120

First Peter
2:22, 85
3:18, 185
3:21, 210
3:21–22, 31
3:22, 48

Second Peter
1:20–21, 12
1:20–21, 2
2:20–22, 114
3:9, 217
3:10, 49
3:11–13, 278
3:13, 49
3:15–16, 287
3:17–18, 288

First John
3:5, 85
3:6-10, 190
4:8, 269
4:16, 269

Jude
3, 26
14–15, 226

Revelation
1:5, 53
1:18, 186
2:2, 115
2:9, 115
2:13, 115
2:19, 115
3:1, 115, 308
3:8, 115
3:15, 115

Scripture Reference Index

Revelation (*continued*)
   3:21, 48
   4:11, 29
   5:11, 33
   6:14, 278
   7:9–12, 275
   10:9–10, 308
   11:19, 154
   14:4, 274
   15:5, 154
   15:8, 154
   21:27, 275

Second Maccabees
   7, 254
   7:9, 254

Subject and Name Index

Though not intended to be exhaustive, this list of topics and names is designed to help you quickly locate key themes, terms, and concepts discussed throughout the book. Organized alphabetically by topic/name and then subtopic, this index includes page references for easy navigation, allowing you to efficiently find the information you are looking for.

Aaron, 95, 127, 135
   Aaronic priesthood,
     125–126, 136, 138,
     145, 147, 154
   anointing of, 177, 209
   the descendants of. *See*
     Aaron, the sons of
   the garments of, 209
   as high priest, 135–136,
     141, 147, 149, 170, 174, 181
   and Hur, 251
   and Moses, 16, 26, 87,
     95–96, 146–147, 150, 171, 212
   offering sacrifice, 84–86,
     140, 174, 207
   the offspring of. *See* Aaron,
     the sons of
   the rod of, 171
   the sons of, 84, 95, 135,
     146–148, 170, 175, 183, 209
Abihu, 86, 95, 148, 207, 214
Abraham, 130, 168, 221,
   228, 231, 233

Abraham (*continued*)
   Abram, 127–128
   the blessing of, 117
   his covenant with God, 231, 300
   the faith of, 116, 121,
     228, 230, 233–234
   the God of, 232–233
   and the Hittites, 232
   and Isaac, 116–117, 122,
     231, 233, 246, 272
   sacrificing Isaac, 116, 118–119
   Jesus greater than, 60, 135
   and Melchizedek, 126–128,
     130, 135, 138
   oath to, 119
   God's promise to, 119–120,
     122, 228, 230–231
   and Sarah, 230, 284
   the seed of, 119–120, 130, 135
   the sons of, 61, 120, 215
   tithing of, 129, 134–135
   and the three visitors, 230, 284

Subject and Name Index

Abram. *See* Abraham

angels
  appearing to Abraham, 284
  appearing to Elijah, 249
  appearing to shepherds, 81
  appearing with God, 43–44
  killing Assyrian army, 251
  surrounding God's throne, 274
  in Jacob's dream, 130, 231
  in heavenly Jerusalem, 274
  Jesus ascending above, 54
  Jesus exalted above, 48
  Jesus lower than, 47, 146
  Jesus not being an archangel, 36
  compared to Jesus. *See*
    Jesus, versus angels
  lacking Jesus's glory, 35
  strengthening Jesus, 98
  submitting to Jesus, 31, 34
  law delivered by, 42
  in lions' den, 247
  LORD appearing as
    angel, 43, 117
  saving Lot, 284
  man lower than, 46–47
  meaning of, 42
  Melchizedek as angel, 128
  as servants of God, 32, 35
  blowing trumpets, 153
  voice of, 33

Apollos, 10–12

apostasy, 107
  and disobedience, 256
  as rejection of God, 110
  atonement for, 213
  cause for, 217
  consequences of, 146
  warning against, 110

atonement
  animal sacrifices as, 92–93,
    141, 150, 174, 179–182, 186
  as covering, 170

atonement (*continued*)
  Day of Atonement, 84, 86,
    121, 169–170, 174–175,
    178–179, 182, 206–209
  of high priest, 84–85, 94,
    170, 179, 182, 207–208
  the sacrifice of Jesus as, 85,
    171, 179, 202
  for sins, 31, 44, 46, 84, 92,
    94, 139, 141, 150,
    170–171, 178–182, 196,
    202, 207
  for unintentional sins, 211

Canaan
  land of, 43, 67–69, 111, 231, 300

Christ
  advent of, 97, 201, 206, 279
  apostatizing from, 66, 114, 271
  blood of, 265
  body of, 198, 202, 274, 286
  church of, 210
  new covenant of, 163, 181, 288
  death of, 44, 48
  deity of, 103
  earthly ministry of, 258
  enemies of, 203
  faith in, 45, 60, 70, 75,
    108, 110, 120, 163, 189
  as firstfruits, 274
  flock of, 294
  as fulfillment of the Old
    Testament, 27, 120, 129,
    141, 152, 179, 197–198, 289
  Jesus as the, 10, 64, 157
  as judge, 188
  knowing, 287
  giver of life, 44, 274
  light of, 15
  as mediator before God, 86, 132
  and Melchizedek, 128–129,
    132–134, 137–138
  mystery of, 294
  name of, 291
  as offering, 138, 140, 290–291
  priesthood of, 138, 190, 306

326

Christ (continued)
  redemptive work of, 163, 181, 183, 185, 265
  reproach of, 238
  resurrection, 30–31, 52, 179, 185
  sacrifice of, 141–142, 195–196, 203
  seated in heaven, 30
  second coming of, 188, 203, 217
  suffering of, 115, 184, 266, 291
  unchanging, 288
covenant
  blood of, 162
  Book of, 162
  Establishing, 44–45, 147, 162–163, 230–231, 277
  of God, 80–82, 155–156, 159, 173, 186, 206, 231, 299–300
  of Jesus, 16, 45, 126, 137, 146–147, 161, 163, 286
  Mosaic, 45
  new, 17, 45, 141, 146–147, 149, 155–157, 159–163, 176–177, 180, 187, 203, 212, 266, 271, 274, 277, 288, 290–292, 298, 306–307
  old, 18, 27, 46, 146–147, 155, 159, 162–163, 180, 187–188, 201–203, 210, 213, 271, 274, 276–277, 290–291
  ratification of, 45–46, 187, 206, 212, 265, 277
  Sabbath as, 81
  Sinaitic, 160–161
  tables of, 171, 174
David
  bowing upon his bed, 235
  chosen by God, 250
  City of, 173
  seeing corruption, 198
  descendants of, 135, 258
  subduing Edom, 234, 270

Subject and Name Index

David (continued)
  expanding Israel, 250
  written upon by God's hand, 153
  as hero of faith, 243
  son of Jesse, 250
  Jesus descending from, 32
  Jesus Son of, 35
  versus Jesus, 146
  killing Goliath, 243
  as righteous king, 61, 246
  first king of Israel, 244
  Messiah Son of, 126, 131
  speaking of the Messiah, 35, 198
  offering praise, 292
  receiving pattern of temple, 176, 307
  persecution of, 197
  promised a Son, 247
  psalmist, 131, 136, 197
  seed of, 131
  shepherd, 250
  as sojourner, 232
  speaking by the Spirit, 35, 49, 131
  preparing for temple building, 153
death
  of Aaron's sons, 148
  of Aaron, 147
  Abel's, 226
  of animal sacrifices, 185
  as archenemy, 51, 203
  for touching the Ark, 170
  for blaspheming against the Holy Spirit, 213
  bodily, 184, 186, 188, 254, 272, 274
  for child sacrifice, 118
  as consequence of sin, 109, 228
  of the cross, 46, 97, 100, 180
  by crucifixion, 265
  as curse, 109
  of David, 153
  defeated through faith, 244

327

Subject and Name Index

death (*continued*)
   to be destroyed, 49
   escaping, 239, 267, 285
   eternal, 238
   fear of, 49
   in God's presence, 86, 121, 139, 169, 178, 191, 207, 272
   for intentional sins, 212
   Jacob fleeing, 231
   of Jacob, 234–235
   of Jeremiah, 256
   Jesus defeating, 186, 203
   likeness of Jesus's, 48, 178
   of Jesus, 92, 180, 184–185, 291
   of Jezebel, 249
   of Joseph, 235
   for violating Old Testament law, 46, 80, 207
   life after, 188, 191
   of Melchizedek, 137
   of Moses, 237
   Nero's, 18
   pangs of, 185
   Paul's, 11
   perfection through, 51
   preceding glory, 52, 54
   reigning over man, 50
   repentance after, 188
   of Samson, 241
   of Sarah, 232
   sharing in Jesus's, 48, 52, 179
   of Stephen, 42, 237
   by stoning, 44, 153, 237, 256
   swallowed up, 51
   victory over, 51, 54, 203

Egypt
   Alexandria, 199
   bondage in, 68, 133
   deliverance out of, 67, 69, 82, 133, 168, 173, 235, 245–246, 249, 271, 300
   Jacob's death in, 234
   Jeremiah stoned in, 255
   Joseph's death in, 235
   land of, 61, 155, 235, 237, 256

Egypt (*continued*)
   LORD's wonders in, 67
   Moses fleeing, 238
   Pharaoh of, 232
   Uriah fleeing to, 256

Ezekiel, the prophet, 205, 295

forgiveness
   through the blood of Jesus, 140–141, 179, 202–203, 276
   of God, 113, 156, 160–161
   of sin(s), 161–163, 179, 183, 187, 196, 202–204, 276

God the Father
   access to, 265
   bestowing glory upon Jesus, 35–36, 52, 95
   believers as children of, 51
   drawing near to, 139
   fellowship with, 180, 207
   Jesus as Son of, 32, 35, 44, 87, 96, 177
   Jesus equal to, 34, 36, 48, 52
   Jesus offering himself to, 181, 291
   Jesus praying to, 63, 98
   Jesus representing believers before, 52, 86, 181
   Jesus sitting at his right hand, 31, 266
   Jesus submitting to, 50–51, 103
   Jesus's obedience to, 96, 99–100
   witnessing to Jesus, 99
   as king of all, 51
   presence of, 121, 171, 181, 187, 205
   priest appearing before, 150
   promising his Son, 131
   raising Jesus from the dead, 32, 179, 185
   seeing him through Jesus, 27
   sacrificing his Son, 119
   speaking through Scriptures, 35
   worshiping, 291

Subject and Name Index

grace, 299
　of God, 44, 52,
　　177, 183, 213, 288–289, 307
　obtaining, 76, 86, 288, 290
　rejecting, 21
heaven
　angels of, 16, 31–32, 35,
　　41, 44, 47–48, 54, 60, 63,
　　98, 126, 145–146, 212, 274
　as spiritual creation, 48, 270
　dew of, 50, 232, 234
　Enoch translated to, 226
　the Father speaking from, 99
　fire from, 185, 249
　God creating, 33–34, 81
　Holy of Holies in, 121–122,
　　181, 191, 204
　Jesus ascending to, 31
　Jesus High Priest in, 85, 95
　Jesus ministering
　　in, 151, 211, 266
　Jesus seated in, 30, 149
　made by God's word, 29
　Moses hands lifted up to, 251
　our names written in, 276
　the new, 49, 278–279
　passing away, 49, 277–278
　stars of, 117
　tabernacle in, 2, 153–154, 181
hell, 64, 189
Holy Spirit
　blaspheming against, 213
　dwelling in Old Testament
　　believers, 292
　fellowship with, 110, 178
　glorified with Father and
　　Son, 48
　being grieved, 213
　inspiring Scripture, 2, 4,
　　179, 298
　Jesus's sacrifice through, 184
　resurrecting Jesus, 53, 184–185
　lying to, 213
　being outraged, 213

Holy Spirit (*continued*)
　performing signs and
　　wonders, 45, 244
　receiving, 77–78, 99
　speaking through
　　Scripture, 51, 115,
　　188–189, 203, 292
　speaking to you, 36–37, 218
　as water, 210
　working in believers, 83,
　　115, 178, 210
Isaac
　with Abraham and
　　Jacob, 130, 168, 215, 230,
　　232, 234
　Abraham offering,
　　116–118, 231, 233, 272
　as son of Abraham, 43,
　　112, 116–117, 228–229
　blessing Jacob, 234, 270
　father of Esau, 269–270
　raised by God, 233–234
　receiving promise of
　　descendants, 231
　receiving promise of the
　　land, 228, 230–231
　sacrificing your, 55
　son of the promise, 234, 246
　the God of, 233
Isaiah, the prophet
　beholding God's glory, 139
　compared to Jesus, 60, 146
　with King Hezekiah, 251
　prophesying of Israel's
　　disobedience, 110–112
　prophesying of Jesus, 51, 85
　prophesying of new
　　creation, 278
　rebuking Israel, 292
　referring to the LORD as
　　shepherd, 294
　sawn asunder, 256

Subject and Name Index

Israel
  atonement for, 85
  believing in Jesus, 157, 160, 163
  as congregation, 85, 206–208, 272, 300
  conquering land, 246
  defeated by Philistines, 241, 250
  defeating its enemies, 111, 240, 242–243, 246, 251
  delivered out of Egypt, 69, 133, 235, 237
  disobedience of, 110, 160, 292, 299–300
  Edom rebelling against, 271
  ethnic, 156, 160–161, 163
  returning from exile, 205–206
  feasts of, 53
  God delivering, 240
  God of, 168, 242, 295
  as God's firstborn, 133
  as God's people, 111, 155, 160, 164, 205–206, 209, 213, 238, 273, 277, 299–300, 311
  high priest of, 132, 147–148
  house of, 111, 155–156
  offspring of Jacob, 234, 270
  as type of Jesus, 133
  judges of, 239–240, 242–243
  king of, 35, 61–62, 132, 234, 249–250, 270
  kingdom of, 242, 258, 271
  land of, 14, 118, 133, 199, 252, 254
  rejecting Moses, 238
  as nation, 299–300
  people of, 81, 84, 95, 118, 150, 160, 170, 173, 182, 208, 212, 234, 242, 249, 271
  prophet in, 61–62
  rebels in, 171
  receiving God's promise, 156–157
  the shepherd of, 294
  sins of, 160, 163, 182–183, 208

Israel (*continued*)
  sons of, 120, 149, 238, 300
  tribes of, 68, 112, 135, 148–149, 156, 171, 174, 234
  in wilderness, 162, 171, 173
Ithamar, 95, 148
Jacob
  with Abraham and Isaac, 230, 232
  at Bethel, 130
  blessed by Isaac, 269–270
  blessing his children, 234
  children of, 234
  deceiving Isaac, 270
  dreaming, 231
  encountering God, 231
  God of, 233
  leaning upon staff, 235
  paying tithe, 130
  as peaceful man, 269
  receiving promise of the land, 228, 230–231
  as sojourner, 215
  standing before Pharaoh, 232
  taking birthright, 112, 269
  threatened by Esau, 112, 130
  worshiping God, 130
James, the brother of Jesus, 8, 18, 245
Jeremiah, the prophet
  covenant promised through, 155–157, 162, 203
  imprisoned, 255
  prophecy of, 154, 255–256
  stoned in Egypt, 255–256
  time of, 155–156
  weak made strong, 249–250
Jerusalem
  Barnabas resident of, 10
  besieged by the Assyrians, 251
  destruction of, 255–256
  earthly, 274
  heavenly, 271, 274–275
  Jesus crucified in, 271

330

Jerusalem (continued)
  Jesus heading toward, 265
  Melchizedek king of, 128–129
  Mount Moriah in, 233
  Mount Zion in (as), 272, 274
  Paul speaking in, 3
  praying toward, 247
  temple of, 17, 247, 254
  walls of, 291
Jesus
  versus Aaron, 16, 150
  advent of, 64, 155, 197, 206
  versus angels, 16, 26, 31,
    35, 52, 54, 60, 145–146
  beginning of creation, 52–53
  blood of, 46, 161–164, 179,
    181, 184, 187, 191,
    203–205, 207,
    209–211, 266, 271,
    276–277, 289, 306
  body of, 151, 202, 306
  church of, 64
  commandments of, 64, 67,
    96, 111, 113, 115, 158, 275, 287
  new covenant of, 17,
    44–45, 137, 146–147, 149,
    155, 157, 161–162, 177, 276
  cross of, 27
  conquering death, 49, 51
  death of, 27, 42, 46, 49,
    178–180, 185, 203
  disciples of, 8, 16, 47, 76, 177
  author of faith, 52, 66, 84, 265
  faith in, 59, 139, 157, 179
  forerunner, 52, 121–122,
    178, 265–266
  glory of, 27–28, 55
  as God, 29–30, 128, 134, 238
  in the Gospels, 67, 78,
    99, 133, 285, 292
  in Hebrews, 26–27, 48, 53,
    63, 66, 76, 86, 139, 146, 298
  imprint of God, 26–27, 29, 223
  and the Jews, 35, 61, 66,
    96, 110, 131, 150–151
  Lamb of God, 92, 311

Jesus (continued)
  and the law, 159, 301
  giver of life, 186
  as Lord, 37, 45, 81,
    86, 98, 111–112, 114,
    233, 265, 288
  as man, 10, 41, 46–49,
    51–52, 54, 81, 85, 94, 97,
    100–101, 134
  and Melchizedek, 133, 137–138
  as Messiah, 10, 64, 101,
    103, 126, 146, 247
  versus Moses, 59–60,
    62–65, 147
  name of, 112
  of Nazareth, 15, 157, 177,
    188, 301
  obedience of, 51, 99–101, 103
  obedience to, 101
  in the Old
    Testament, 37, 146, 159,
    197, 298, 301
  priesthood of, 95, 126, 142, 307
  redemption of. See Jesus,
    salvation of
  the reproach of, 115, 238,
    265, 291
  resurrection of, 31–32, 53,
    184–185, 203, 210, 294
  sacrifice of, 31, 126,
    138–139, 141, 147,
    161, 179–181, 184–185,
    187, 202, 264, 266, 290–291
  salvation of, 42, 46, 52,
    60, 191, 264–265, 299, 301
  Savior, 114–115, 158, 288
  seated in heaven, 28–31,
    149, 181, 202, 266
  second coming of, 203, 217
  great shepherd, 259, 294–295
  Son of David, 32, 131, 135
  Son of God, 15, 26–28,
    32, 35–37, 41, 53, 63–64,
    66, 84, 99–100, 119,
    146, 177, 185, 206–207,
    211–212, 301
  sovereignty of, 48–49

331

Subject and Name Index

Jesus *(continued)*
  suffering of, 51, 55, 92,
    97–98, 151, 187
  superiority of, 26, 34, 36,
    60, 62, 126
  as Teacher, 291
  trials of, 265–266
  Word of God, 4, 44, 177
Joshua
  son of Jehozadak, 277
  son of Nun, 60, 82, 239
    burying Joseph's bones, 235
    entering Canaan, 69
    having faith, 45, 68
    spying out Canaan, 68
judgment
  breastpiece of, 149
  the eternal, 108, 115,
    157, 188, 226, 277, 299
  of God, 64, 67, 70,
    112, 188, 213–214, 217,
    226, 228, 238, 300
  of king, 246
justification, 44, 61, 109–110,
  158, 276
life
  of Abraham, 228, 233
  book of, 275
  of Christ, 159, 197, 274
  of David, 197, 235, 243
  after death, 188, 191
  earthly, 134, 254
  end of, 129
  eternal, 75, 113, 158, 187,
    189, 203, 254
  of Jacob, 232
  of Moses, 235, 237–238, 248
  in new creation, 52
  newness of, 52, 179, 254
  returning to, 185, 253–254, 274
  risking own, 170, 207
  unholy, 269
  way leading to, 113

Matthew, disciple of Jesus, 98–99,
  111, 133
  the Gospel of, 2, 180, 285
Melchizedek
  blessing Abraham, 125,
    127–128, 130, 135
  greater than Abraham, 135
  meeting Abraham, 127–128
  appearance of, 127
  descent of, 129, 133–135
  as divine appearance, 128–129
  as historic figure, 129, 134
  identity of, 127–129, 132,
    134, 137
  mention of, 128, 131
  name of, 128
  order of, 99, 126–127, 131,
    136, 138, 146, 149–150
  priesthood of, 126, 135, 137
  theme of, 121, 132
  as type of Christ, 128,
    132–135, 137
Messiah
  and Melchizedek, 129
  David speaking of, 35
  descending from the tribe
    of Judah, 137
  Jesus as, 101, 247, 301
  as priest-king, 131, 135
  priesthood of, 132, 137–138
  promised, 35, 103, 126,
    131–132, 146, 258
  receiving God's oath-
    promise, 125, 131, 136–138
  Son of David, 35, 131
  suffering of, 101
  triumph over his enemies, 131
Moses
  anointing Aaron, 209
  building the
    tabernacle, 152, 169,
    175–176, 209, 307
  and the burning bush, 42, 233
  as child, 237
  chosen by God, 171

Moses (*continued*)
  fleeing Egypt, 238
  in Egypt, 237–238
  escaping the edge of the
    sword, 248
  God speaking to, 169
  communing with God,
    61–62, 65, 152
  obedient to God, 62–63, 65
  reflecting God's glory, 27
  in Hebrews, 60, 221
  inaugurating the Sinaitic
    covenant, 54, 147, 162
  instructed by God, 63, 87,
    93, 118, 149–150, 153, 170–171
  instructing
    Israel, 68, 77, 84, 160
  Jesus superior to, 16, 26,
    59–60, 62–65, 96,
    146–147, 150, 212
  prophesying of Jesus, 63, 101
  in Judaism, 61, 147, 150
  killing an Egyptian, 237–238
  law of, 61, 147, 265
  receiving the law, 42–44,
    147, 160, 173, 272
  writing the law, 160
  prophesying of Israel, 234
  greatest prophet, 60–62
  as servant, 62–64, 66, 146
  shown pattern of the
    tabernacle, 152–153
  speaking in faith, 249
  in the wilderness, 79, 177, 251
Nadab, 86, 95, 148, 207, 214
offering
  of animals, 182, 201, 289–290
  atonement, 84–85
  body and blood of
    Jesus, 138, 141, 187, 202,
    289, 306
  bread and wine, 138
  burnt, 84, 116, 201–202,
    243, 249, 290–291
  freewill, 291

offering (*continued*)
  gifts, 292, 295, 306
  by the high priest, 149, 187, 306
  of strange incense, 87, 207, 214
  Jesus as, 138, 140, 171,
    184–185, 187, 196, 202, 306
  meal and drink, 291
  offering a sacrifice, 84,
    93–94, 117, 140–142, 150,
    202, 242, 249, 283, 291,
    306–307
  peace, 291
  of praise and
    thanksgiving, 283, 291–292
  sin, 85, 93, 150, 170, 174,
    182, 208, 212, 290–291
  trespass, 211–212
  true worship, 291
Passover
  Feast, 53, 147, 242
  lamb, 238
  meal, 161–162
  Sabbath following, 53
Paul
  as author of Hebrews, 8,
    10–12, 295
  in dating Hebrews, 18
  New Testament author, 8
Peter
  New Testament author, 8
  in dating Hebrews, 18
priesthood
  Aaronic, 95, 125, 136
  of Christ, i, 17, 91,
    95, 126, 132, 135,
    137–138, 140, 142, 145,
    211, 276, 306
  human, 140–141, 177
  in the Old
    Testament, 18, 84, 87,
    126, 138, 140–141, 147, 168
  Levitical, 135, 137
  of Melchizedek, 126–127,
    132, 135, 137–138

Subject and Name Index

priesthood (*continued*)
  in the New Testament, 141–142, 307
promised land
  entering, 59, 81–82, 235, 238
  rest in, 82
redemption
  day of, 213
  hope of, 217
  of Jesus, 42, 182, 185, 299
resurrection
  of believers, 48, 52, 274
  of Jesus, 31–32, 45, 48, 53–54, 185–186, 198, 210, 274, 291, 294
righteousness
  before God, 110, 301
  of God, 207, 279, 301
  of Jesus, 48, 95, 139, 179, 181
  of the law, 157
  obtaining, 180, 288
  perseverance in, 116
  way of, 114
  by works, 110
Roman Empire, 215
sacrifice
  of Abel, 225
  abolishing, 140
  acceptable, 54, 141, 225, 283, 285, 290, 292
  animal, 87, 150, 163, 180, 186, 188, 197, 201–203, 254, 289–291, 306–307
  blood of, 86, 162, 170, 179, 181
  of Cain, 225
  child, 118–119, 300
  on Day of Atonement, 209
  of deliberate sin, 211
  human, 118–119

sacrifice (*continued*)
  of Jesus, 17, 31, 46, 126, 138–139, 141–142, 147, 161, 163, 167, 170–171, 179, 185, 188, 190, 195–196, 201–203, 205, 207, 213, 276, 290–291
  of New Testament, 16, 138, 307
  of praise, 292
  in Old Testament, 138, 140–141, 159, 183–185, 197, 204, 211, 249, 290–291, 306–307
  ordinance of, 225
  to pagan gods, 256
  offered by priest, 84, 93, 149–150, 168, 202, 306–307
sacrificial system, 17–18, 142
salvation
  author of, 52, 265
  of believers, 26, 51, 121, 140, 164
  eternal, 101, 141
  by faith, 141, 157
  God's plan of, 80, 155, 298
  wrought by Jesus, 16, 31, 42, 46, 52, 60, 126, 183, 188, 190, 264
  losing, 87, 214, 216, 269
  of recipients, 16–17, 42, 190, 196, 211, 263–264
  requirements for, 60, 140–141
  urgency of, 113
Sinai
  the covenant at, 160, 162
  the law at, 274, 300–301
  the Mount of, 42, 69, 271–273, 277
  the wilderness of, 44, 69, 206, 271, 273
sin
  atonement for, 31, 44, 46, 85, 139, 141, 150, 171, 178–180, 182, 186, 196, 208

Subject and Name Index

sin *(continued)*
consequence of, 47, 49, 69, 115, 156, 178, 209, 290, 299
covered, 170, 191
falling into, 29
forgiveness of, 141, 156, 160–161, 163–164, 179, 187, 196, 202–203
of the high priest, 84–85, 93–94, 182, 207
against the Holy Spirit, 213
intentional, 212
unintentional, 93, 212
Jesus without, 85, 94, 99, 266, 290
of the land, 209
lifestyle of, 110, 114, 189, 269
of man, 29, 48, 158, 279, 300
offering, 84–85, 93, 150, 170, 174, 182, 208, 212
of the people, 92, 160, 163, 170, 179, 182, 202, 208, 291
removal of, 183, 188, 209, 264, 298
repentance of, 264, 266
sinful nature, 85, 94, 178, 207
transfer of, 291

Solomon
moving the Ark, 173
in psalms, 246
son of David, 153, 235
the Temple of, 154, 233, 247, 307
wisdom of, 246, 250

tabernacle
built by Moses, 63, 150, 176
defiled, 184, 208
design of, 141, 152, 167–169, 176–177, 307
during David's reign, 173
earthly, 65, 150, 152, 169, 181
exclusive to Israel, 150
filled by God's glory, 177

tabernacle

tabernacle *(continued)*
furniture of, 152, 167, 175, 177, 208–209
heavenly, 149–150, 154, 176, 181
served by the high priest, 31, 187, 202, 290
Jesus as the new, 44, 177–178
standing when Hebrews was written, 179
replaced by the temple, 168
theme of, 168–169
veil of, 121
in the wilderness, 154, 173

335

Finished by the grace of God

—David Adeeb

www.ingramcontent.com/pod-product-compliance
Lightning Source LLC
Chambersburg PA
CBHW020311010526
44107CB00001B/69